P9-AOJ-821

CHAPTER ONE

AYISHETU BUGRE SANK TO THE RED GROUND IN A DEFERENTIAL squat, her dark eyes avoiding the jeering men and women around her. The heat pressed down like an open palm as she focused instead on the packed red dirt that led to a ragged grouping of white-washed mud huts. Men with wiry white whiskers and puffy hats slapped their right hands together, then touched the center of their chests in greeting as they gathered around her, pulled by the gossip that whizzed through the ramshackle town.

From a distance the village looked as though it had been built from toadstools. Pumpkin-colored mud huts domed with dried grass blended almost perfectly with the red laterite soil. Fierce dry heat usually kept their movements slow and deliberate, but the men carried a kind of buzzing energy as they circled the kneeling woman. Their faces were trenched like worn tires, severe and unsmiling. They waited for their village chief to emerge from inside a painted mud hut, where he was pulling off a dusty outfit not unlike silk pajamas and replacing it with more regal and voluminous robes.

The woman before them was uncommonly beautiful, with deep brown eyes and thick, full lips. Ayishetu guessed she was forty-two, but it was impossible to know for certain. She had raised eight children through the usual cycles of hunger and illness and was now helping raise three grandchildren. A renowned maker of shea butter soaps and lotions, who had once organized her neighbors into money-making cooperatives, her unlined, heart-shaped face was the perfect advertisement for the benefits of her buttery smooth creams.

If she burned with rage and indignation, it was difficult to tell. She sat ducking her head so her face would reveal nothing. In her hands she cradled a small white chicken barely a few months old. The pullet's beady eyes shifted with fear, much like Ayishetu's darted from the ground to the crowd and quickly back again. Its heart raced, pulsing in her hands. Her own heart thumped nervously in her chest.

Perhaps three thousand people live in this maze of cramped mud compounds, built on a swath of dry, rocky West African land that only begrudgingly offers up yam or maize. On most days men wait out the hottest part of the day, lounging beneath shade trees in swirling, dress-like boubous and faded Muslim caps. Their many wives move with quiet grace, bowls of water balanced on their heads and silent babies strapped to their backs. The village was a place of stereotypes brought to life, where the word *primitive* bubbled to the lips. Life could be unspeakably hard and cruel in northern Ghana, full of hardship and loss. Survival and devastation were separated by a hair's breadth. Misfortune fell without reason or warning, a mosquito's bite robbing one family of a cherished child while mysteriously sparing another.

Ghana had seen troubled times since winning independence from the British more than fifty years ago, including two decades lost to corruption and coups, but it was considered one of the most stable, productive countries of West Africa. Once called the Gold Coast for the rivers of precious metals that ran beneath its red soil, it was a darling of foreign donors, attracting more than one billion dollars each year in foreign aid. Its capital city had a shopping mall and a movie theater; Internet cafés abounded, crowded with boys playing online video games and lanky teenagers penning love notes to girlfriends overseas. The country had one of the fastest-performing stock exchanges, a handful of Hummers cruising its highways, and a bevy of megachurches, but its remote rural villages were still held in thrall by dark magic and the accompanying vise grip of superstition and paranoia.

It seems too fantastical to believe, but in the country's more remote villages people say women like Ayishetu rise on dark and ominous nights with a ravenous appetite, toss a magical blanket over the sleeping forms of their husbands, and leave the physical realm to go hunting for souls. They turn themselves into fireballs and streak across the night sky, perching with their hungry covens atop the tallest trees and feasting on the flesh of their latest victims. They could spirit away a cowife's womb, shrink a man's genitals, cock and aim their mystical guns. Their black magic is intangible, invisible, mysterious: a woman's spiritual fingerprints can be seen only by the clear eyes of a powerful diviner, a mystic man sifting through cowrie shells, buttons, nuts, bolts, and coins, looking for answers sent from the ancestors, who sat at the right hand of God, manipulating the fortunes of those who dishonored them.

Spiritual exploits have physical consequences. By morning exhaustion is etched on the faces of the victims, who cannot sleep for the torment. It is said that what happens in the spiritual realm spills over to the physical one; what happens under their victim's skin is what kills them: the blood turning to water, a missing uterus, a stone planted in the bladder, a chain of subconscious decisions that leads to a deadly car crash.

The effects of Ayishetu's suspected nighttime antics could be clearly seen by anyone.

Her niece, barely sixteen and already a mother, had begun to swell and bloat. She was burning with fever, hardly able to stand. Although a white doctor at the nearby hospital said she shouldn't eat salt, her family continued to cook as usual, filling soups and stews with cubes of flavored monosodium glutamate. They were convinced their daughter's illness had murkier origins: they were certain Ayishetu had captured the girl's soul, trapped it in the body of an insect, and was using it to torture her. Among themselves they whispered, tallying reasons for the attack.

Their suspicions were made public on a day Ayishetu had spent
quietly walking the rows of her husband's fields in the grinding
equatorial heat, planting soybeans by hand from a chipped tin bowl.
When she was called to his home, her brother-in-law announced
that his daughter had been calling Ayishetu's name. She'd been
identified, he hissed. He was convinced Ayishetu was spiritually
poisoning his daughter's soul, sneaking in the dead of night to the
girl's side and harassing her to death. He demanded that she release
his sick daughter. Ayishetu told him she didn't know what he was
saying.

His breath carried the ripe funk of grain alcohol as he called for
Ayishetu's blood, threatening her with a long knife known locally
as a cutlass. Neighbors and relatives grabbed him, convinced him
to calm his temper and instead send her away, up the crumbling red
road to a nearby village called Gambaga. In the courtyard outside
the palace of the old chief, the matter could be settled for once and
forever.

Gambaga's chief, the *gambarana*, was thought to be descended
from a long line of women and men born with the power to effortlessly cross between the physical and spiritual realms. He was
renowned for his ability to communicate with the ancestors and
to use their guidance to determine whether a woman was wicked
or innocent, all through the sacrifice of a chicken. The ancestors
were like guardians, omniscient and wise. It was paramount to offer
sacrifices that would honor them, and in some communities they
were consulted on issues both large and small. Because they guided
his decisions, the chief's word was final; there was no avenue of ap-
peal, no other soothsayer who would dispute his verdict. To be declared guilty by him was to face banishment, to be forced to leave
the safety of one's family and to start again under the permanent
stain of the chief's ruling.

And so, in the narrow courtyard where Ayishetu knelt, where
hens scratched for food and dogs shook off their fleas, not far from
where hundreds of exiled old women husked bags of corn and shelled
endless bowls of peanuts, an ancient, otherworldly court convened.

Children danced with excitement, half-dazzled by Ayishetu and her supposed powers. They raced from schoolyards, finding courage in the growing crowd, to see the kind of woman their mothers and fathers had warned them about since they were infants. Ayishetu kept her covered head bowed, but she could feel the crowd growing around her. A cacophony came from onlookers debating the relative merits of the case: her husband's wealth, their prosperous farm, and their plentiful sons were offered up as evidence of her dark powers. How else could she have garnered such things?

Ayishetu's husband, skinny and small with long white bristles sprouting from his chin, stood and faced the assembled onlookers. He was timid, his ear-pleasing melody of Mampruli vowels barely intelligible above the din. Because he was the eldest of five sons, his father's lands had passed into his hands, and though he had neither oxen nor machinery to make his farming easier, he and his wife had prospered. In no other context would they be considered rich, but in their tiny village they'd managed to build a large compound and fill it with sons. Ayishetu's husband could see it was a lifetime of re-sentment that had prompted his four brothers to bring this trouble. They were jealous of his twenty acres of land, his plentiful harvests, his relative wealth, and his good fortune to father four strong boys.

He gestured at the chicken his wife held in her hands. If she was innocent, he declared, the spirits of the ancestors should show they believed her to be harmless by guiding the bird to die on its back.

If the accusation was true, he continued softly, the fowl should die with its beak in the soil.

"Have you all heard?" the *gambarana*, the old chief, asked impa-tiently. His grim face was its usual mask of ferocity. His throne was a rough pallet of goatskins, his palace a collection of mud-daubed rooms roofed with long grass. His cheeks had collapsed with age, the skin around his eyes withered and wrinkled. His teeth were gone, worn to yellow nubs by a combination of heavy drinking and dental care that consisted of occasionally chewing on a pencil-size bit of branch.

He was an illiterate farmer who had once found occasional work as a security guard and, years before, sometimes joined the paupers and debtors who made their money by sitting in the sun breaking apart rocks with homemade hammers. That was all left behind when he was chosen to rule from the chief's goatskins in an age-old process guided by the ancestors. Now he had more than ten wives and a color TV.

His renowned powers commanded respect; his short temper ensured fear. He could channel centuries-old spiritual powers and call on the ancestors to determine Ayishetu's guilt or innocence. A bird's death at the hands of the *gambarana* could sentence a woman like Ayishetu to living in exile in the collection of mud huts behind his home. There, a woman who had spent her life under the care and command of her father, her uncles, her brothers, and then her husband and sons would be seen as belonging to the chief. She would eke out an existence alone, away from family and children, begging work from farmers for survival.

At the time of Ayishetu's trial there were already nearly two hundred such women living on the edge of town. Rituals could cleanse them of their dark magic, ceremonies could make them wards of spiteful spirits that would hunt them down and kill them if they harmed another. Once purified they were theoretically free to go, but few women felt they could leave. Their families made it clear that they had nowhere to stay, and their communities promised brutal physical punishment should they return uninvited. One woman had had her left ear cut off; another had returned from her home village with an ugly scar where her skull had been cleaved with a sharp knife.

Now it was time to decide whether Ayishetu would join them.

The wizardly old *gambarana* reached for Ayishetu's bird. He raised a long knife to its throat and slit it, tossing the bird onto the grimy ground near his predecessor's grave while watching for signs that the ancestors were manipulating its movements. It struggled and flopped, squawked without sound, spraying trickles of blood from the wound at its neck. For a moment its black eyes blinked, seemingly in disbelief at this turn of events. The fowl landed on its

back, a sign the ancestors believed in Ayishetu's innocence. Then it gave a final heave and flipped onto its front.

A bird that landed on its back exonerated Ayishetu. Dying on its beak was a conviction.

Already Ayishetu's niece had handed the chief a fowl of her own. Held upright by two men standing on either side of her, the pale girl's physical state was damning testimony on its own. She could barely steady her head, barely open her eyes, barely croak out the words. I have seen this woman hunting me, she whispered, pointing to Ayishetu. She is hunting me and I know she is going to harm me. If this is not true, the girl breathed, let my fowl not accept.

The chief once again called on the spirits of the ancestors to direct the bird. If it landed on its back, they believed the girl's accusation. If it landed on its breast, she was telling tales.

Her fowl also struggled in death, lying first on its back, then flipping onto its front.

Men who had squeezed into the few patches of shade strained to see how the birds landed. Children, chests heaving, eyes dancing with the thrill of running and hopping to escape the unpredictable trajectory of the dying birds and their jets of blood, now looked up at the men. They remained mostly silent and confused. Neither bird had died well. Both had flipped and flopped, landed on their backs, then nestled their beaks in the ground.

What was the ancestors' message? Neither had convicted nor acquitted the woman, and throughout her trial Ayishetu had said nothing. She did not beg forgiveness, shout about the unfairness, trade insults with the family who dragged her to this place, nor offer explanations for the events that led to her brother-in-law's allegation. She knew she could not speak in front of these men without risking further accusation, so she knelt, mute and blank. Culture had fit her with a muzzle and she wore it now.

With barely a word or gesture, the *gambarana* sided with her niece. He selected a man from among the group, one of the many men who basked in his power, shared his many bottles of hooch, and leached small bills from his savings. The *gambarana* ordered this

man to take Ayishetu back to her village, with strict instructions
to find and release the girl's soul. It was likely hidden among her
possessions, perhaps trapped in the body of a beetle or a cockroach.

And so, inside her cool, dark room, Ayishetu's hands, heavy and
thick like a man's, scrabbled through a sack of millet grains the size
of pushpin heads looking for the insect believed to be the vessel that
held the girl's soul. They were calloused, these hands, rough and dry
with the scars of farmwork. She wore a loop of beads at her throat
and a circle of glass beads at her wrist, but it was the dime store
ring, mashed to a smaller size and worn around her wedding ring
finger, that drew the eye. It was iridescent blue and flecked with gold
sparkles; a gold dollar sign shone out from its face. It too dug deeper
and deeper into the sack, desperately searching.

The frantic hunt turned to a tall clay pot of white corn kernels.
Ayishetu's hands slashed through the corn, lifting and spilling the
kernels with a sound like gentle rain. Her search had a frenzied energy she did not feel. Her chaperone, a tall man in traditional dress,
lifted his chin of white bristles at her in a gesture meant to renew
her focus on the search. He stooped next to her, overturning pots,
scattering plastic bowls, and hurling tin plates with the carelessness
of a child.

Her food stores had given the room a faint, yeasty smell. The
thick walls, shaped from mud and straw and baked in the intensity
of the oppressive heat, muffled the shouts and arguments happening outside her door. Ayishetu didn't want to hurry; she didn't want
to leave. The smooth floor of her dark room, barely ten paces wide
and perfectly round, felt cool on her bare feet. The thick thatched
roof was impenetrable by either the African sun or occasional tor-
rents of rain. Sweat beaded at her neck; it was too stuffy to remain
in the room in the middle of the day, but she would rather stay than
face the consequences of the chief's judgment.

She stood briefly, drew out her colorful fabric in both hands,
and in a gesture repeated dozens of times each day rewrapped it
around her dark dress and rolled its ends firmly in place. In one sudden, graceful motion she was back on her knees circling her arms

behind the tall pots. A flurry of movement caught her eye. Yakubu, her chaperone, clamped his hands around the cockroach and bolted out the door. Ayishetu hung back, one thought clanging through her head in a numbing chorus: *They are wrong, they are wrong, they are wrong.*

She dipped her head through the low doorway and walked head down into the courtyard. The suddenness of the sun made everything seem bleached out and too white, but Ayishetu could see that while she had been searching among her cooking pots and bags of grain, girls with babies on their hips and boys with the seats of their pants worn to transparency had gathered at her family's door.

Word spread quickly, invisibly, drawing farmers from their fields and women from their places at the hand-cranked water well with the revelation that Ayishetu had returned, convicted. There was tremendous noise as neighbor shouted at neighbor. Even the women, normally silent and unseen, hollered insults. The women Ayishetu had once warmly greeted, the women she had helped to get their soaps, lotions, and grains to market, now distanced themselves from her with every shout. Arms flailed wildly as men roared at one another, each besting the other's bravery with loud threats of how they would handle the wicked woman in their midst.

Instinctively Ayishetu cowered behind Yakubu's thin frame, unconsciously shrinking her own body in the hopes it could disappear. Yakubu was loyal to the chief and could hardly be considered her defender, but he was all she had. She couldn't see her husband or any of her children.

Lured by the news that their accusations had proved correct, Ayishetu's four brothers-in-law appeared at the family's nine-room compound shouting for blood. They stank of *akpateshie*, a locally brewed gin that burned the back of the throat, warmed the belly, and had the potency of jet fuel. Another pack of maybe twenty teenage boys followed them, some carrying sticks, others with homemade, short-handled hoes slung over their shoulders.

Yakubu handed her brother-in-law the cockroach cupped in his hands without ceremony or explanation. It was the color of earwax, the size of a stick of chewing gum. It was understood that the roach contained his daughter's soul. Although the angry man took it, he dropped it on the ground without glancing at it, shouting that it meant nothing, fixed nothing, saved nothing. Ayishetu snaked around Yakubu, using him as a shield, as her brother-in-law poked his long knife at her chest.

Yakubu hustled her out of the compound and down the footpath worn in a meandering line through the waist-high fields of corn that led to the rough, red road. Ayishetu's twenty-year-old son, tall, lean, and rippling with muscles, pleaded with his uncle to let him put his mother on a bicycle and deliver her away from the village. He refused, practically spitting with rage as he screamed about the dangers she held for the community, the wrongs this woman had committed, the ways she had tricked them, gaining their confidence and trust only to stalk their dreams and hunger for the souls of their children.

The mob had marched for only minutes, hurling insults and abuse. Ayishetu can barely remember it, barely piece it together, what happened first, what came next, her hands a blur of motion as they recreate a pattern of bruises and fractures. Her husband's large farm had disappeared from view when Ayishetu felt the first stick land with a dull thwack atop her head. The bloodthirsty boys knocked her down, waited until she got up, and knocked her down again.

The knob of a hoe handle, a thick knuckle of smooth, pale wood, landed with a sickening crack below her left eye. Its impact reverberated to the cartilage and bone in her nose, exploding blood vessels and causing a plume of red to gush down her face, throat, and chest. For a moment she was nowhere, neither conscious nor unconscious. Then a pulse of solid pain brought her back to the present. She found herself again sprawled on the sandy road, her manly hands, with their henna-stained fingernails, wrapped protectively around her head.

Her heart pounded. She gulped air, trying to catch her breath with the stunning realization that her husband's brothers, her family, these boys—they were going to kill her. They threw rocks, knocked her on the head with sticks an inch thick. They slapped her, punched her with closed fists, yanked off her head wrap and pulled at her coarse dark hair. She struggled to stand, but another mighty swing of the solid bulb of wood landed on the side of her head. Another fell on the small of her back. One more on her shoulder blade sent her tumbling headlong to the side of the road.

It didn't matter how the birds died: her community had already convicted her and were determined to impose a death sentence.

Ayishetu was a witch.

CHAPTER TWO

I'D FIRST LEARNED OF THE WITCH CAMPS WHILE READING A human rights report authored by the U.S. State Department. It detailed the unimaginable treatment the accused women received, hidden away at these remote camps and struggling to survive without the security of family. But bizarrely Gambaga's witch camp was also listed in my travel guide to Ghana as a sight to see for travelers visiting the country's desolate northern region.

What I knew of witchcraft came from fairy tales and movies. Witches were broom-riding old women with green-tinged complexions and noses like sprouted potatoes. They wore pointy black hats and would terrorize children, threatening to cook them up and eat them. I knew that when the New World was young a wave of hysteria had swept through a Puritan American colony and led to the burning deaths of dozens of women and children blamed for worshipping the devil and bewitching their neighbors. I pictured the classic scene from *Macbeth*, the dangerously windswept moors where a gaggle of women gathered around a huge bubbling cauldron in a raging midnight thunderstorm to cast spells against enemies. When I first tried to imagine Gambaga's witch camp, I simply substituted Shakespeare's trio of Scottish women with African women in bright wraps and headscarves.

I was curious to see something associated with folk legends

and horror stories from the Middle Ages alive and well in Africa. The same kind of voyeurism likely drives most Western visitors to seek out the hard-to-reach camp. The Bradt travel guide calls the Gambaga camp a "genuine humanitarian dilemma," but clearly the novelty outweighs the distressing idea of a modern-day colony of witches. Indeed it makes for an unusual tourist attraction, given that the main feature is a collection of old ladies husking corncobs and cracking peanut shells. It is like something out of the *Twilight Zone*, a living, breathing museum, a zoo where the inhabitants are human. For a bit of money, and with the assistance of a translator, the camp's exhibits come to life, recounting in short, disinterested sentences the dream or accusation that drove them out of their villages.

Most cultures have their version of witchcraft, a destructive mysticism so attuned to nature it can control and manipulate the future. But none is so tied to a place and a people's identity as African witchcraft. Its stranglehold on the continent is as hard for an outsider to understand and appreciate as its rituals and traditions. It moves, in some ways, like a microscopic virus. Unseen, unbidden, and unconcerned with class divisions, income levels, or educational achievements, the belief in witchcraft brings sickness, death, and destruction to livelihoods and family bonds, requiring only the slightest exposure to spread from compound to compound.

And yet despite its very ancient and often dark aspects, witchcraft is too often offered as a stock African stereotype and made light of throughout the rest of the world. An emaciated, eccentric monkey using scoops of vivid fruit flesh to paint mysterious symbols on trees and rocks played Disney's version of Africa's witchdoctors. Even the Nigerian film industry cranks out hundreds of campy, low-quality movies filled with images of half-crazed old ladies chanting and cackling fireside during the night's darkest hour. In reality, even in Nairobi, Johannesburg, and Lagos, three of Africa's biggest and most cosmopolitan cities, the belief in witchcraft simmers just below the surface. Believers can be found in virtually all corners of the continent and beyond, out in the di-

aspora where traditions have been transplanted along with their
practitioners.

In central Africa, Congo, and Angola children are tortured and
turned out on the streets for displaying witch-like traits. They are
beaten or abandoned for possessing a disquieting nature, a physical disability or malformation, or a tendency to misbehave. Twins
and triplets and those who lose their mother in childbirth are particularly suspicious. In Liberia and Sierra Leone secret societies are
blamed for bodies found emptied of their organs. Spiritual imams
known as *marabouts* in Senegal and Guinea claim they can create *juju*
for invisibility or invincibility. Voodoo found its birth in Togo and
Benin. The religion is still strong there, but bears little resemblance
to the voodoo of Haiti, with its secret societies and trance-laden
ceremonies. Neither version of the religion looks anything like the
Hollywood version of soft dolls and pushpins and zombies rising
from the earth to feast on human brains.

Trivializing witchcraft belies the violence that accompanies it.
Albinos have been murdered in Tanzania and Rwanda by thugs
collecting organs for witchdoctors willing to pay for the spiritual
powers an albino's heart and liver supposedly contain. In oil-rich
Gabon twenty-three elderly men and women were put to trial for
practicing witchcraft, only to be released nearly a year later, when it
was decided that the evidence against them was insufficient. Witch
hunters backed by armed men ransacked small villages in The
Gambia, compelling nearly a thousand people in the tiny country
into captivity. They were reportedly force-fed hallucinatory concoctions in an attempt to identify a witch the country's dictator blamed
for the death of his aunt.

If they weren't beaten to death, stoned, or lynched, women like
Ayishetu were chased out of their villages and banished. Unused
to fending for themselves and dogged by persistent rumors of dark
powers, many women found refuge in one of six isolated colonies
for suspected witches in the most remote corners of northern
Ghana. Ayishetu's husband left her to live in Gambaga, the mystical
town with a reputation for witch finding, where her fate had been

decided by the inconclusive death throes of a chicken. Her husband
pedaled there on his bicycle at least once a week, each time promising to bring his wife home as soon as tempers in their own village
had cooled.

FOR MY FIRST JOURNEY TO THE "WITCH CAMP" WHERE AYISHETU
lived I traveled with Grace, a charismatic Christian newly graduated
from one of Ghana's journalism schools, and Joanna, an elementary
school teacher from Brooklyn visiting Ghana for three months on
an Amnesty International scholarship. I was in the country working with a nongovernmental organization devoted to increasing the
quality and quantity of human rights journalism. It was supposed
to be a six-month hiatus from my newspaper job back in Toronto, a
chance to train local journalists in the investigative techniques used
to substantiate reports of human rights abuses and assist them with
sensitive interviews.

It's considered impolite to talk about witchcraft; in fact most
Ghanaians living in the country's south bristled at my inquiries.
They couldn't understand my fascination with what they consider
a black mark on their country and thought my questions were just
a way to belittle something they publicly dismissed as an embarrassing and hopelessly backward tradition still practiced among the
ignorant, pagan class.

Ghanaians, like all of us, are shaped by their landscape and
history. Rich in gold and a veritable hothouse of fruits, vegetables,
and cocoa, Ghana has never experienced war; its people live with
the legacy of slavery, but without the scars of conflict. Ghanaians
will invite perfect strangers to eat from their plate, encouraging the
unsuspecting foreigner to dip a mound of doughy *fufu* made from
pounded tapioca plants into a pool of fiery *shito* paste, laughing
merrily as the tears begin to well up in the stranger's eyes. On my
first night in the country I stepped beyond the heavy gates of our
compound and into a moonless night, navigating the empty street
with the aid of a flashlight. It was quiet and intensely dark. I was
in search of beer—brave enough to venture down the block, but

anxious enough to want to drink at home. As I rounded the corner, where cornstalks filled the empty plot, my eyes began to adjust
and I realized I wasn't alone. Men and women sat on stoops and
porches, away from the stuffy stillness of their sitting rooms and
kitchens. Their skin was so dark it blended into the night.

At the bar men sat at plastic tables positioned under the weak
street lamps and drained sweating bottles of beer. Unswervingly
loyal to whichever party shares their ethnic roots, Ghanaians are
quick-witted, silver-tongued, and mad for politics, making their
radio talk shows a heated, often ribald theater of jokes, rants, and
double entendres. The bar's patrons erupted into occasional fits
of infectious laughter as they argued in Twi about the state of the
country's politics. The bar's owners eventually became like a second
family to me, but in those early days I hastily bought eight beers for
myself and my housemates and carted them away with the warning
that I needed to return the liter bottles or risk losing my fifteen-cent
deposit.

I was back the next day, not for the money but for the street
theater. Duncan's Drinking Spot had prime roadside real estate.
I sipped a sugary orange Fanta as I watched women wearing impossibly constructed dresses and head wraps unhurriedly sashay
home from church, handkerchiefs at the ready to mop the sweat
from their foreheads. With time I learned to navigate those streets,
joking with the touts who sold handicrafts on the main thorough-
fare, stopping women who sold pineapples from a platter atop their
heads and deftly relieved the fruit of its tough exterior with a sharp
knife. Within days I was waving down *tro-tros*, the stripped-down
minivans crammed with extra bench seats that passed for public
transport, and making my way around the congested city.

The immediacy of life in Ghana was exciting and addictive, but
I was surprised at the casual references to curses and witchcraft.
After a squabble over a taxi fare my friend Moses, a man in his thir-
ties who worked on computers and had traveled outside Ghana to
Dubai and Hong Kong, urged me with all seriousness to top up the
driver's tip, lest he take his complaints to the witchdoctor. My Gha-

naian friends initially snickered at my typical Westerner's interest in witchcraft, but deeper conversation made it clear that their minds had been conditioned to see witchcraft where I couldn't.

Even those I considered pragmatic and progressive repeated outlandish rumors with the conviction of truth. Urban legends quickly became gospel. At a party I was told that mobile phones displaying a 967 number could ring with such high-frequency signals that the brain would hemorrhage when the call was answered. Twenty-seven people had died this way, I was warned. Tell your friends! It sounded like the plot of a bad horror movie, but the rumor took on such strength that MTN Areeba, the largest cellular network in Ghana, released a statement saying it had conducted a "full scale national and international priority investigation" and had "confirmed that these rumors [were] completely unsubstantiated and [had] no technological evidence to support them."

No numbers exist on deaths or injuries related to accusations of practicing witchcraft, but a quick scan of the continent's headlines suggests its toll is deadly. Most communities rid themselves of witchcraft by attacking its alleged practitioners: sisters in South Africa hacked to death with dull farm instruments by irate neighbors; a chief killed by his angry villagers in Malawi; nieces in Kenya stabbed to death; a woman hacked to death with an axe in Zimbabwe; an abducted baby found decapitated in Uganda, its body discovered on sale for use in witchcraft rituals. In Ghana girls and women were sometimes denied food and water until evil spirits had been starved from their bodies.

The country's witch colonies were actually established as an alternative to the violence. The idea was to provide a safe haven where accused women could live while a spiritual leader harnessing the power of the ancestors leached the witchcraft out of them. In theory once a woman's powers have been fully deadened and she's been threatened with a swift and brutal death at the hands of the ancestors if she practices again, she can eventually return to her community. Gambaga's camp, like the five others hidden in Ghana's northern region, is not technically a prison. The women are free to roam the village, forage in the nearby bush, and return to their families. There are no fences to keep them in or wardens to monitor their movements. Fear of retribution is enough of a motivator for the women to police themselves.

In the 1990s more than eight hundred women and a handful of men were living in two remote witch camps. Charities responded by providing boxes of used clothing and hosting conferences on eradicating witchcraft accusations and village-level workshops where men and boys were warned that they would be charged with murder or assault if they attacked suspected witches. It seemed to be for naught. In 2003 Ghana's Commission on Human Rights and Administrative Justice, a government-funded watchdog group, discovered that the number of women banished to camps was actually growing. They'd discovered a third witch camp and estimated that more than a thousand women and a smattering of men were living in exile. In its report for that year the U.S. State Department suggested that aid groups had already switched their focus from reducing accusations to simply supporting the accused women already living at the camps. They provided food, medical care, and "other support"—vague bureaucratese that could mean anything from bicycles to latrines.

By the time I moved to Gambaga in 2007 the numbers had swelled again, tripling to more than three thousand. There were rumored to be six camps hidden in the country's rural northern region. They may have begun as a kind of sanctuary, but the camps certainly weren't solving anything.

IF AFRICA'S OUTLINE CAN BE SEEN AS A RIGHT-FACING SKULL, with South Africa its jutting jaw and Uganda's Lake Victoria its empty eye socket, Ghana can be found at the base of the head, a neat rectangle in one of the world's poorest regions. Its capital, Accra, sits with its back turned to the pounding waves of the Atlantic, enveloped in a soup of heavy humidity and diesel fumes, a maze of one-story homes and modern high-rise office buildings, greasy auto repair yards, sushi restaurants, fast-food plazas, and Lebanese-owned supermarkets selling caviar, feta cheese, and stuffed olives.

Life is lived outside. Drivers of the yellow, red, and black taxis navigate open sewers and tides of foot traffic with one hand on the horn, trolling for fares. Men dressed in impeccable business suits carry on mobile phone conversations so loud it seems the message will reach its destination by volume alone. In person they greet one another with a "slap-and-snap" handshake, a loud clapping together of palms ending with a snap as their middle fingers pull apart. Boys with T-shirts depicting the rapper 50 Cent lean out the doors of the *tro-tros*, chanting a nasally "Circ! Circ! Circ!" as they swirl one finger in the air, a sign they're headed for the city's main traffic circle. Joanna, Grace, and I met there to catch a *tro-tro* headed north to the country's witch camps.

I was working with Grace at a local newspaper and figured we would write a feature-length article detailing the conditions of the camps and the absurdity of the accusations. We would of course argue for the camps' closure. What I knew of Gambaga's camp was gleaned from the guidebook and U.S. State Department reports. I'd learned it housed anywhere between 150 and 200 women, who came from as far away as Togo and Burkina Faso. There was also a church-based aid group attached to it. The Bradt guide told me the rest:

> In most parts of northern Ghana, it doesn't require any effort— just a bit of misfortune—for a woman to find herself stigmatized as a witch. It is customary, for instance, for a charge of sorcery to be leveled at an elderly female relative of anybody who dies prematurely of measles, epilepsy, malaria, cholera or any other disease, while elder wives are also often accused of casting a spell to make their polygamous husband impotent or his younger wives barren.

"Rural women continued to be banished by traditional village authorities or their families for suspected witchcraft," read the 2007 U.S. State Department report.

◆

Most accused witches were older women, often widows, who were identified by fellow villagers as the cause of difficulties, such as illness, crop failure, or financial misfortune. The women did not face formal legal sanction if they returned home; however, most feared that they would be beaten or lynched if they returned to their villages. Fearing violence against them, many women accused of being witches did not pursue legal action to challenge charges against them and return to their community.

The report spoke of a thirty-five-year-old man accused of stabbing to death his wife, whom he suspected was a witch. An American documentary film about another witch camp showed a Ghanaian man on death row, convicted of shooting his mother to death after she landed, still in the form of a fireball, atop his only child and burned most of the little girl's body.

Accra's dozens of newspapers would occasionally mention witchcraft. A bevy of bare-breasted older woman earned a front-page picture for shouting curses at police officers inside a station where their young relative was being held for impaired driving. A disheveled, disoriented woman who outsmarted a closed gate, a dozing watchman, and a locked door was called a witch after she wandered into the marital bed of a suburban couple. Elsewhere she might have been labeled mentally ill, but here her crash landing was considered witchcraft.

The stories occasionally veered into the ridiculous. The newspaper where I worked with Grace carried a story revealing that Ghana was playing host to an international conference of witches from the United States, Spain, Iran, Nigeria, and India. The event's organizers promised that participants would cull more than a million people worldwide that year alone, through the spread of HIV, tuberculosis, car crashes, floods, gas explosions, and building collapses. Documents obtained by the paper quoted the witches' agenda: "In the first quarter of our calendar year we are to infect 110,000 people (both married and unmarried) with HIV/AIDS through sex, 4,000 with tuberculosis, 6,000 with high blood pressure, and 2,600 with blindness, while 11,000 pastors and preachers will be destroyed, 220 marriages broken, and 100,000 wombs destroyed."

An Accra radio station once caused a frenzy when they reported that a listener at the main bus station had seen a woman and her lover physically locked together in the midst of sex. The mind conjured a Venus fly trap clenched around a hot dog. The radio station suggested only a blanket covered the unfortunate couple as they were wheeled on a makeshift wagon toward a bus. They were hoping to somehow sneak onto the bus, still melded as one, and travel north to convince the woman's suspicious (and clearly intuitive) husband to lift a curse triggered by infidelity.

I dismissed this as the product of a slow news day. (Crowds of curious people descended on the bus station hoping to catch a glimpse of the couple, but dozens of radio stations and newspapers later reported with obvious disappointment that there were no further sightings.) I believed witchcraft was born and sustained of Africa's poverty, its lack of health care and sanitation, its dearth of education, women's rights, and population control, even its corruption. I thought the solutions could be found in the same places: belief in the supernatural would be eroded by the science and logic that comes with greater development, functional courts and cops, and more education. Cleaner water and better hospitals, clinics and access to medicines would reduce the illnesses and deaths attributed to witches. Witchcraft would become a footnote in history if there were fewer strange deaths to explain and more logical ways to explain them.

So, armed with what I knew from the guidebook and the dry language of the U.S. State Department report, I found myself traveling north to Gambaga with Joanna and Grace, who explained that her Christian faith made her immune to a witch's attacks. Still, she refused to shake hands with the accused women.

ACCRA SEEMED TO STRETCH ON FOREVER, AN ENDLESS LOOP OF low-slung, half-finished concrete buildings topped hopefully with lonely staircases that would one day, when money permitted, lead to a new addition. They were filled with shops, some selling fabric or pirated DVDs, others outfitted as bright pharmacies or hardware stores crammed with stepladders, buckets of nails, and thick rolls of mesh wire. It was almost too much to take in. At the choked traffic circles teenage boys threaded through the crawling cars, hawking everything from inflatable plastic globes to puppies, newspapers, and waxy, bitter chocolate bars impervious to the African sun. Stopping at a red light opened endless shopping possibilities, from pens to barbecue lighters to rat poison—all the latest in cheaply manufactured Chinese goods.

We were surrounded by food, the antithesis of the overwrought food-aid-for-starving-Africans commercials. As we moved north each little town seemed to offer a roving buffet of cassava chips, salty popcorn, fried turkey tails, dense loaves of tea bread, or sweet green oranges, all of it balanced on women's heads moving through the stalled traffic. Boys on bicycles outfitted with coolers sold small plastic bags of frozen strawberry-flavored yogurt. Stalls with names like "In God's Hands" or "Jesus My Savior" or "Don't Mind Your Wife Chop Bar" offered takeaway containers of salted boiled eggs, spaghetti, and stir-fried rice served with dollops of searingly hot *shito* paste. Almost everything was tinged red from the ubiquitous palm oil.

We drove into the center of the country, where Ghana's hot, wet climate acts as a kind of hothouse, the perfect environment for a cornucopia of fruits and vegetables, from papaya to passion fruit. It's the ideal growing conditions for cocoa, whose brown pods fuel Ghana's economy. As we drove into Kumasi, the yeasty, slightly unpleasant smell of drying cocoa beans permeated the vehicle. We lumbered up the paved road and into lush forest, catching fleeting glimpses of the red, rectangular mud homes hidden among dense plantings of palm, mango, and banana trees. Towering cottonwood trees watched over it all, their leafy branches reaching high above spindly trunks anchored by a fortress of exposed roots.

The further north we drove, the more the world changed. Time seemed to wind backward, from the modernity of Accra to the colonial architecture of Kumasi and up to the medieval mud huts of the north. My head bobbed as the gentle rocking of the van and the heat of the day put me to sleep. I awoke to the sound of honking horns as we sped into Tamale, the north's largest city, where men in long, impossibly white Islamic shirts pedaled creaking bicycles. Somewhere we had crossed an invisible line, passing from thick green forests into the sparse and grassy savannah, from the south's exuberant Christianity to the north's reserved Islam, from urban streets choked with cars to wide lanes clogged with bicycles. It was hot but dry. In the south beads of sweat slithered uncomfortably down one's spine, but here they evaporated almost immediately.

We sped through town to a lonely turnoff at Walewale, an isolated transportation hub for travelers heading into northern Ghana's more remote communities. There we were handed wooded tiles as tickets and told to wait for the next *tro-tro*. In the south the vans often seated seventeen, but in the north they carried at least twenty, sometimes twenty-five passengers. A lean, older man with rotted teeth and eyes rimmed with kohl took the seat next to me. Behind him a woman with a long, white headscarf edged with embroidery and cheeks nicked with scars balanced a huge metal bowl on her knees.

We were three women traveling alone, none of us able to speak any of the north's languages, but we were treated warmly and watched over by our fellow passengers. A schoolteacher carrying a black briefcase offered his hand in greeting, telling me, "You are welcome!," as though he was the *tro-tro's* host. He smiled broadly when he heard I was traveling to see Gambaga's witches, telling me he was unafraid of the women—not because he didn't believe in witchcraft, but because he was a newcomer to the village, assigned by the government to the remote post, and his different ethnicity made him immune to the witches' attacks.

The vehicle wouldn't move until all the tickets were sold, and it took nearly an hour for the "mate," the fare collector, to find enough passengers so we could set off on the road that connected Gambaga with the outside world. The dirt track felt corrugated. Rain had worn a rippled pattern onto its surface, while an abandoned maintenance contract had left it ungraded. The driver plowed through thick stones or skidded across bare earth baked hard by the sun. The van filled up with dust as we drove in and out of deep ruts. The journey from the main bus station in Accra was maybe 350 miles, but bad roads crowded with heavy, plodding cargo trucks, a schedule that moved on the driver's whims, and decrepit vehicles prone to breakdowns meant that even under optimum conditions the drive to Gambaga could take at least eighteen hours. It took us nearly two days to finally reach the village, where we were dropped at the roadside near the Gambaga police outpost, exhausted, dehydrated, and tinged red with dust.

It was as if we had slipped through a time portal. In the dying orange light of an October afternoon flowering vines snaked around the cone-topped mud huts. We stepped into a *National Geographic* photo of quintessential Africa. Men with flat-topped Muslim caps rode unhurriedly by on their rickety bicycles, ferrying two or three colorful hens strung out upside down from the handlebars. Some carried a sheep bleating above the rear tire or a bale of long grass balanced between their knees. Children rode two or three to an adult-size bike, one perched on the crossbar to work the steering, another pedaling furiously, too small to both sit and ride. Those without brakes were given away by the soles of their plastic sandals, worn to wafers by the foot dragging it takes to bring a bicycle to a stop. It was exhilarating to be in a place that seemed so untouched.

CUSTOM DICTATED THAT, FOR OUR FIRST VISIT TO THE WITCH camp, we present ourselves and our intentions to the village chief, the *gambarana*, and seek his permission to enter the camp. Secretly smug at the idea that we would soon have one of those unbeatable travel tales so competitively told on the expatriate cocktail circuit—"Once, when I was at an African witch camp . . ."—we followed a teenager named Hassan through the narrow dirt alleyways framed by the high mud walls of the village's compounds to the chief's palace.

The country's statistical service measures poverty using a person's possessions—sewing machines, stoves, refrigerators, fans, radios, video players, televisions, cameras, electric irons, bicycles, cars, or mobile phones—to calculate wealth. Poverty might be better illustrated by the coins jangling in one's pocket, but in the most recent census, statisticians found that 66 percent of homes in the rural grasslands could afford to own a bicycle, but fewer than 1 percent had a car; 6 percent owned a fan; 3 percent owned a refrigerator, stove, or mobile phone; 68 percent had a battery-operated radio, but only 6 percent had a television. Few families have the extra cash to invest in expensive electronic conveniences in places where there isn't even a socket to bring them to life. Only 40 percent of Ghanaian households are hooked up to the nation's power grid.

Added up and crunched into quotable figures, most northern families spend an average of seventy-eight cents every day on food, clothing, and shelter, less than Americans spend on two first-class postage stamps. Many eat only what they can grow; money generated from the sale of what's left over—an armful of yams, a basket of corn, a recycled liter bottle filled with fermented palm wine— amounts to less than three hundred dollars each year.

It wasn't a place for pretension. Hidden behind the village's yellow Catholic church, the *gambarana*'s palace was made of mud, brushed with white paint and fronted by a shade made from woven branches. A few stumps and logs had been placed underneath the awning for seating. A slab of unadorned concrete made for a kind of throne. Inside the front room of his round palace plastic lawn chairs were gathered up and deposited in a semicircle around the *gambarana*, a thin and fierce-looking man who got up to change into his royal robes when we asked to take his picture. Hassan acted as our translator; two of the chief's young sons, dressed only in holey underpants, watched curiously, understanding nothing we said but offering shy smiles in response.

The *gambarana* returned wearing a flowing white robe with an elaborate geometric pattern stitched around the collar in green, burgundy, and yellow thread. He carried a tall walking stick made of dark wood, its handle adorned with a leather-wrapped talisman. On his head he wore a small blue cap, a light-colored amulet stitched on the front. He had tossed a rainbow-hued bath towel over his shoulder. He sat before us on a white-and-brown speckled goatskin with his legs gathered under the roomy robe, his voluminous sleeves swallowing his arms and hands.

The *gambarana*'s famed ability to control witches is celebrated each year at a festival in a neighboring town. The hierarchy of the area's chiefs is somewhat complicated, with small village chiefs falling at the bottom and one divinely chosen tribal chief reigning supreme. In the middle are the tangled branches of numerous royal families, all fighting for the chance at the power that comes with being named chief of a town like Gambaga. The Mamprusi people who live in Gambaga actually think of the *gambarana* as female because the first one was a woman, a *zobzia*, or light-skinned, red-headed woman who was thought of as a kind of magical albino. The oral history says the area's ultimate tribal leader was meeting with his elders in the hills separating Gambaga from the next village, in a place where witches were once outfitted with heavy, red-hot chokers and killed, when the *zobzia* emerged from the bush, her red hair flaming. She was accompanied by a sole drummer, who tapped out a talking rhythm meaning "Are you the only one who eats?" The woman threatened the spiritual leader with a spear, taking aim while singing.

The elders begged her to spare his life, making promises of shared power if she would save them the embarrassment of losing their king. She made only one demand: the paramount chief would collect up his dozens of wives and hundreds of devotees and move away from her territory. She would identify and battle the witches who turned themselves into fireballs and lit up the night sky. She would keep them from roaming the spiritual realm, where they could kill and cannibalize their enemies and offspring. Her treatments would bring her wealth and prestige, allowing the women to return home cleansed. In return she would allow the tribal king to live. He had to leave, she complained, because since he'd moved to

Gambaga she was no longer getting paid to deal with the witchcraft cases she once had.

One of Gambaga's primary schools is today named Zobzia. It is said that her descendants inherit the genes that rob them of melanin, with every generation producing at least one light-skinned, almost yellow-tinged baby with a soft dusting of curly reddish hair and nearly white eyelashes.

The *gambarana* we met, who was black-skinned and gray-haired, made sure to tell us through a translator that, though he might judge them to be witches, the women living in Gambaga's camp were not prisoners. They were able to come and go as they pleased, he said, but their families didn't want them; they were witches whose people wanted to kill them. We were not the first Westerners to travel to Gambaga, and the *gambarana's* defensiveness made it clear he'd faced uncomfortable questions and criticism from previous white visitors. He wanted to make sure we understood his motives. He was protecting the women, giving them a safe place to stay. Hassan explained that the chief gave the women a portion of the corn and millet he harvested so they would have something to eat.

The *gambarana* would tell us nothing of the ceremonies he performed for the women, nothing about where he got the power to control them. He seemed to speak no English, but carefully monitored the translation nonetheless, barking his corrections and clarifications whether they were needed or not. He unabashedly asked us for money, *kola*, in exchange for taking his picture. *Kola* refers to kola nuts, the bitter, slightly stimulating pink nuts that grow throughout the northern region. Tradition demands that visitors pay homage to the authority of a chief by presenting him with a gift, and in the north it was once custom to present an almond-shaped kola nut, which was then shared with the visitor as a sign of welcome. Although the nuts are still widely available, the tradition has evolved. Over time, and particularly for white visitors, *kola* has come to mean cash.

For some chiefs, charging *kola* was one of the only ways to earn extra money. Four out of five northern men feed their family by farming, having few other means to actually earn an income. Only about 5 percent of all northerners with jobs are considered professionals, administrators, or clerical staff. Teachers and nurses are lumped in with fishermen and *tro-tro* drivers, and together they make up 10 percent of the northern region's workforce. A fraction find work at hotels or restaurants. The remainder who aren't classified as farmers claim to earn an income doing small trading, selling firewood, charcoal, or credit for mobile phones, although these jobs are really done only by women and children. It's a hand-to-mouth existence, and the resulting poverty can be seen in the constellation of bald ringworm scabs crowning the scalps of schoolchildren, the wadded up plastic bags bound with loops of string that stand in for soccer balls. It's the faded "Fabulous at 40!" and McPherson family reunion T-shirts that the young men wear. It's the sloped floors and plastic kettles of water at the communal bathrooms, the women paid the equivalent of a quarter to carry away sloppy buckets of human waste.

We slipped the *gambarana* 50,000 cedi notes, then worth about five dollars, and he sat unsmiling as we took several snapshots in the dimly lit room. I noticed a Sanyo TV set sitting in the corner, a jarring sight in a room made of mud. Out-of-date bank calendars with similarly unsmiling figures dressed in voluminous robes lined one wall. Although we had learned very little, the interview was over and the money was paid, so the *gambarana* granted us permission to speak with the women. I walked away feeling slightly unsettled, as though we had just paid admission to a man who clearly profited from his collection of outcasts, women whose very status as exiles depended on his mysterious powers. It made me think of psychics advertised on late-night infomercials who collected $2.99 for each minute of their advice. The whole camp made me think of an old age home, a place where families could dump their mothers and grandmothers when they became too expensive to feed or too difficult to manage.

We were no clearer on what happened to bring these women to the village, nor what happened to them when arrived, nor if or how they managed to leave. I hoped those answers would come from the women themselves.

There was almost nothing to denote that the tight circle of huts where they lived was different from the rest of the village, except that the mud homes were more compact than the rest, populated only by women and surrounded by mud walls built low enough that neighbors could easily spy in. Spectacularly ugly turkeys with their bald blue heads, wattles of red flesh, and vulture-like plumage pecked at the detritus strewn around the camp, fighting with ducks for a drink from puddles laced with green algae. Although Gambaga is a district center and was once the epicenter of a powerful kingdom fought over by German, French, and British colonialists, its glory has long since faded, leaving rivers of pungent sewage running past crumbling mud homes. There were no doors on which to knock, so Hassan, still acting as our translator, let out a low "Ko-ko-ko" to signify our arrival at the home of Hawa Mahama, the *magazia*, or queen.

The title Queen of the Witches fit her not because of her awesome powers but because of her regal bearing. In my memory Hawa is tall and statuesque, moving with quiet grace around the compound she shared with three other women. She'd been selected by the other accused women to represent their interests, a mirror of the kind of hierarchy that existed outside the camp and a measure of familiarity for its residents. Hawa's shoulders hunched with age. She didn't know how old she was and couldn't remember how many years had passed since she had arrived at the camp. Maybe a decade, maybe two. More likely three or four. Her two sons had been young boys when she left them; now they had two wives each and sons of their own. Hawa wore no earrings but had a string of pale orange beads looped around her neck. She wore a long dress fashioned from a brightly patterned orange-and-blue-splotched African fabric and a green patterned head wrap that hid her graying hair.

A wooden bench was taken from a nearby compound and we sat in Hawa's courtyard in a semicircle, the perfect parody of the "broken telephone" game. Questions asked in my Canadian accent were repeated by Grace in Twi, a language widely spoken in the south, then translated by Hassan into Mampruli, a northern dialect spoken by a few thousand people living in the relatively sparsely populated region. The chief sent a minder, perhaps to monitor our questions but more likely to monitor the women's responses. We were halfway through the interview before I realized that Hawa could not see much more than a few inches in front of her nose; her eyesight was clouded by untreated glaucoma. Crouched on a roughly hewn foot-high wooden stool in the middle of her court-yard, Hawa faced a barrage of questions from an audience she saw only as a blur of shapes and colors.

She spoke softly of a long-ago dream. Her nephew woke one morning and told his father he had seen Auntie in his dream and she'd been trying to strangle him. The boy's premonition was enough for Hawa's brother to accuse her of witchcraft. The strong-willed woman, a popular praise singer who performed at dozens of ceremonies and funerals, lived at the time with her husband and two sons in a village about a half-hour's drive from Gambaga. It was a place with a health clinic and a sprawling primary school but little else. Hawa didn't bother with a trial; her brother's reaction to the dream was enough to convince her that he believed she was a witch. She didn't agree with the accusation, in fact she had no memory of ever wanting to harm the boy, but she walked away from her family, determined to live free at the witch camp rather than under a cloud of suspicion at home.

Behind her four women took little notice of their queen's story as they cracked peanut shells. Without the support of their fami-lies the old women were left to fend for themselves. The chief may have given them a portion of his harvests, but they had to work to survive. They were hired out as farmhands, wandering up and down the rows of corn and bean fields, sometimes dropping seeds into dibbed holes, sometimes chopping weeds from the parched ground. Sometimes they sold water at the market; other times they sat in tight circles, trading gossip as their gnarled fingers husked corn or groundnuts, the peanuts that were a mainstay of the Ghanaian diet. They were responsible for collecting their own firewood and finding their own water for bathing, washing, and cooking. After I moved to Gambaga I would sometimes see them in the muted gray of the predawn darkness, their silhouettes moving in a silent line toward the bush, some of them carrying enormous baskets atop their heads, others balancing bamboo poles several times longer than their diminished frames. Before the heat of the day set in they used the bamboo to shake sausage-shaped *dawadawa* pods from the trees. Over days they ground and dried the beans into a protein-filled mud-colored paste with a pungent, foul smell reminiscent of the odor that wafts from a teenage boy's sneakers.

I had expected the women to admit to some curious coincidences that couldn't quite be explained, to tell breathless tales of dramatic escape from lynch mobs and angry crowds of pitchfork-wielding neighbors. I was disappointed. There was no talk of potions or cauldrons or late-night chanting under stormy skies. There were no confessions to mysterious deaths, unexplained phenomena, or spooky coincidences. There was only flat, emotionless talk of polygamous marriages populated by jealous cowives, of unhappy daughters-in-law, paranoid neighbors, or strange dreams involving sheep, insects, or vultures. An illness or death may have prompted the accusation of witchcraft, but none claimed responsibility for causing it. No one spoke of the chicken sacrifice the chief used to reveal that a woman was a witch. Everything interesting was taboo and therefore secret. The women wouldn't talk about how they came to possess witchcraft nor what the chief did to rid them of it.

To me, informed as I was by a guidebook and the U.S. State Department, the witch camp was a black-and-white issue, a clear human rights violation. The women were denied the right to a fair trial. They were denied the right to live where they chose. They were denied the right to live without violence. At a time in their lives when they should have been hollering after their grandchildren, resting under the shade of the mango trees while they watched their daughters and granddaughters perform the hundreds of tasks that keep an African compound functioning, these emaciated women were working as hard as newlyweds or new mothers. I wondered about the kind of people who could banish a woman because of a dream. Were they unaware that malaria could cause vivid dreams? Or were they simply cruel, showing no remorse or mercy for the women they exiled?

Hawa haunted me. There was something about writing a story like hers that deadened my ability to go back to my job as a health reporter, to writing about the latest cholesterol medications or the West's obesity epidemic. I was convinced, however naïvely, that if a light simply shone on a problem it would somehow convince those willing to care to connect with those who needed it most. I returned to Toronto to stay only long enough to prepare to leave it. I moved back to Africa—the entire continent—and made a slim red backpack my home. I fell into a pattern of travel and writing: to Kenya for cows dying in a drought, to Sierra Leone to attend a diamond university, to Tanzania for tea with AIDS orphans. In Toronto I had moved on autopilot, shuffling through my day without thinking too much about it. But this life required constant focus. It was a visual feast, an assault, a constant challenge to keep up. Walking down the road was like running the gauntlet. Touts called for attention, taxis swerved in hopes of picking up a white passenger, fat market ladies with thighs like rugby running backs presided over massive piles of green pineapples and mountains of plastic flip-flops. Children posed, clapped, shouted: *Mzungu! Obruni!* White man!

There was something about the place, about its stories, that pulled me in, kept me chasing the next *tro-tro*, *matatu*, or *car rapide* into the bush. As friends paired off, settled down, and spoke hopefully about babies, I began to see the parallels to Hawa's decision to leave what she knew and seek a different kind of freedom rather than live a diminished life at home. An accident of birth had put me in a place where I was raised with confidence and determination, with curiosity and drive. But her traits were mine. She was a witch; I was merely independent.

I saw it simply: poverty drove Hawa's family to make an accusation that would force her from the village. Ignorance kept them from understanding that a boy's nighttime visions were nothing more than feverish dreams. An absence of clean water left them open to water-borne bugs like giardia and cholera, whose symptoms could quickly turn fatal. A lack of proper medical attention made them and their loved ones vulnerable to a host of invisible and deadly parasites whose origins were not easy to track.

Elders were supposed to be regarded as wise sages to be revered and respected. It was supposed to take a village, one that included seasoned mothers and grandmothers, to raise a child. Witchcraft, and these witch camps, were a perversion of all that.

When people asked why I stayed in Africa I spoke of Hawa. I wanted to understand what separated us, what made us the same, what really triggered these accusations, why there was such a permanent and pervasive belief in witchcraft. I wanted to know who these women were and what they had done to earn the wrath of their accusers. I wanted to know more about their so-called victims. What was it about these hidden, rural communities that made witchcraft so prevalent? I suspected that these camps had become convenient dumping grounds for old ladies who'd outlived their usefulness. Did people really believe in witchcraft, or was it just superstition?

It hadn't really occurred to me that something concrete fueled this belief, that there was a more basic reason for the persistent belief in witchcraft: things happened in the dark nights that made people afraid.

CHAPTER THREE

ON THE NORTHERN EDGE OF GAMBAGA TOWN, AWAY FROM THE low-walled huts where the women are kept, a bizarre black rock stretches out like a large pond flash-frozen in a windstorm. Pocked and chipped, seemingly charred by the fierce equatorial sun, its dark complexion competes with the rust-colored paths meandering through the vivid green Guinea grasses that swallow sound with their swaying. A stone shaped like a crocodile presides over the blackened rock pond. Time has eroded its snout, rendering whatever sharp teeth it once had smooth and harmless. It looks less like a fearsome river dweller and more like a well-fed lizard. Time has also eroded the details of the legend of the croc, but it remains one of Gambaga's 133 spiritual protectors.

Every night, as I attempted to digest stories told during the day of spiritual cannibalism, of curses that could cost a student her eyesight or ignite the pages of the books she read, I walked alone among the fields of skinny corn stalks to reach this natural statue. I could hear but not see the boys hidden in the bowl of cornfields, racing toy cars fashioned out of empty Coke cans. In the distance I could see girls walking silently through their games, enormous baskets of laundry balanced on their heads. Most nights I was startled by the sudden appearance of farmers quietly returning home from a day in the fields, their bare feet sure and silent as they picked their way through the rocks, carrying handmade hoes slung over their shoulders. They would greet me with a routine set of questions about my health, my family, my home, and my husband, and I would reply to each with a nasally "Naaaaa," meaning all was fine. I knew I was not alone. And yet when I caught sight of shirtsleeves fluttering in the breeze, the waving arms of an industrious scarecrow, the hair on the back of my neck would stand on end.

This creepy feeling was most palpable at night, when the moon stayed low to the horizon and clouds moved dark, heavy and ominous, like silent bulky battleships across the sky. On more sinister nights, with nearby Gambaga village darkened by power cuts, the dust kicked up in the breeze, reaching out and pulling back with ghostly fingers. Sometimes in stages, sometimes with the foreground lit more intensely than the background, sheets of heat lightning would give off a lilac hue that painted the leaves twisting in the breeze. The country was in the grips of a devastating drought and newly planted crops were shriveling beneath the soil. Acacia seeds shook in their pods in cruel imitation of a hard rain, the trees silhouetted in flashes to the left, to the right, directly overhead, spotlighting the underbellies of swooping bats. So much lightning, yet so little noise.

There was something to this place that could be felt but not seen.

SIMON NGOTA ARRIVED IN GAMBAGA IN THE EARLY 1990S, HIS facial scarring and his language marking him as a stranger from further east, where the red rocks of Ghana's northernmost escarpment run to the Togolese border. Simon was raised as a Catholic, and after his father died while Simon was still a boy local priests paid for him to be trained as a catechist.

Christian religions had once rooted out witches and heretics in Europe and America, publicly tortured them and burned them on stakes, but most African churches didn't preach against the existence of witchcraft. In some of the megachurches in Accra, under the vast domes where evangelists described themselves as bishops or prophets and didn't align themselves with Protestant or Catholic churches, parishioners would actually be pulled from the congregation and labeled as witches. A popular church service televised on Sunday mornings garnered huge ratings by drawing tearful young women from the audience, then beginning the healing processes with the laying on of hands and shouted commands for the offending demons to clear off.

The church, whether Catholic or charismatic, was seen as offering protection from witches, so followers had nothing to fear. Again and again Christians told me they believed in witchcraft but didn't worry about it, leaving a gruesome mental picture with their reassurance that their safety came from being "covered in the blood of Jesus."

Simon was such a good student that his mother worried he too would take the vows of a priest, never marry and never provide her with grandchildren. But the lonely life of a cleric didn't interest Simon; in fact he had the forethought to keep all of his report cards so he could one day show his own children that he had been "a bright, conscientious student who made good decisions."

In his heart Simon is a farmer, a man whose best days are spent crop-touring from the driver's seat of a slow-moving vehicle. In the late 1970s he was hired to teach blind men to farm in a remote northwestern village by laying out yards of string knotted with bits of nutshell. He guided the men with his voice, encouraging them to tuck seeds into the ground when they felt the next nutshell marker. He was so successful at improving their onion production that Ghana's former military dictator awarded him with a medal. Since he'd arrived in the village alone, the village's chief, a Muslim man with eight wives and fifty-four children, offered to have one of his daughters cook Simon's meals, clean his house, and wash his clothes. Evelyn was a tall, soft-eyed, sweet-tempered teenager, and Simon spent his nights flirting with her under the pretense of learning the local language. Soon he couldn't imagine life without her. He paid for her to attend sewing classes, which Evelyn abandoned with relief when she fell pregnant. Simon's first wife had stayed behind in his ancestral northeastern village, where she nursed a sickly new-born. She agreed to the polygamous marriage and bore the former Catholic catechist more children, but she hasn't shared a home with Simon since. Evelyn converted to Christianity and became her co-wife. When Simon began working at the witch camp in Gambaga, it was Evelyn and their infant daughter who moved with him to the concrete blockhouse built specially for the little family on the westernmost edge of town.

Simon was hired to work for the Presbyterian church, at what the church dubbed the Gambaga Outcast Home, more cleverly called GO Home when the chief was out of earshot. His job was to sort out what transpired to bring the women to the witch camp, then advocate for them to be returned to their families and villages. He would travel to impossibly remote villages, to sit with chiefs and accusers and family members and try to convince them that the accused woman no longer posed any danger. He felt sorry for the women, he said, and believed they needed to be shown compassion. His willingness to work with the accused women had the village believing he too was a powerful witch.

Outside the small house there was enough acreage to plant corn or beans and a yard large enough to keep hogs and dogs and a few *jatropha* bushes, whose branches Simon chewed to pulpy slivers to clean his teeth. Steps from his backdoor he built two even smaller concrete rooms, one outfitted with a thick padlock to store food rations and the other painted deep blue and decorated with posters warning against lynching suspected witches. Two showed a woman being beaten by young men with sticks and rocks and warned, "This could be your mother." Another cautioned that lynching and brand-ing are crimes, that anyone found beating up old ladies could face assault charges. The last reminded readers that all women deserve love and respect. The figures in each were pinched-looking, with squinty eyes and twig-like limbs.

Over the years Simon had designed a standard set of questions, approaching the women and their banishment with the kind of clinical detachment he thought befit social workers. His disinterest in the nature of the accusation squelched the salaciousness of the process. He wanted to know the banalities on which the woman's return hinged: Was the accuser still alive? Did the accusation prove true? Was it possible for a son, brother, or husband to argue for the woman's release? Could he provide protection and support for the old woman after she returned home? In a little more than a decade Simon had reunited more than two hundred women with their nervous families, making numerous trips to assuage fears of further attacks. He organized workshops that brought together traditional leaders in all their finery, gave speeches to discourage violence, and arranged seminars about fevers and malaria and the effect they could have on one's dreams. His predecessor had lasted only a few months before she ran from the village complaining of the chief's moody temper; Simon had worked for thirteen years with the *gambarana*, using the sort of diplomatic skills made famous by his fellow countryman, former United Nations secretary-general Kofi Annan.

Simon described himself as a social worker, and although he didn't have the credentials to make the claim experience had taught him more about witchcraft accusations than anyone in the country. "I am one of you," he would tell traditional leaders attending his anti-witchcraft meetings. "We are not against anything but violence. Sometimes the young people want to beat the old ladies. It is better to refer these cases to your chief and, if he decides, to send them to Gambaga." He would nod at them reverently. "That is what I came to take the opportunity to tell my fathers, who are my elders."

Evelyn taught me what she knew about witchcraft as she went about her daily chores. She had once dreamed of a black cat, she told me while crushing hot peppers against the rough surface of a mortar stone. In her dream she picked up a broom and began beating the cat, only to jump back in surprise when it transformed into one of the women living at the camp. Evelyn believed the woman haunted her dreams out of jealousy; Simon may have cared for them in the way of a doting husband, but she was his real wife. On another day, while Evelyn sluiced compost for the family's pig, I was reminded that witchcraft meant worshipping a fallen angel. Dripping laundry provided the backdrop to another day's conversation, this one about a witch's tools. Evelyn snapped sheets as she spoke of the bowls, knives, or cloths that helped a woman transport herself to the spiritual realm, fly across the sky, or hurt her victims.

Now a mother to four children and likely somewhere in her forties, Evelyn still prayed five times a day, sending her list of wants and needs to Jesus. She worried about me being unmarried and childless and told me often that her prayers were for Jesus to send me a husband and a half-dozen babies. She had to borrow money to buy her daughter's schoolbooks but splurged on beautiful blue batik fabric to make into a short-sleeved jacket and matching long skirt for my birthday. When I tried on the outfit I discovered that she had very thoughtfully sewn in pregnancy panels and a forgiving elastic waistband, "just in case!"

She had not carried a child to term in six years, and it weighed heavily on her. She longed for another baby and prayed fervently for it each day, even though her husband was nearly sixty and already had ten children, some with children of their own. It upset them both, this mysterious infertility. They were clearly able to make children, but for some reason Evelyn's last two pregnancies had ended in miscarriage. They were both strong and healthy; they worked hard and were respected by their neighbors. They attended the Presbyterian church every Sunday and raised their children to be God-fearing. Neither could understand why they'd lost the ability to make a baby.

Simon referred to his heyday as "back when there was hair," when he sported a clownish cloud of wiry black hair. Now he kept his receding white hair cropped close to his skull. He had the slight potbelly of a man well fed, but money slipped through his fingers. Simon's house contained almost no furniture, just a few mattresses on the floor, a couple of plastic chairs, and a wooden dresser piled high with folded laundry. A large TV sitting in the corner was fried during an electrical storm, but he had never found the money to repair or replace it. His children, like all children, seemed to be in constant need of medications, schoolbooks, money for uniforms, a new pair of shoes, or a less-worn pair of trousers. Maintaining his aging red motorbike and keeping the family fed seemed to eat up his wages.

Although the Presbyterian church once paid him a decent salary, tensions led to his funders pulling their support. An expert came to review the project—there was some concern about a Christian organization working with a chief who called himself Muslim—and in the midst of the dispute Simon lost the vehicle provided for the project. We agreed that in exchange for his help with my research I would buy back his beloved truck, a beat-up thirteen-year-old Hilux held together by duct tape and prayer, so rusted it looked like it had been shot up in a gun battle, and give it to Simon and his family.

Simon handled the vehicle gingerly, refusing to go much beyond forty miles an hour, accelerating only when he was about to be overtaken by another car or when I'd look pointedly at his right foot. Whenever we chanced to reach our destination without a tire puncture or oil leak or the truck bursting into flames, as happened twice in our travels, Simon was moved to offer thanks to a higher power. "We praise God for delivering us safely," he'd murmur as he gently switched off the engine.

There was something about riding in the old truck that put Simon in a confessional mood. As he settled into fourth gear the flat, dry landscape and furrowed fields rolled past, looking bruised under a punishing sun. Puddles of dark shadow pooled under the outstretched arms of the occasional almond tree. He told me he was considering taking another wife. Evelyn didn't want another cowife, but he wanted more children. His first wife could no longer produce children and he was beginning to suspect that Evelyn couldn't give him any more either. I tried to gently dissuade him from fathering more children, pointing to his age, his finances, and the fact that he was already a grandfather. I saw children as an expense, whereas he saw them as insurance.

His willingness to work with me put the accused women at ease. They trusted and respected Simon and had come to see him as their husband, telling him their stories and secrets. They would often wake him at 4 a.m., tapping at his screen door in the darkness to ask for a lift to the hospital or money to pay for medication. I also needed Simon to make sense of witchcraft. He could help unravel the proverbs and riddles that couched talk of witchcraft and travel with me to the other camps hidden in Ghana's northern region. He introduced me to Carlos Akuka, a teacher in training at the college in Tamale who considered himself born-again and avidly attended the Presbyterian church. Carlos spoke five languages and became my translator. I also became his student: in dozens of candid conversations about his own experience of witchcraft, he taught me more than I expected about the depth of the belief.

Simon identified more than a dozen women whose stories he wanted me to hear. There was Ayishetu, chased from her village by a violent mob, whose life was destroyed by the accusation that she practiced witchcraft, and Winangi, a tiny splinter of a woman who'd gone seeking witchcraft to protect herself and her children. She pleaded with her husband to move her to the camp when she felt she'd lost control of the dark gift. A smart businesswoman named Asara had ended up at the camp when a debtor accused her of causing a meningitis outbreak. Napoa, mannish and grumpy, readily identified herself as a witch and caused fear among the other women living at the camp.

Simon wouldn't say whether he believed in witchcraft. He dreamed of starting his own charity to help reunite the women with their families and planned to set it up somewhere with fertile fields, away from the chief and his temper. Whenever I asked whether he believed the women were witches, he diplomatically dodged the question. "Whether you accept it or you don't accept it, the issue is still there," he said. "However you think about it, you have to accept it because it's generally accepted in Africa."

THE GAMBAGA OUTCAST HOME, AS THE WITCH CAMP IS MORE formally known, traces its roots back several generations to a time when it was commonplace to simply kill a suspected witch, some-

times by fire or stonings or beatings or other torturous tests intended to reveal whether a woman possessed witchcraft. The *zobzia*
and her descendants were renowned for their ability to identify and
control witches, but the village became a safe haven only a few generations ago, after an accused woman threw herself at the mercy of
the town's Muslim cleric, the current imam's great-grandfather, as
he walked with his entourage to the neighboring town. The con-
demned woman clutched him about the knees, a daring move since
almost no one was permitted to touch the region's spiritual leaders,
and sobbed that she and her young son were about to be killed. She
begged him to spare her life. The imam had the woman and her son
swear on the Quran that they wouldn't commit witchcraft again,
then sheltered the woman at the mosque. She earned her keep as a
cleaner and her son became a Muslim scholar. Within a few years
the grounds of the mosque were crowded with banished women.

They were moved to the colony and placed under the *gambarana's* control after a dispute between the imam and the *nayiri*, the
region's ultimate tribal leader. I was told the *nayiri* had also grown
tired of being woken by the call to prayer and saw the loss of the free
labor of the accused women as a fitting punishment for the noisy
mosque.

The call to prayer still reverberates over Gambaga, book-ended
by an air-conditioned administrative building to the east and, to the
west, a sleepy police checkpoint that is the legacy of the surprisingly
violent and volatile tribal skirmishes that have plagued the north
for decades. Gambaga's paved main street takes ten minutes to cross
on foot, fifteen minutes in the heat of the day. At the western end
of town is a tiny post office, a low-slung jail with windows the size
of shoeboxes, a soccer pitch where donkeys, goats, and sheep graze,
the bright yellow Zobzia elementary school, and a library full of
outdated Dutch and English children's books. At the town's center
is a bank with a Western Union outlet, where transactions move in
only one direction: in.

Life revolves around the market, a collection of wooden tables
where salty seasonings, canned tomato paste, and rice, cassava, and

yams are traded for a few pennies. Ingredients of everyday survival are sold in single servings to put their cost within reach. Coins are traded for quick-burning candles, thumb-size bags of salt, palm-size bags of laundry soap, a single egg, three tablespoons of vegetable oil, cigarettes by the stick, rice by the cupful, or clean drinking water doled out in stretchy plastic bags. Most people eat what they grow and pray for enough surplus to fund life's extras, but they survive only because emergency food relief arrives during the aptly named lean season. Only the occasional hum of a motorbike, the vibrant, synthetic materials of the secondhand clothing, and the blaring, tinny noise of a handheld radio break the spell of what could otherwise seem like medieval times.

WITCHCRAFT IS ANCHORED IN THE IDEA THAT WE LIVE IN TWO worlds simultaneously: the world we see and the unseen world that flows around us. Spirits that can be appeased and directed populate that second realm. The two worlds spill into one another; disharmony between the two can cause life in one to end in the other. Without a healthy spirit the physical self will die, and vice versa.

Because this spiritual energy moves through people and objects, a spirit might take up residence in the dense branches of a tree, a slow-moving turtle, or a crocodile-shaped stone like the one that protected Gambaga village. To honor and satisfy the spirits with sacrifices and ceremonies is to position oneself to receive their blessings. Shrines are erected as places where offerings and sacrifices can be made in hopes a spirit will direct its energy to the prosperity, good health, and good fortune of those who worship it.

It's believed that all people are bestowed with a particular gift, whether strength or intelligence, a clear singing voice, a talent for carving, the innate knowledge of herbs, or something more nebulous, such as a closer relationship with the spiritual realm. The gifts are interdependent—one relies on the gift of another to survive—but those with the ability to see into the spiritual realm and slip easily between the two worlds are considered born leaders and often become chiefs. They excel at ruling the people around them because their divine gift allows them to travel into the spirit world and seek the wisdom of the ancestors. The powers of these born leaders are seen as protective; they are used to promote harmony between the two worlds, to interpret the wishes of the ancestors and direct the sacrifices and rituals meant to honor them. But the natural world is a place of balance: if there are forces in the world working for something, it stands to reason that there are equal but opposite forces working against it as well.

Witchcraft was once seen as purely divine, a gift passed through the family line that flourished under the tutelage of those who also possessed it. But the upheaval and chaos of the slave raids and the swift societal changes brought by white men with ledgers and laws changed how people perceived this gift. As society became more secularized and resources grew scarce with the pressure of one community bumping up against another, it became more difficult to find favor with the ancestors. By rewarding those willing to work as accountants or clerks colonialism broke down the rigorous African hierarchy that held villages and tribes together, eroding the traditional authority and respect shown to chiefs and elders. People resorted to using mystical powers to ensure they would thrive.

The easiest way to success was to clear the path of competitors. It wasn't so much a means of protection as a way to make your own family or farm stronger than your neighbor's. Talismans stuffed with herbs, blessed with incantations, and stitched up with animal skins were worn as a sign of the protection of powerful witchcraft, or *juju*. More dangerous were the invisible talismans said to be tucked up inside witchcraft's most powerful practitioners. They were carried inside the body, where they could not be dislodged. Deadly witchcraft became a means to command power and respect.

There developed a notion that one could acquire witchcraft instead of being born with it, but the dark, self-interested craft, focused solely on destroying enemies, came at a terrible cost. Witches were spiritual cannibals, capturing souls in the spiritual realm to feed the insatiable appetite that came with initiation into a coven.

At night they roamed the rocky grounds of the spiritual realm, feasting on the flesh of their victims. In northern Ghana those victims were most likely to come from the witch's own family. They dreamed they were being tormented, chased by sharp-clawed birds, or herded like cattle or sheep. Victims of witchcraft looked for signs of attack: bite marks still pressed faintly into the flesh or seeping wounds that refused to heal. They grew thin and listless. All were signs that a witch was slowly siphoning a person's spirit. Spiritual death was quickly followed by physical death.

Witchcraft gradually divided into two opposing camps: the herbalists or witchdoctors, who used their natural abilities to divine and cure, and the witches, who used their natural abilities to hurt. Over time it further divided along gender lines: men were leaders and healers, and, with few exceptions, women were witches. Because a witch's attack could be fought off only with more powerful witchcraft, victims sought the help of powerful witchdoctors. These men peered into the spiritual realm to see who was responsible for "catching" the soul, then provided *juju*, items or mantras imbued with magic, as protection in these pitched spiritual battles.

Witches are not easily recognized, but certain traits are interpreted as signs of spiritual powers. They are usually women, frequently crippled or disfigured, often elderly, ugly, or prone to strange behavior. The mentally ill are possessed. Even the brave, aggressive, and demanding are worthy of suspicion since it's commonly assumed their confidence comes from their powers. Because anyone can buy witchcraft, everyone is suspect.

It's difficult to speak of fireballs and elderly women committing spiritual cannibalism without sounding sensational, skeptical, or absurd. That is part of the reluctance to speak about witchcraft. Colonial administrators once used the belief to justify oppression, arguing that people who believed in the invisible magic of witches could not be rational enough to govern themselves. It plays to all the worst stereotypes of Africa, suggesting an exotic mysticism that preys on primitive thinking. In a society where there are no coincidences, where every action is linked to one that came before it and no death is considered accidental, witchcraft provides an answer to the very difficult question "Why?" In such a place witchcraft is a necessary element of understanding the unfolding of one's fate. It's a complex way of thinking that links the spiritual and physical worlds, giving people a sense of their place in the universe and a set of social rules and values that allow them to survive powers both seen and unseen that work both for and against them.

CHAPTER FOUR

My translator, Carlos, disagreed with the gingerly way I conducted my initial interviews with the accused women living at the Gambaga camp. I wanted them to trust me enough to open up to me, to tell me how it felt to be labeled a witch, how it felt to watch their family and neighbors turn against them. I wanted to know whether they felt the accusation was fair or based on a simple misunderstanding, or whether it was something more.

Mostly I wanted to keep an open mind. I didn't believe the women actually flew through the night to feast on the flesh of their children. I thought their dreams were the same as mine, images created by a mind struggling with worry or anxiety. I was more interested in what motivated people to make an accusation and what happened to a woman who accepted the judgment of a dead bird. I went to the women bearing no gifts and offering no cash, although I suspected experience with other journalists and budding anthropology students had taught them that they would eventually be rewarded. I wanted the women to speak to me simply because they wanted to, because they saw me as sympathetic. Carlos, an exceedingly polite evangelical Christian who laughed easily and never tired of trying to convince me to join him in church, believed my sympathy was misplaced. He goaded me during interviews, pressing me to ask tougher questions. "Maybe you could ask her how she chooses her victims and how she kills them," he suggested during one interview.

Carlos's heart would not be softened, no matter how pitiful the story. To him every woman in the camp was a witch delivered to the *gambarana* for a reason. He wanted me to clear from my eyes the romance of the north's exoticism and see the reality around me. "In the local context the person you can trust the least is the person closest to you," he said. Distrust and paranoia had deep roots. The person who makes him most suspicious is also the person he considers his best friend. He lowered his voice: People poison each other here in the north. It happens a lot. That's why a person offering another a cup of water will drink from it first, he said, to prove that there is nothing wrong with it. It's wise, he counseled, to be wary whenever someone brings you food.

I shouldn't be deceived by the simplicity of life in the north, by the mud huts and the low-tech farms, he warned me. A dangerous knowledge was hidden in these rural villages. It was like moving to a shiny new subdivision and realizing that all my smiling neighbors hid a sinister secret. I asked how he could live in a place with such mistrust. "Somehow," he answered, revealing nothing.

I brought up Hawa Mahama, the beloved and blind old *magazia* who had attended Carlos's church, arriving every Sunday to sing with gusto from the white plastic patio chairs that stood in for pews. Surely she was only a sweet old lady who'd fallen victim to circumstance, I said. His face split into a wide grin, thinking I was joking. That's what they want you to think, he said.

Carlos could take my gentle ribbing about witchcraft; he could see the contradiction in distrusting one's best friend. When my mind simply couldn't see beyond the irrationality of a particular accusation he could laugh with me. But he took the threat of witches seriously. He taught me that witchcraft could be picked up anywhere. It could slide down the coil of DNA shared between a mother and her daughter, pass in a quiet moment from a midwife to a newborn. It could be instantly transferred on a slick of sweat, coated on a coin found in the street, ingested in an otherwise innocuous snack offered by a stranger. It could be passed without a person's knowledge, her dreams suddenly cluttering up with strange and violent images, without any sense of where it came from, how to use it, or how to get rid of it.

To Carlos the dangers were everywhere. I should never give money to someone I didn't know, he advised, nor accept money from a stranger. "That might be the start of many woes," he said, explaining that passing money to beggars was known as "the debt of my hand." The bill could easily be carried off to the fetish priest to make *juju*, leaving the do-gooder to watch helplessly as his good fortune was transferred to the beggar. "Your star that is bright could be made dim through the acts of the fetish priest," Carlos said.

I had already learned that witchcraft was mostly confined to women. Men who possessed special powers used them to build up their reputation. If they relied on *juju* to find their success they were revered, even feared. If they were particularly powerful they hung a shingle and advertised their services as a witchdoctor, promising herbal remedies and spiritual muscle.

Most women banished to the Gambaga camp claimed to know nothing of the supernatural, shrugging their shoulders with innocence when asked about witchcraft. They blamed their exile on a jealous cowife or a sickly child. Women sent to witch camps were usually widows or women who'd passed into menopause without the blessing of a son. Some were unusually good with money and often found themselves accused of witchcraft when it came time for family or neighbors to repay loans. A few had lost favor in their family because they spoke up for themselves, demanding property or other inheritances due to them. Most were seen as quarrelsome, causing problems for their husband and his other wives. For someone raised outside a culture permeated with witchcraft it was easy to believe that the witch camp was nothing more than a convenient place to send difficult women. Then I met Napoa Dermongso.

Napoa's dreams had always been dark and restless, filled with violence and danger. Late at night, in the dark recesses of her mind, splinters flew as trees were felled. In her dream state she picked up a

heavy axe and gleefully smashed logs into matchsticks. Vultures circled in the bluish midnight light overhead, shrieking as they ripped
at the flesh of their terrified victims. Talons tore into screaming
pigs. Fallen cattle or sheep lay dying on a rocky riverside landscape
that was both disturbing and familiar.

Napoa saw herself roaming freely among the mayhem, always in
high spirits and in the company of the same handful of people. She
woke in the morning with the hazy, cobwebby feeling of a drunk,
exhausted from the carefree carousing of her dreams. In the first
moments of wakefulness the night's exploits came slowly into focus,
like the twist of a camera lens.

During the day she raised her children's children and her cowives' children, washed and mended clothing, carried water and
wood, tended fields, turned the crops into weighty meals and precious food stores. During the day she was like every other married
woman in her tiny village, sharing her husband and their compound
with a handful of cowives. There was little to set her life apart from
the women around her. But she spoke wistfully about her dreams
the way a junkie describes a heroin high: the nights were an explo-
sion of eye-popping color, debauched, leering faces, a scramble of
high-octane excitement. Invincibility. Power. Pleasure. The insatiable appetite. That gnawing, desperate need for more, more, more.
And then the morning would creep up, guilt dragging like a heavy
yoke, anchoring her to her nighttime deeds.

Most nights her cowife's daughter nestled beside her on a thin
plastic mat, sleeping soundly as the older woman dreamed. The girl
adored Napoa and followed her everywhere, quick to offer her help,
a shy smile on her face. Napoa loved her as though she had carried
the child in her own womb. The girl had been born to the third of
Napoa's five cowives, but it was Napoa she called mother.

The girl was ten when she first appeared in Napoa's dreams.
Napoa counted her own age by the number of chiefs she had survived and figured she was about fifty, since she'd outlived five traditional leaders. She had an anxious, mannish face and wore a
kaleidoscope of colors: a housedress awash in red roosters, a peach

skirt, a string of small yellow and green beads, a faded white head wrap. A deep scar swooped across her left cheek. She had large arms and masculine hands and was missing her top teeth on the left side. When asked about her children, she answered, "Alive."

In the dream Napoa saw herself transform the girl's spirit into a fowl and her own into a hawk. Then, following the bird's natural instinct for prey, Napoa went hunting, tearing through the dark sky over the rocky ground of the riverbed, wheeling over slow-moving cattle and sheep, intent on the tiny chick. When Napoa awoke, shivering, she sadly told her husband, "A hawk has caught a certain fowl."

The little girl grew lean; within three days she was dead.

Napoa believed she'd killed the girl she once loved like a daughter using a dark magic that had plagued her since her teenage years, when she first began dreaming of dangerously thrilling, heart-pumping nighttime feats of destruction that seemed, in the heat of the moment, to have no consequences.

Napoa kept to herself around the witch camp. A woman who shared her compound needled her, interrupting with snide insults as Napoa told her story. Napoa's face remained blank, as though she had long ago built up a barrier against the woman's words. Her lips pursed as questions were put to her. An inappropriate chuckle, a kind of tired, bemused laugh, escaped from her as though she could not quite believe the things she was being asked nor the things she was saying.

"People know that she still practices the witchcraft," Carlos translated for her. "She can dream and see herself. When she dreams, the craft can take her to a particular location where she sees herself perform or doing certain bad acts she herself doesn't like. She can see herself going to the children and harming the children, which she doesn't like. She sees herself in the company of cattle or sheep, and the witches will be roaming together. She sees herself at the riverside, on the rocky ground, which she doesn't like. She doesn't like it because she thinks it's better to lie at a particular spot and enjoy your sleep rather than roaming around. She can just see herself holding meat, not knowing what kind of meat that she's holding, and she can just be walking and see a particular company and then they will give her meat. She doesn't have any knowledge about it."

Carlos interpreted the dreams: the witches transformed their human prey into sheep and cattle. The meat the women held represented their victims' souls. They were most likely to attack their own family, he said, to prove their loyalty to their coven. The "particular company" portioning out the meat in her dreams were the women who were part of Napoa's coven.

Napoa had been sent to live at the Gambaga camp twice before, exiled first by her eldest son after he complained that she was stalking him in his dreams. She couldn't remember how long she stayed before her husband arranged for her release, but the second time she was sent home without performing the final sacrament, a traditional ceremony involving the slaughter of a sheep and the ritualistic shaving of the woman's head. Napoa begged her family to return her to Gambaga to perform the ritual, believing that her witchcraft would return without it, but they refused. They had already paid the *gambarana* for her liberation and feared he would charge an even larger sum for the ceremony.

It worried her, Simon said later, the idea that she was still imbued with witchcraft. "She thought she would be able to be rid of it, but she went home and it was still there." When I next met with Napoa, Simon offered to translate and their familiarity seemed to make her speak more openly. After the little girl died Napoa voluntarily returned to the witch camp without protest, her heart heavy with guilt. "She didn't want to get the girl," Simon translated. "She loved that girl so much. She was so dear to her. She was always in her room; they were all calling her mother. She didn't like doing that thing."

When they are sentenced to live at the camp the women take part in a complicated ritual in which they're given a concoction of bitter, often nauseating herbs to drink. It's hoped that inducing vomiting will dislodge whatever magical amulets or charms an accused woman might be hiding and that might be the source of her power. Splashes of alcohol are spilled on the ground to marry the woman and the village's spiritual protectors together. She lives with the knowledge that if she practices witchcraft again the spirits will hunt her down and kill her. It is this belief, that the women can be controlled by violent, vengeful spirits, that makes the witch camps a viable alternative to lynching.

Napoa, however, saw these spirits as large snakes, and in her dream state she simply hopped over them on her way to the rocky riverbed. She claimed that she owned no talismans and had no idea how she came to possess witchcraft in the first place. Her mother was accused and sent to be tested before the *gambarana* when a man from their village became sick, so she figured she might have been born with it. Simon grilled her on this point, as he was convinced she was hiding something that helped her perform witchcraft, even though they had twice cleaned and cleared her hut in the witch camp. She insisted she was hiding nothing and would gladly have given it up if it meant ending her torment.

Then she remembered dreaming when she returned home from her first stay at the camp that she was conversing with "a certain man," a man belonging to her coven whom she refused to identify. He threw something in her mouth, which lodged in her throat. It happened so quickly she wasn't able to refuse or prevent it. Her powers grew. Now when she dreams she sees herself watching her children at their homes and knows she is still doing witchcraft. She fears that the dreams are a premonition that she is unwittingly planning an attack against her children.

"So you see, it's not easy to get rid of because it's not on the outside," Simon said.

She laughed resignedly when I asked why she swallowed whatever the man threw. "It's not how we're sitting here," Simon translated for her. "It was a spiritual thing. He threw the thing in her throat, and it's not like she can say no. It's spiritual. They were conversing and it happened very fast."

Napoa had not had a peaceful night's sleep at the camp, confessing that she knew from her dreams that she was still "roaming everywhere," a euphemism for carousing with her coven. When she woke up she sat looking sour-faced and glum in the doorway of her small, blackened hut. Simon was so worried about her he talked about arranging for a psychiatrist to visit. It was a nice thought, but amounted to empty words. The church was barely paying Simon, and even though I saw him slip the occasional bill to women needing medication or taxi rides to the hospital, there simply wasn't enough money to consider consulting a psychiatrist. The majority of the country's doctors are based in the south, and besides, the Ministry of Health has only two clinical psychiatrists, one-tenth of what is needed.

"The way it is, she cannot think of going home again," Simon said. "Her children don't visit here, they fear her. She herself does not want to go. If there's a way for her witchcraft to be reduced, then her brother says she can go to [live with him], but she doesn't know how she could do it."

ALTHOUGH SOME WOMEN, LIKE NAPOA, DREADED THEIR ABILI-ties and desperately wanted to be rid of them, others actually sought out witchcraft. It was strange to live among women whose lives had been shattered by dark magic and hear the claim that anyone could, or would, willingly acquire it. Until I lived in the north and saw firsthand the hardness of a woman's life I couldn't understand why anyone would want something that came with the risk of unwit-tingly using it against one's children. Witchcraft brought with it the ethical dilemma of whether one could live with the guilt of actually using its powers to harm. It also arrived with the nagging anxiety that it would never be enough, that an enemy would be armed with something more powerful, more destructive. But witchcraft could be purchased.

Winangi Azum went in search of witchcraft as her husband slid into a haze of alcoholism, fearing that she and her children were vulnerable to curses cast by her in-laws. She had been married to a chief, but when that man died she married a farmer with a fondness for palm wine, who grew millet, maize, groundnuts, and yam. He added another wife, then another. Winangi shook her head when asked whether she agreed to the polygamous marriage; she and her cowives fought constantly. She bore her husband eight children, including two sets of twins, but because she was a widow her husband did not treat her with the respect of a senior wife, and neither did her cowives.

"She and the rival were always quarreling, quarreling," Simon said for her. "But her husband loved her so much before they came."

Winangi wore a loop of green and blue beads at her throat, and another of yellow and red. Two rings circled her middle right finger, and giant gold hoops were threaded through her ears. She had browned teeth, but a complete set. She pointed to a scar that left a raised bump on the leanest part of her right shin, a sore that she scratched and scratched until it became swollen and infected. She sought treatment from a witchdoctor in the nearby town of Nakpanduri, who told her that if she'd been a child she would have been killed by the infection. It was obvious she was strong, he said, and he offered her the chance to become even stronger, using witchcraft.

That was perhaps thirty years ago, about the time she first noticed that her husband "suffered from problems when he was drunk." He was abusive to the children and insulted her, she said. His brothers had given her herbs to bathe him in, a common kind of folk remedy, but she began to suspect that they were the problem. Her brothers-in-law were using the herbs to bewitch her husband until it seemed he was mentally ill. Paranoia drove her to find the witchdoctor and invest in protective black magic. "She felt that if she doesn't also make herself strong, they may also try to hunt her and her children," Simon translated for her.

Winangi was thinking of her children when she gathered together a fowl, a sheep, a cloth of mixed colors, and the equivalent of about eight dollars, an amazing sum back then, especially for a woman. After a visit from the witchdoctor, during which he slaughtered the animals Winangi had assembled, she could suddenly see into the spiritual realm and soon found she was traveling in her sleep. It was the classic sign of witchcraft, and for years Winangi considered it money well spent. Her children grew. Her cowife moved back to her parents. Then Winangi felt control of the dark gift slipping away. She traveled to Nakpanduri to learn how to regain it, but by then the old witchdoctor had died. With time she began seeing her sleeping children in her dreams. When her son caught sight of her in his sleep he angrily accused her of trying to harm him.

"She wouldn't have taken it if she knew," Simon explained. "She didn't know she would 'chop' her children."

Winangi came to live at the camp at her own insistence, seeking to clear her head and calm her jittery nerves. She had a sense that she was being chased and couldn't sleep. "Her heart was panicking," Simon explained. "She was very, very lean, and anytime she would try to sleep she would see things are standing in her room around her, trying to grab her."

Months after arriving at the camp she was still quite thin. She sat in Simon's tiny blue office like a schoolgirl, her knees tucked up under her chin. Winangi had first come to my room at the guesthouse at the edge of Gambaga, knocking on the screen door shortly after four in the morning. It was the quietest part of her day, before the rest of the camp awoke, before she got too busy with planting or weeding, the manual jobs she took on to survive. Simon had accompanied her, and he called softly through the window, his voice drifting into my dreams. I groggily asked to meet later, after the afternoon's call to prayer, when I was awake.

One had only to look at the lives of northern women to appreciate why, despite the fear of being unmasked, of being killed or banished, of the worry that one would lose control, as Napoa and Winangi had, and turn on a cherished son or daughter, witchcraft still held a particular kind of lure. Northern women are praised when they're respectful and industrious, but a woman's status in the community depends on her age, the number of male children she's raised, and the importance of her husband. If he is a chief she automatically feels the respect of her colleagues. If he is a lazy drunkard who squanders the family's fortunes she feels the sting of disgrace.

Women have no ability to speak for themselves, no avenue to influence the decisions being made for them. When quarrels arise among women competing for attention and desperate for respect, they have no obvious path to resolution. Culture doesn't allow them to take their problems to the chief, nor are they permitted to sit at the traditional court and ask for a solution. If a premature death, the arrival of a new wife, or an intractable disagreement pushes a woman away from the safety of her husband's compound, her father's home, or her brother's farm, she is as vulnerable as a newborn.

Babies born in Ghana's northern villages are usually doused in water infused with herbs and blessed by traditional healers, or witchdoctors, hours after their birth. The babies wear belts of little leather squares stitched up around herbs and small scrolls decorated with ancient mantras, talismans meant to protect them from evil spirits. From the time they're born they are immersed in witchcraft. The charms don't always work their magic: northern Ghana is one of the world's deadliest places for infants and toddlers. UNICEF estimates that with their little bodies weakened by chronic hunger 76,000 Ghanaian children, more than 10 percent of babies born in the country each year, will succumb to any one of a long list of viruses, parasites, and other invisible killers before their fifth birthday. Their mothers are equally at risk: between 28,000 and 117,000 women are left disabled each year from trying to carry on their husband's line; one in thirty-five will die in the effort. Statistics are so imprecise because so few women in rural regions actually deliver their babies in places where medical information is recorded. It's thought that another 1,400 to 3,900 Ghanaian women will die within forty-two days of giving birth.

A girl born mewling and unwanted into the already crowded mud hut of a hungry northern family at the height of the lean season will learn how to balance water in a bucket on her head before she learns the letters that make up her name. At an age when she still shares a sleeping mat with her siblings, when her spine is still soft and growing, a girl born in the north will often be sent south to work as a housemaid for a rich relative or live on the streets and work as a *kayayo*, a kind of porter ferrying the heavy loads of truck drivers and bulk buyers from the truck to the market stall and sometimes back again. She will literally use her head to earn her keep. Mere pennies will amass over weeks of grueling work, and they will quickly be eaten up by her daily costs: food to eat, a place to sleep, a few moments of peace in the public bathroom, a bucket of water to bathe and rinse her clothing.

It can be dangerous, back-breaking work, but for most northern girls it is the only way to build the capital they need to make themselves eligible for marriage, the only way to equip their kitchens with flat wooden spoons, deep tin cooking pots, and colorful plastic buckets. They'll grow up on the streets, sleeping like a litter of kittens huddled into one another for warmth and protection, before returning to their father's village to be traded for a decent dowry.

Even the northern Ghanaian girls lured into the classroom by promises of Dutch food rations or bicycles donated by a Kiwi soprano singer are more likely to get pregnant and drop out than graduate from high school. In the time I lived in Gambaga only 575 girls across the entire country were enrolled in secondary school. Fewer than 10 percent of all women born and raised in northern Ghana are able to read or write.

Born into poverty, bartered into polygamy, treated as little more than beasts of burden, useful in the absence of machinery and essential to the manufacture of more sons, many women living in northern Ghana are entitled to little more than a lifetime of servitude. It's no wonder that, like Winangi, they reach for whatever lifelines they're offered. Socially powerless and facing a hard life lived on the shaky ground of polygamy, women reach for witchcraft's promises of power and respect, for the guarantee of protection in a world they have been raised to believe is too dangerous or unwieldy to be lived in alone.

W<small>HEN A GROUP OF SEVENTY-TWO</small> P<small>RESBYTERIAN</small> "<small>PRAYER WAR-</small> riors" arrived in Gambaga one muggy April day Simon approached the church's young pastor to ask whether they might help Napoa rid herself of witchcraft. The disciples were thought to be infused with the power of intensive prayer, the kind said to produce miracles. They had been credited with healing sicknesses, chasing out evil spirits, and producing "breakthroughs," all through the power of prayer.

"In Ghanaian culture, in the African setting, we believe that a person's blessings can be hindered by another person, another presence," Pastor Richard Kumah said. A breakthrough meant literally breaking through that obstacle.

Napoa no longer controlled her magic; witchcraft controlled her. "According to her it's like a force on her to do certain things. When she is sleeping, voices will come on her and say, 'Let's go.' At times she doesn't want to go, but it seems like a force, so she has to go," Kumah said. The same mischievous spirits that cause fornication and drunkenness, even smoking, could be blamed on witchcraft, he added. "You can see the thing is destroying you, but you can't stop. Some people who have been sick for a long time will go from hospital to hospital, from herbalist to herbalist, but there is no cure. Some are chronic, but some may be backed by evil spirits."

Kumah was a slim man with a kind smile, a soft voice, and a thick moustache. He was born in a village in the northern part of the Volta region, the first of his mother's three boys, who were joined by the eight girls and six boys born to his father's other wives. "We are a football team," he joked. His parents were traditionalists, making sacrifices to their ancestors. But there were too many children and they were poor farmers, so the children were parceled out to the family's wealthier cousins and relations. He was in primary three, the equivalent to the third grade, when he was sent to live with an evangelical uncle in Tamale. It was his first introduction to organized religion and it changed the direction of his life, leading him to university and a life of relative prosperity as a minister.

Bible verses and proverbs framed in faux mother-of-pearl finish hung on the walls of the Gambaga manse where he lived. A poster-size portrait showed Kumah in a dark suit and his glamorous wife in a frothy white wedding dress. He opened our interview with a prayer, asking that God be at the center of our discussions and that we be able to "communicate effectively so that our aims are achieved."

When Napoa came seeking her deliverance, the faithful gathered with the prayer warriors for three days at the yellow concrete-block Presbyterian church. They began at eight in the morning and stayed until noon, praying solidly, sometimes together, sometimes in noisy bunches, sometimes producing a fuzzy drone as each muttered his or her own prayer. The pastor and the warriors continued through the day, even after the sun had set, drawing together as many congregants as they could. Sometimes, hoarse, dehydrated, and at the edge of exhaustion, they quit as late as 10 p.m. On those nights the prayer warriors helped to swell the pitch of the prayer, then spread out to guide the congregants in their prayers. Some laid their hands on a person's head. Others touched an ailing body part. Many simply prayed from a distance.

Gradually, as the intensity grew, people began wailing, "behaving abnormally," Kumah said, collapsing or swaying. They would be carried forward and helped through their deliverance, their bodies jittering and shaking as the warriors prayed over them. When they came back to consciousness they sat up feeling energized. Most wept. Some said they felt as though a heavy stone had been lifted from their body. Others saw visions. "Some will talk and say it's a spirit in them," Kumah said. "At times we will shout at the spirit and tell it to come out."

Evelyn had participated in Napoa's deliverance. As she told me about that night at the church she ran her hands through a bowl of soybeans, digging out the deformed and disfigured in preparation for the next day's planting. She vividly remembered Napoa's torment. "When God's prayers came to her, you see she started talking. Confessing, confessing. It's a problem, really!" Evelyn said.

During that first evening of prayer Napoa began swaying and moaning. The prayer warriors collected her and privately questioned her about what was bothering her. She told them she was disturbed by a spirit. She had killed so many people, she said. Her last victim, a little girl she loved so much she was like a daughter, haunted her. Confessions came spilling out of her. Napoa told them she had used cutlasses and knives. She roamed by a sinister riverbed with a group of equally dark-hearted people and occasionally found herself holding mysterious cuts of meat. She could not control it. She feared for her two surviving children because when she slept she could see herself standing over them and was desperately scared she would kill them too. She begged the others to confirm her visions. "'You see these people, they are attacking me!' she said. But no one would see anything," Evelyn recounted, shaking her head.

Napoa told the prayer warriors that she had turned a man into a stick, then chopped him to bits with a cutlass. At the first blow he had "turned back into a human, thrashing to die." A man Napoa "worked with" in the spiritual realm butchered him and distributed the meat. They always gave her such a small portion, she complained. She believed the dead man was the chief of her village. Someone in the congregation remembered that the man had in fact died sometime in the previous year.

Napoa told them that she had a special mat, and when she slept on it she flew. She also had special dresses that allowed her to fly, and a special cloth. The warriors told her to gather up all of the things that were affected by witchcraft and bring them to the church. They would burn them and pray over her, helping her seek her deliverance. She came carrying a heavy sack filled with a small aluminum pot, a plate, and a bowl. These she used for cooking and eating the flesh of her victims, she said. She also brought the dresses, African print dresses that reached to the floor, that helped her to fly. These were doused in kerosene and set aflame. One of the prayer warriors began a prayer, and as the flames danced the people fell into a trance, muttering their prayers.

They were praying for the things to be soaked in the blood of Jesus, to be purified and sanctified through his blood. They asked that any link between these items and this person be broken and that the tools be rendered powerless. They asked that any power behind these things be destroyed in the name of Jesus. When the fire died down they dug a hole and buried the ashes and the blackened pot, plate, and bowl.

Napoa was unmoved, the pastor said. Evelyn remembered she sat looking bewildered as the prayer warriors prayed over her. She muttered about how the spirits bothered her, how they came to her in the night and wouldn't let her sleep. Kumah could see that three days of nonstop prayer made no difference. Napoa later told Evelyn she felt her witchcraft grow even stronger.

"She was lying down at night, and by the time she realized— her friends, those who were working with her, gave her some of their things because she had burned hers—and she will be hunting people," Evelyn said, clucking her tongue in disapproval.

The prayers didn't work because they didn't destroy all of her tools, the pastor explained, comparing it to taking only a half-dose of malaria medication. The parasite isn't destroyed; in fact, because it has tasted the medicine meant to destroy it, it builds immunity and grows stronger.

Kumah believed that Napoa kept a calabash hidden somewhere, and that it was the secret source of her power. Inside the calabash, a bowl made from a dried gourd, was a mixture: "fingernails, hair, bees, cowries, blood and many other strange things. This is where they generate their power from," he said. "The more complex the mixture or concoction, the more powerful you become.

"She said it's at home," he added. "She can't go because they will kill her and she says even if we were directed we couldn't find it. We believe she was not fully delivered because that thing is still there."

When a group of white pastors from Accra visited three months later Napoa again appeared at the guesthouse begging for their help. They again told her to bring the tools of her dark trade and they would pray over her. She came bearing a cloth and told them she used it to help her fly in the night.

"She used to go out in the night operating with that cloth," Evelyn said, flinging one of her son's small T-shirts over her head. Its armholes hung around her ears. "She would cover herself like this and turn into anything and fly away."

They burned the cloth, but Napoa felt she was still flying. Evelyn couldn't understand why the old woman's continued practice hadn't led to her death.

"Others too, they will attempt and they will die, but nothing happens to her," Evelyn said, setting aside her tin of soybeans. A woman had come from the camp to tell Simon that she saw Napoa in her dreams. Practicing witchcraft while living under the threat of the town's spirits seemed impossible, but other women confirmed that they too had seen Napoa in their dreams and took it as a sign she was still a witch who roamed in the spiritual realm. It was the audacity of practicing right under the *gambarana*'s nose that made it so difficult to believe.

"As she's confessed like this, maybe she regrets and with the prayer she feels badly about what she has done and will ask for forgiveness, seriously," Evelyn said. "I don't know what they will do about her case. All these prayers and she's still doing it."

Evelyn supported her husband's work and lived, for the most part, without fear of the women banished to the camp. Like most northerners she accepted the idea that the spirits can kill witches who pledge their allegiance but continue to practice. It's what allows the camps to exist; it's what prevents accused women from being lynched, stoned, or beaten to death. But Evelyn's next words made clear how easily that faith could erode. She saw only one solution for completely ridding a woman of witchcraft. "As for witchcraft," she said, returning to her bowl of soybeans, "they cannot remove it from you. They cannot remove the witchcraft from you except for death."

ON A RARE DAMP AND CHILLY MORNING, LONG BEFORE THE SUN had considered rising, Simon came to collect me on his motorbike. We were going to interview Napoa's husband in her home village of Baralong, about an hour's drive from Gambaga. We set out early in hopes of catching him before he headed out to his fields.

Even on his motorbike Simon drove at a sedate pace, shouting questions over his shoulder about my family. I seemed to grow in his esteem when he learned that my parents were hobby farmers. As I was telling him about their mules and cattle and crops, we suddenly turned from the main dirt road down a faint path beaten into the grass by surefooted goats and graceful women with heavy loads on their heads.

There are no roads leading to Napoa's remote village; how Simon ever managed to find it is a mystery. As we crunched our way up a hill the path disappeared, covered over by thick rocks, gnarled tree roots, and wide puddles. All around us men hunched over hoes in their fields as schoolboys armed with branches beat oxen dragging plows. At times I had to get down from the bike and walk; the trail was so bad it became too treacherous for both of us to ride. Baralong actually means "they shall not cross," a reference to the shelf of rocks separating the village from the outside world, specifically the slave raiders whose greedy need for human slaves forced this isolation.

After more than an hour we drove into a valley where green fields radiated out from a small cluster of mud huts. It was as though we had journeyed to a secret place, known only to those who had been shown the way. We hobbled off the bike next to a large compound and stepped across a wobbly, bleached stone covering a large bowl made of the dried rind of a gourd, a type of *juju* meant to disarm evil spirits. I ducked through a narrow walkway into a huge courtyard painted whimsically with flowers. They looked as if they'd been drawn by a child's hand, with triangles for leaves, a button stamen, and a bubbly ring of circles for the petals. Papaya plants towered overhead. Doves cooed as they pecked at stray millet seeds spilled onto the courtyard.

Only three of Napoa's five cowives remained, and they busied themselves with cooking. One pounded a massive mortar and pestle while another dumped a huge cauldron of raw rice to dry on the ground. A little girl dressed in a pink sweater devilishly stalked the doves, a stick held high over her head.

Sule Dawuni made Napoa the first of his wives decades ago, never suspecting she practiced witchcraft. "If you see a snake, you won't catch it," he said by way of explaining that, obviously, sane men don't chase women who are known to bewitch them. Dawuni was a slim man wearing a shiny pastel-green boubou and a traditional olive-colored cap with white stars threaded around it. He grew millet, maize, and groundnuts, raised guinea fowl and sheep, and supplemented his income by plowing fields with his team of big-headed oxen. He was considered rich, even though he eschewed cash and preferred bartering. Silver and bronze rings circled the third and fourth fingers of his left hand; three vertical lines were carved into the flesh under both of his bright brown eyes.

Five years after they were married, after Napoa had given birth five times, her mother was sent to live in Gambaga when a man fell sick and she was accused of causing his illness. Neighbors soon began to suspect that Napoa might have inherited her mother's dark gift. Then she confessed to "catching" her own son by capturing his soul in the spiritual realm and trapping it in the body of a cockroach. "The child hasn't died, but he never recovered to his normal state," Simon translated as the boy, now a grown man searching for a wife of his own, stepped into the compound as though conjured by talk of his curse.

The boy fainted, his father remembered, and when they took him to the hospital the doctors told them he was "low on blood and water." The boy remained at the hospital for a month. It wasn't until Napoa had been tested by the traditional fowl-slaughtering ceremony and made to return home to release her son's soul that the boy began to recover. Like Ayishetu, Napoa was followed from Gambaga by someone from the *gambarana*'s palace, who watched as she shifted and searched through the clay pots piled in her room and eventually emerged with a cockroach. The bug was simply released, Simon explained. Removing it from the woman's possession was enough to free the soul.

Although the young man looked well-muscled and strong, he told Simon softly that he could not work for long nor handle the sun. He had trouble controlling the plow, he said, and felt unusually anxious and nervous, as though something was always worrying him.

Napoa's husband blamed her for the death of twenty children born into his household, both his own children and his grandchildren. It seemed she carried death in her pocket and proximity alone could provoke an attack. One of Dawuni's grandsons slept in Napoa's room, and the next day he was found dead. When the ten-year-old son of one of Napoa's cowives fell sick while attending school they assumed he was suffering from malaria, but Dawuni said the doctors found he too was short of blood and water. It was a puzzling diagnosis; I'd never encountered it before, but I heard it often during my time in the north.

Again Napoa was sent home from the witch camp to find and release the child's soul, but the night she arrived no one could sleep, and in the morning the child died. "The minute you start catching your people, you can't do any good," her husband said. He didn't see witchcraft as an entirely negative thing and believed there were some who used their gift to safeguard their family and promote its prosperity. "Those who use their witchcraft for positive purposes, they never catch anyone," he said.

A year earlier, after the crops had been harvested and spread out to dry in the compound, the *gambarana* had sent a representative to Dawuni's house to warn him that Napoa had confessed to catching her own husband. They wanted to temporarily return her to the village to find and release his soul, but her husband refused to let her near him. He figured his wife only wanted access to the compound "to commit further crimes."

"If she dares enter here, she won't come back [to Gambaga]," he told Simon. He preferred to die rather than let Napoa near his wives and grandchildren. She had turned too many of his children and grandchildren into memories and left her own son too weak to farm. To his father the damaged young man was as good as dead. "I will kill her," he vowed. "She has already killed her son."

Napoa's husband also believed his wife's power came from a calabash filled with strands of hair, blood, nail clippings, and herbs buried somewhere near the house. No one had been able to locate it, despite a desperate bid to dig up patches of the surrounding fields.

Her husband had done everything he could think of to rid her of the witchcraft. He had repeatedly sent her to the *gambarana*, spending more than a hundred dollars on ceremonies, concoctions, and his wife's upkeep at the camp. It was a substantial investment, considering he dealt mostly in trade, not cash, and, like most of Ghana's rural farmers, he had little savings. He made her drink nauseating herbs, hoping she would dislodge and vomit whatever evil talismans were hidden inside her. He had paid for all kinds of *juju* men to visit, some traveling from as far away as Togo.

Dawuni himself had been to dozens of soothsayers, witchdoctors with the ability to see into the spiritual realm, and they all said the same thing: "Don't joke around with her." They too were in awe of his wife's power. He was covered in protective *juju* but knew she could easily overpower it. Dawuni and Napoa had even traveled to the Tongo shrines, a mystical grouping of stones near the Burkina Faso border reputed to be inhabited by a powerful witch-hunting spirit. Her husband shrugged his shoulders and sighed with exasperation. Napoa still practiced. He knew she was unable to sleep, and he seemed to take some satisfaction from the idea that the souls she hunted were now haunting her.

His son handed Simon a live guinea fowl as a gift. Baralong had sent dozens of women to Gambaga over the years and Simon had become a regular visitor to the village, where he gently lobbied for the women to be welcomed home. Dawuni treated him like a cherished friend. He was no stranger to Simon's persuasions, but the farmer had made it clear that he felt safer with his wife at Gambaga. He laughed and clapped his hands at the inanity of the idea that he would accept her back now. "When you quarrel with someone, it is better if they are away than living with that person. If they're far away, it's better," he said. "They can do something and you won't know." Like drop poison in your food, he added darkly.

"Her gift is exceptional," Simon translated. "He's tried the *gambarana*, he's tried Tongo, but where will he go again? As there is no way of curing her witchcraft, there is no way of her coming home again."

CHAPTER FIVE

I FOUND MY NOTEBOOK FILLING UP WITH VIVID STARS. ARROWS and question marks were scribbled onto the lined paper in moments of intense frustration and confusion as my interview subjects attempted to speak of witchcraft without actually speaking of witchcraft. I left the marks as reminders to go back, ask again, get some clarity. I was confused by talk of talismans and dreams, puzzled by what was happening in this world versus what was happening in the spiritual world, baffled by the mechanics of movement between the two. Instead of speaking clearly about witches and victims, people would speak guardedly, and cryptically, of cattle, sheep, riverbeds, snakes, or insects. I was impatient to learn the secrets that most of the accused women took to their graves.

"Sometimes they will never tell you the facts," Simon warned me at the outset. "It's like a secret to them. There are some societies that are secret. If you are not a member of that society, you will never know the details of it. That's why we conclude witchcraft is a mystery."

In a polygamous culture where women are seen as servants, coaxing stories out of the accused women often meant interpreting riddles delivered in Mampruli or Dagbani, obscure dialects spoken only in the northern region. Napoa compared me to a midwife, saying, "No one could feel shy on the day of delivery." Simon translated the translation: "She thinks you can help her, so she is telling you her secrets in order for you to give her the best help you can."

A woman who had been raised at a remote camp after her mother was accused of witchcraft spoke even more enigmatically. "If a rabbit is lying under a shrub, anything that threatens the rabbit, it's that same thing that follows the rabbit and kills it," she said, leaving me dumbfounded. When I turned to the translator he told me the woman meant that if she left the camp and returned to her mother's village, she would be plagued by suspicion and rumor because her neighbors would assume she had inherited her mother's witchcraft.

Another woman, a native to Gambaga who stopped to eavesdrop on an interview, laughed uproariously when she heard of my interest in witchcraft, then anxiously backed away from my questions. She told me firmly, as virtually all of the accused women did, that she didn't know anything about witchcraft, offering as her reason, "I am not one of them." She was not a witch, she insisted, so how could she know anything about witchcraft? "If I don't control the way I talk, they will send me to the chief," she said. "Why should I know anything about it when I am not one of them? If you say there is witchcraft, then they will want you to prove it."

Other than polite greetings I spoke no Mampruli or Dagbani and was completely at the mercy of my translators. When Carlos returned to school Simon arranged for his neighbor's son, Kizito, to take over. Thoughtful and quiet with the "ch-ch-ch" chortle of an old man, Kizito planned to attend agricultural college in the fall. I had hoped to hire a woman, figuring she would connect more easily with the accused witches, but couldn't find one with suitably strong English living near the village and willing to converse with suspected witches.

Unused to speaking for themselves, most of the accused women had no idea where to begin. My first few interviews were disastrous. I would return to the guesthouse and transcribe the tapes, cringing as the words were rewound and replayed—again and again and again—and still I understood virtually nothing. Complicated queries were answered with one word. Open questions that were designed to invite narration left the women bewildered and uneasy. Carlos and Kizito were often embarrassed by my obvious confusion over what to them must have seemed the most obvious concepts about witchcraft, such as the dreamscapes, the telltale signs of an attack, even the physical attributes of a witch, things they had learned as toddlers. They giggled into their hands at the frankness of asking an elderly accused woman whether she believed in witchcraft or whether she felt she had committed witchcraft. Such questioning was so culturally inappropriate—and so unlikely to produce an honest answer—that it was only my white skin that allowed me to get away with it.

I spent large chunks of time unraveling relationships in a place where friends were called brothers, *father* was a term of respect, not necessarily an indication of paternity, and women with five daughters were described as childless. ("Oh, we don't count daughters," Simon said cheerfully.) A woman might say she had ten children, only to reveal later that although she had delivered ten children, only two of them had survived. Or she might say she had twelve children, neglecting to mention that only three of them were born to her; the others belonged to her cowives, but as the first wife she could claim them all as her own.

To work out a woman's age I relied on her memory of significant events in the country's history: if she remembered the details of Ghana's achieving independence, she was more than fifty; if she remembered the details of the first military coup, she was more than forty. Several follow-up interviews were required to pinpoint the chronology of events in a place where time was of little importance, where the passing of the day was measured by the muezzin's calls and vague dates were distinguished by times of heavy rainfall, plentiful harvests, devastating droughts, or sudden changes in the political landscape. The women's faces held few clues, falling into one of two categories: their skin was either smooth and youthful or shriveled and collapsed like an apple doll.

To build rapport with the women I spent a few afternoons with them shelling peanuts and, on lazy Sunday afternoons, went to the camp's version of a beauty parlor to have my fingernails painted with a mixture of green herbs that bled a rust color. The women were curious about my age, whether I was married, why I lived apart from my husband, and how many children we had. Much scandalized tongue clicking followed my confession that I was neither married nor a mother. "Oh! Oh! Oh! You've got to try," came the translation. "You must try to marry!"

To fill in the details of Ayishetu's accusation I spoke with her four times and interviewed her husband, two of her sons, and her daughter. We spoke with her village chief, her husband's uncle, and Yakubu, the minder sent from the *gambarana*'s palace to supervise the retrieval of her niece's soul. It took roughly six hours just to piece together the fact that Ayishetu was actually accused of witchcraft twice and sent to stay at Gambaga both times.

I asked for an interview with Ayishetu's son, who, I was told, played something of a hero's role, riding in on a bicycle to save his mother from her beating. I found myself sitting in a large circle with Kizito, Ayishetu, her twelve-year-old son, and an uncle who lived in Gambaga village and spoke fairly good English. We spoke for nearly an hour about what the boy remembered of his mother's accusation, about the things he saw and the people who participated. Then I asked about his role in her rescue.

"They were sitting in the evening when they called their mother a witch. The next morning they said their mother had bewitched the uncle's daughter," Kizito translated.

"Who is 'they'?" I asked.

Blank stares.

"When you say 'they' called her a witch and 'they' were sitting, who are you talking about?"

Translation from the uncle: "The 'people' called her a witch. 'They' refers to the family."

"What people?"

"The uncles."

"The boy's father's brothers?"

"Yes."

"Same mother, same father?"

"Yes."

"And where are the brothers when this happens?"

"In their compound."

"'Their' being the boy's father's compound, or the uncles' compound?"

"His own father's compound."

Ayishetu cut in: "They didn't send me to the chief's palace, but told me to go straight to Gambaga."

"Again, who is 'they'?"

"Her accusers, her junior husband."

"Her junior husband?"

"The husband's junior brother."

Okay. I take a deep breath. "So, what next?"

"They came with cutlasses and guns and asked why they hadn't left."

(Aaargh! Who is "they"?)

I asked where Ayishetu was when this happened.

"Gambaga."

"Wait," I said. "I thought we were talking about the day she was beaten in the village. What happened on the day she was beaten?"

"Oh, the boy wasn't there."

I looked up from my notebook. "Sorry?"

After several minutes it emerged that, as Ayishetu was being beaten, the boy escaped to his grandparents' house, but days later he happened to be passing on his way to the farm to see the damage to his parents' house when he heard that his mother had briefly returned to the village. And then it turned out she was accused again, by a woman who was a friend of the uncle—

I interrupted. "Friends like you and I are friends?" I asked Kizito. "Or friends like, you know, friends who sleep together?"

"Just friends. But everybody believes [the friend] is possessed by fairies."

"Oh yes?"

"Yes."

"Okay." A minute or so passed as I stared at my notebook, massaging the bridge of my nose, wondering how the story had managed to get so far off-track. "Okay, so," I gestured at the boy, trying to keep a grip on the interview. He was painfully shy, barely spoke above a whisper, and rarely looked up from his scabby knees. "Where is he, what does he see when his mother is being beaten?"

"He wasn't there."

"He wasn't there? This boy?"

"Yes."

"I thought this was the son who came on the bicycle?"

"No, that was his brother, Abdullai."

It was frustrating, and there were moments when it became clear the women were lying, telling me half-truths, or deliberately leaving out details that might have been considered incriminating. There was nothing to be done but keep making those vivid stars and arrows, go back, ask more questions and seek more clarity, even if sometimes I felt I was being led down a rabbit hole.

IN ANCIENT TIMES GHANA WAS A NAME THAT BELONGED TO THE carpet of sand dunes that lay about five hundred miles north of the country's present-day border. It was a place where trains of hundreds of camels laden with salt and gold skirted the Sahara, arcing toward the vibrant souks of North Africa. Slave raiding, water shortages, and land disputes pushed tribes south into what is today considered Ghana's northern territory. The land was rocky, grassy, and dry, overrun with flying insects that could infect the blood of bulls and crawling insects that could pick the carcasses clean. But it was virtually empty, and according to legend feuding brothers relied on magical signs to show them where best to settle their families and followers.

The area was already home to small seminomadic groups of farmers who built their mud homes, surrounded them with tall walls, added rooms as the families grew and prospered, then abandoned their settlements when the land grew tired or water grew scarce. These people were not considered tribal; they may have shared geography, but they were not necessarily linked by language or culture, they didn't always come from the same familial line, nor did a chief or set of elders rule them. They were considered fierce and independent, answering to the ancestral gods they carried with them across the savannah and whatever spirits they discovered attached to their land. For the most part the seminomadic farmers ignored one another until circumstance pressed one group against another, triggering a pattern of war and assimilation as old as time.

That changed in the middle of the fifteenth century, as the Age of Discovery was under way in Europe, when Mamprusi brothers from farther up the Volta River moved south, successfully waging war with virtually all of the area's existing inhabitants. Some were pushed off their land; others were forced to feed their new Mamprusi rulers with a portion of their harvests.

A fearsome and infamous slave raider known as Babatu had already descended from the north with his brutal personal army, capturing whole villages as slaves to be swept north to the continent's famed Muslim cities, or east to Dahomey, present-day Benin, where they were seen as fodder for the macabre king's human sacrifices. From the south came mounted Asante warriors, who slaughtered anyone who stood in the way of their kingdom's growth. Defeated northern chiefs were ordered to pay tribute to the Asante king in the form of kola nuts and human slaves.

Fear and desperation saw neighbors turn against each other in an effort to spare their own kin from strangers arriving on horseback looking for able-bodied men and women. Families began carving identifying lines or swoops into the cheeks, foreheads, and chins of their members so they could recognize one another when they met as slaves. Men either pushed their wives and children deeper and deeper into the isolated bush or became part of the mass of bodies shackled at the neck, sold at the markets, and force-marched to the coast.

It's not known exactly how many northerners were shoved into the dank dungeons of the Portuguese, Dutch, and British slave-trading castles and sent overseas to the brutality of the New World's sugar and cotton plantations, but northern Ghana was already depleted and fragmented when British colonial agents appeared in the late 1800s. A medical officer who arrived in the northern territory in the dying days of the dry season wrote that he encountered villages paralyzed by hunger. The people he found were exhausted, dispirited, and succumbing in great numbers to river blindness, sleeping sickness, influenza, meningitis, malaria, the kidney or liver ruin of bilharzia, and the bone pain of yaws. Most, he reported, were on the brink of starvation.

Colonial archives would suggest that the British were most concerned by the nudity of the northern tribes. They focused on creating order out of what they saw as chaos, lumping together people whose languages sounded similar and randomly appointing men to rule them. It laid the foundation for explosive feuds and the corruptive influence of political power, but the immediate impact seemed lost amid the furious pace of change. Northern tribes were pressured to put on European-style clothes, attend church, settle with only one woman, and live by the bewildering ordinances of British rule.

Administrators planned to transform the area's piecemeal farming into an export economy, but they quickly learned that little could be done to make life easier. The dry savannah could not be coaxed into giving much more than it already provided. Colonial bureaucrats tried growing cotton, manufacturing salt, and smoking fish, but the harsh climate, rocky landscape, and innumerable pests and parasites thwarted virtually every economic venture they could dream up. A railway and mineral mines were nixed when it was determined that their astronomical construction costs would leave them unprofitable. Poor water sources meant farmers could keep only a few cattle and goats, even though colonial veterinarians had managed to eradicate rinderpest and control sleeping sickness. Even a colonial effort to abolish tolls charged against nomadic Fulani farmers moving their cattle south proved disastrous. The farmers

considered the tolls a payment that protected them against marauding cattle rustlers; without the tolls they no longer felt it was safe to
pass through northern Ghana. Colonial administrators, then development experts, exhausted every potential avenue to bring sustainable economic growth to the north. They concluded that without
better irrigation and more mechanized farm equipment, such as
tractors, fertilizer spreaders, and plows, northern Ghanaians—like
so many other rural Africans—would likely never move beyond
subsistence farming.

NABOLE'S ASSEMBLYMAN CAME TO MEET US, APOLOGIZING FOR
his tardiness even though we'd arrived in his village unannounced.
Nabole was home to Ghana's most remote witch camp, a colony
that sprang to life in 1994, in the midst of one of the north's blood-
est battles. More than any other village I visited, Nabole illustrated
why the north held so many reasons to believe in witchcraft.

To get there we drove more than three hours from Gambaga,
turned off an empty stretch of pavement, and nosed our beat-up
silver truck down a rutted path overgrown with patches of tall grass.
We were miles from anywhere. The rumble of cargo trucks crawling
along the highway had been left far behind, replaced by the drone
of hidden insects and the shimmer of heat waves rising before us.
Along the way we picked up two older men walking in tall rubber boots along the roadside, who said they knew the village. Their
faces were a canvas of tiny pinprick scars swirling around their eyebrows and cheekbones. I was traveling with Simon and Kizito. In
the wet season the road leading into Nabole disappears under wa-
terways swollen with rain. Although the rains hadn't started yet—
they were, in fact, worryingly late—we sent Kizito out from the bed
of the truck twice. With his feet bare and his pant legs rolled over
his knees, he waded into the wide puddles to test their depth and
decide whether we could charge our way across.

There are more than seventy-five languages spoken in Ghana, a
sign of the tribal fractionalization that existed before colonial set-
tlers arbitrarily threw borders onto the map. Kizito spoke five lan-

guages, three of them so closely related it was difficult to tell them apart, as well as English and the language of his mother's people, the more northern Frafra. In Ghana's northern region, an area about the size of the state of West Virginia, ethnographers have recorded more than thirty local dialects, meaning a half-hour's drive in any direction brings a change of language. Neighbors sometimes can't speak with neighbors. At Nabole Kizito busied himself taking pictures with my camera, since there was nothing he could translate. The Konkomba language is unlike any other in the north, and he couldn't understand a word.

Konkombas are known as one of Ghana's most fearsome northern people, often described as volatile, stubborn, and practically ungovernable. Simon, ethnically a Kusase, claimed it was nearly impossible to have a civilized pint of beer with a Konkomba man. With enough alcohol flowing through his veins, Simon claimed, a Konkomba man will invariably start throwing punches, and he won't stop until his knuckles have broken bones or drawn blood. The Konkombas are isolated, he told me, and they prefer it that way. I read that they purposely built their tumbledown huts a few feet farther than an arrow's trajectory away from their neighbors, then allowed grass and bush to grow up as camouflage. The paranoia, isolation, poverty, and boredom that seemed to blanket the north made their villages ripe for accusations of witchcraft.

"These people," Simon said as we drove into Nabole, his voice heavy with dismay. "What help does the government give them? Are they even part of Ghana?"

Nabole's two dozen mud homes were virtually swallowed up by tall grasses. The sky was like a turbulent sea, low and gray and mottled with clouds that stubbornly refused to release the rain within them. It was so desperately hot that only the flies buzzing around the open-air butcher seemed to move with any energy. A man with a cigarette dangling from his lower lip languidly stripped a dead goat of its skin and meat. Its skull and hooves had already been cut away and were left sitting tied together beside the meatier remains of the carcass. We slowed our truck next to a thin girl in a long floral dress sitting bored-looking and lonely atop a flat stone, to buy fifteen cents' worth of peanut-flavored snacks. Aside from the raw goat meat it seemed to be the only food on offer in the village. We dropped our scarred guides outside the town's drinking spot, called Being a Man is Not a Day Job. A man so drunk he stumbled straight into the tail end of our truck waved us toward the grouping of huts that were home to the women accused of witchcraft.

"Look at him," Simon said, disgusted. "And he's a Muslim."

"That's right!" the man belched, clearly ignoring the tenet of Islam forbidding the drinking of alcohol. "I'm a Muslim, so no one can talk nonsense to me!"

Nabole felt lawless and wild, with drunks stumbling around and the danger of quick tempers and even quicker fists hanging over it all, as heavy and threatening as the clouds overhead. Even the women scurried around shouting roughly at one another. "You see, they are not friendly like in other villages," Simon remarked. It was true. There was something depressing about Nabole.

We waited in the shade of an almond tree for the assemblyman, the only man in the village who spoke enough English to help us. When John Gmajo Nloi appeared, he was dressed in one of his best outfits, a loose-fitting peach-colored shirt and matching pajama pants tie-dyed to form a kind of bull's eye of olive dye around his knees. He regretted keeping us waiting, but he'd been out at another village, offering an apology. I figured I'd misheard until John explained that in Konkomba custom, if a man elopes with a woman he must send someone to the woman's family as his emissary to apologize for taking their daughter without paying for her first. It was an education in exactly how much wives and daughters were viewed as property. I had seen how hard they worked to keep their families fed and clothed, but I hadn't realized exactly how little influence women had over their own lives. They could be used and traded depending on their father's greed or their husband's whims. John had gone to a neighboring village on behalf of his brother's son, for tradition demands that the man making the apology must be of high standing. He is usually sent loaded with gifts of food and drink, but the woman's family doesn't always accept the apology and may come to collect their daughter. In fact a man may have to send gifts two or three times before the clandestine marriage is finally accepted.

John's eyes, obscured by a thick pair of glasses, were deeply hooded, giving the impression that he was about to fall asleep. It was difficult to tell whether his glasses were set askance or whether there was something off about the alignment of his eyes. He didn't so much speak as exclaim. His nephew's new in-laws told him that if the family had sent anyone else, "they would have put me in chains and sent me to work in the fields!" They had a long list of grievances and did not accept the apology, but instead demanded that their daughter be returned. The men from John's family are rough with their women, they complained. Sometimes men in their own village have tried to apologize and John's family refused them, coming instead to retrieve their daughters.

"They say he should pay for this girl with cash money!" John said. He figured he would have to make at least a second trip. It was better to try again than to leave bad blood between the two families. Whether the young couple was in love was irrelevant.

We'd come to the village to speak with the accused women, but John wanted to tell us the story of how he nearly died at the hands of a witch. It was one of witchcraft's many quirks that there was nothing extraordinary about an educated man of high standing believing in witchcraft; education was no barometer of belief.

John remembered that stars still hung in the predawn sky as a line of primary school students, some wearing faded orange dress shirts and torn brown short pants, marched across the tall grass of the Nabole schoolyard, praise-singing for the coming day. One of the schoolyard singers looked to the sky and shrieked. A fireball loomed over the makeshift choir, blazing with an ominous orange glow. The children scattered, running away blindly. They knew a fireball was a witch's disguise. But John stumbled and landed hard on the grass. Within days he fell sick with an illness that caused him to swell and bloat.

John puffed out his cheeks and moved like a spaceman without gravity, theatrical flourishes to show how his arms and legs had ballooned and his stomach stuck out. He put his hands to either side of his head, moving them about three inches out from his ears. "My face was out to here," he said.

The other little boys who were in the field that day also fell mysteriously sick, some with diarrhea, some complaining of headaches, some thrashing about in the night with fever. The compound where John lived with his father's other wives, his aunts, cousins, grandparents, and half-brothers and sisters was hard hit. "Maybe fifteen or sixteen children died in my house that year," he remembered.

When he became too sick to be cared for at home his teacher convinced his parents to send him to the hospital, a two-hour car ride away. His parents were convinced their little boy was on death's door when word arrived that one of his schoolmates had died, but on his deathbed had accused "a certain old woman" of cursing the boys. She was killing the others, John's schoolmate rasped. He urged the village to kill her before she could kill them.

"She put me up in a tree," John said, pointing up at the thin leaves of a neem tree swaying in the afternoon breeze, a visual aid for the next part of his story. John's family and fellow villagers went to the woman's house in a mob and "beat her from A to Z." The bruised and bloodied old woman eventually led them to a tree, not unlike the neem tree before us, where they hacked away with machetes until it fell. Although it was healthy, with many branches loaded with leaves, the inside was blackened and hollow. Once opened, insects came spilling out of its remains, and as they flew away the woman called out the name of each child the bugs represented.

Almost immediately John's health began to improve.

He figured he spent about six months in the hospital. "I could have died!" he said, shaking his head at the wonder of it—not at the idea of falling victim to witchcraft but at all that could have been lost if the old woman's attack had been successful. "She could have killed me, me who went to school and became an assemblyman!"

JOHN'S POLITICAL DAYS COULD NOT HAVE BEEN DEVOTED TO DE-velopment. The village's concrete schoolhouse was only partially sheltered by a collapsed roof. The boarded-up health outpost, a tiny room painted white and coated with patterns of dust, decayed in the dry heat behind a heavy padlock. As in so many other tiny northern villages, Nabole's homes were made of what comes cheap: red mud bricks baked under the intense African sun that were held together with a thick paste of rich red soil and covered with long grass that had been harvested with a scythe, bound with twine, and bleached a dull gray by the same strong sun.

The northern territory had always seemed like an afterthought, even in the days when the colony was known as the Gold Coast. After experimenting with growing cotton, salting fish, and min-ing minerals, the British government seemed prepared to aban-don the north as a liability. Then the call came for men to work in the Tarkwa gold mines. Once again able-bodied men became the north's most valuable export. Northern chiefs were paid to provide recruits and the government turned a blind eye to the coercive hand they used to persuade their village's young men to join the long line of economic migrants walking the three hundred miles south to the gold fields around Kumasi. Northern fields of maize, sorghum, and millet lay fallow as young men chased their fortune in the south's canopy of cocoa trees or in its gaping gold and manganese mines. The north's missing men, and subsequent missing harvests, exacer-bated the already precarious food supply, deepening a debilitating cycle of hunger and poverty.

By the time the country was declared free from British rule in 1957 a north-south trading route had been cut through the dense forests and paved, running from the southern ports up to Tamale and beyond to Ouagadougou. The ribbon of road brought more goods north and triggered mass migration south as northern farm-ers realized they could work the cocoa plantations, then hop onto a vehicle and be home within a few days for their own harvests—a vast improvement over the weeks spent walking from the mines to the fields.

Ghana's beginning was heralded as a sensational start for sub-Saharan Africa's first independent country, but its earliest president, Kwame Nkrumah, envisioned a united Africa where all countries were freed from colonization. Grandiose projects connected to that dream—such as the headquarters of Nkrumah's Organization of the African Union, a multimillion-dollar building that was never used—nearly bankrupted the country without bringing real development to the people. Nkrumah set an early and unfortunate pattern among African politicians, beginning his career as a hero and ending it in a haze of paranoia and dictatorship. While on state business in Vietnam in 1966 he learned that he had been overthrown by the military.

The early pride of Africa for its smart meld of British bureaucracy and African leadership, Ghana became like a top-of-the-line motorcar whose owners drove it too fast and ignored its intricate inner workings. By the 1970s a bloated public service and an arrogant political leadership had drained Ghana's national purse with corruption and nepotism. Bureaucrats grew fat on the profits of the country's struggling cocoa farmers. Cracks began appearing in the country's fledgling economy. The north's old rivalries found a new platform in party politics, entrenching old quarrels. Land rights plagued virtually every community. As the economy crashed, men who'd spent decades in the south returned to their northern villages expecting to take over the farms of their fathers and grandfathers, only to find their fields had been expropriated by other families.

By the 1970s northern men who traveled south did so only for adventure; there were barely any jobs to be had. The country's currency crisis, ignored for more than a decade, meant businesses could no longer find the foreign exchange they needed to buy imports. Besides, officious bureaucrats looking for a bribe made it nearly impossible to secure a legitimate import license. The currency crisis also caused exports to tumble; in five years, from 1975 to 1980, the amount of minerals, timber, plywood, and cocoa being sold to the international market dropped by a third.

The breakdown spread. Without imports industry couldn't secure materials. Factories sat idle, their employees going months without paychecks. Water plants couldn't secure parts for repairs, and soon crowded cities faced severe water shortages. Without parts greasy auto repair shops could survive only by patching up thread-bare tires. The metaphor of the neglected luxury vehicle became reality: 70 percent of the country's cars and trucks were grounded waiting for repairs; the remaining vehicles were often stalled at gas stations, waiting in long lines for the next shipment of gasoline to reach the pumps.

The country's inflation rate climbed to a staggering 130 percent, worsening an economic disaster already exacerbated by two consecutive crippling droughts. A cutthroat black market in produce smuggled in from Nigeria, Togo, or neighboring Ivory Coast made the capital's largest food market a den of thieves. Ghanaians were starving by the time the charismatic flight lieutenant Jerry John Rawlings, a twenty-three-year-old Ghanaian of mixed Scottish heritage, stormed the government palace in 1979 and toppled the government. Stores lined their shelves with all the items needed to prepare and cook meals, but no food. That was rationed and distributed by chit, meaning increasingly thin Ghanaians, their collarbones protruding in what became known as the "Rawlings chain," whiled away their days waiting in long lines to receive bags of maize.

In the north long-simmering tensions bubbled over. Population counts in the 1960s showed that the north was so sparsely populated there were just eight people per square kilometer, but twenty years later double that number were living in the same space. Old enemies chafed against one another, a situation made worse by returnees, creating a dangerous friction that erupted in 1984, just as the country succumbed to its third coup. In the decade between 1984 and 1994 six northern tribes squared off in eleven major conflicts. Peace agreements were brokered and broken with dizzying speed. Ethnic groups piled on a mutual enemy, only to break ties and battle one another when an ally showed weakness. The country's military leadership, already facing the more pressing concerns of serious drought, widespread hunger, and a complete breakdown in the currency and economy, dispersed army personnel but mostly left the conflicts to play themselves out.

Four coups had rocked Ghana in only fifteen years. In order to secure aid Rawlings was finally forced to concede to World Bank and International Monetary Fund demands to open state-run companies, agencies, and mines to foreign interests. As the political landscape stabilized, foreign donors began pouring money into development projects, and economic structural reforms recharged the country's industrial, manufacturing, and banking sectors. Money was secured for tools, pesticides, and fertilizers for the agricultural sector. In relatively short order roads and telephone systems were upgraded. Donors cobbled together eighty million dollars for a northern electricity program.

By the 1990s democracy had eluded twelve of fifteen West African nations, but Ghana had managed to climb up from the bottom third of the United Nations index of human development. Liberia and Sierra Leone were in the headlines for their vicious civil wars, yet Rawlings made history in 2001, when the former military dictator heeded the wishes of voters and peacefully handed control of the country to the opposition party. Democracy was reborn.

With its salt ponds and healthy deposits of bauxite, gold, manganese ore, and other minerals, Ghana became one of the safest places in the region to conduct business. The south powered ahead. The north, however, languished, and the Guinea Fowl War exposed just how contentious northern rivalries had grown—and how easily Ghana could follow its neighbors into gruesome civil war.

The dispute began at the market but spilled quickly into the streets. In the early months of 1994 young men set up random roadblocks and patrolled them using AK-47s. After ten days of fighting Ghana's leaders declared a state of emergency, temporarily suspending a constitution that was only two years old. Army officers took up defensive positions. Tanks rolled down the main street of Tamale, the north's biggest city, where an estimated 100,000 people sought refuge from the fighting. In all, between 150,000 and 250,000 northerners were chased from their homes in the skirmish. Some four hundred villages were utterly destroyed, the mud bricks of family compounds broken and burned. At least two thousand people were killed.

It was 1994, but the Konkombas fought with weapons that belonged to another era. An account of their fighting tactics, published in *Africa Report*, described contingents of Konkomba men on bicycles attacking villages in the early morning hours.

> These bicycle warriors strike the thatched huts of their enemies with burning arrows, forcing the inhabitants to flee. The terrified victims are then shot with lethal poisoned arrows dipped in snake venom. Then, a second formation of warriors appears—made up of children in the front row firing gunpowder as a decoy to draw and exhaust enemy fire. Fast behind the decoys follow armed men firing real bullets. Behind them come ululating women, cheering the men on. The women carry pick axes to bury their dead and they are said to attack any cowards who try to turn back.

The tactics were terrifying and ferocious. The animosity that prompted the Guinea Fowl War could still be felt at the village level, in places like Nabole, where old grudges held firm. Millions had been spent on peace-building programs to heal the north's deep divides, but they couldn't quite erase a mentality that had built up over decades of hardship and neglect. Families living in villages like Nabole were forced to rely on one another to survive, and that bred vulnerability, jealousy, and resentment. There was never enough water, enough food, enough men, or enough money, and the ties that bound these tiny villages together were stretched so thin, pulled so taut, that the slightest social misstep caused them to snap.

It was the Internet age, but northern villagers still lived, and fought, as in feudal times. Their health was ignored, their education all but absent. Their water came from wells and boreholes; their villages were lit by the soft glow of kerosene lamps. There still wasn't enough water, food, money, or men. History, insecurity, poor living conditions, and rampant jealousy and paranoia coalesced to form a perfect breeding ground for fear, mistrust, superstition, and witchcraft.

CHAPTER SIX

GHANAIANS WHO FELT DEFENSIVE ABOUT THEIR STANCE ON witchcraft liked to remind me that the last woman to be executed in Europe for practicing witchcraft died a little more than two hundred years ago, proof that Western belief in witchcraft was hardly ancient history. Europeans living in the fourteenth and fifteenth centuries saw witchcraft everywhere; thousands of women and hundreds of men were blamed for stirring up bad weather, cuckolding husbands, shrinking genitals, stealing wombs, and killing children, among other misfortunes. Estimates on how many women were killed during the witch hunts vary wildly, from 40,000 to more than 100,000, but the torturous deaths of at least 12,000 women are well-documented in transcripts of their court cases.

While the term *witchcraft* may have been coined as shorthand for describing pagan healers, Europe's witch hunts had the blessing of the Catholic Church. It was by papal order that most countries convened witch trials. Inquisitors usually referred to a book written by the pope's investigators, a handbook for identifying, interrogating, torturing, and punishing witches, known as the *Malleus Maleficarum*, or "The Hammer of Witches." The book made clear that the new definition of a witch was a woman who'd been seduced by the devil. Investigators were instructed to shave a woman bare to look for the devil's marks. The women were then tortured with nails, thumb presses, vises, iron collars, among other disturbing devices, and ordered to provide the names of the other women in their covens. Then they were burned, strangled, decapitated, or drowned, often in public and usually naked.

It was known as the Dark Ages for a reason. Farmers and villagers were born into the lower class and stayed there, largely illiterate, malnourished, and saddled with more children than they could afford to feed. Feudal families survived with subsistence farming, paying heavy taxes to kings, princes, or dukes for the privilege of working their land. Disease was rampant; the plague killed millions, often in a matter of days, as it swept across the continent. The gruesome illness, with its oozing boils and painful death, was held out as a sign of God's wrath. It was the Church, in fact, that held most people in its grip, with the promise of paradise in the afterlife or an eternity in hell.

It was also a time of enormous change. During the two hundred years that made up the most intense period of witch burnings, Europe moved into the Age of Enlightenment, surviving plagues, war, the decline of paganism, the Inquisition, the splintering of the powerful Catholic Church, and the emergence of the Protestant faith. In those two centuries Europeans developed the cannon, the printing press, the mechanical clock, eyeglasses, and distilled liquor. Christopher Columbus discovered America; Portuguese ships landed on the African coast.

Belief in witchcraft waned as medical discoveries increased, as education became more accessible, and as the Church relaxed its stance on the Devil's power. Changes to politics, the erosion of the feudal system, and the beginning of the industrialized age softened social hierarchies, meaning that fortunes were less tied to birthright and more apt to change with education and hard work. Autopsies helped doctors across Europe understand what was happening inside the human body and how disease could upset its normal function. They learned about brain function, dissected organs, and charted the passage of blood. They learned to read for signs of infection in phlegm, blood, and bile. The relationship be-

tween sanitation, drinking water, and disease outbreaks became better understood. New treatments were based on science, not superstition.

The growth of scholastic thought brought philosophy to the fore, allowing rationalization to trump the supernatural. Critical thinking encouraged the exploration of more rigorous alternative reasoning and more plausible causes for misfortune. As Europe's educated elite sought to differentiate themselves from illiterates, it became embarrassing to admit to superstitious beliefs.

SCIENTISTS IN AMERICA AND EUROPE HAD FIGURED OUT HOW to harness the unusual abilities of their witches to produce telephones, fax machines, and airplanes, Wuni Zakari declared. He was a teacher and the *rana*, the chief, of remote Mozio village. Each time he was transferred to teach at a new school he married a new wife. Six times the Mozio *rana* had been moved around the region, and we spent half a day driving to three of his homes, meeting three of his wives, before we finally found him watching a soccer match at the local high school in Nalerigu, just four miles from Gambaga.

He envisioned a very different kind of witch camp, seeing potential in the witches' power. Because witches could fly, morph into animals, or disappear, the Mozio *rana*, and others like him, believed they could be used for good instead of evil. "If in Africa we could do that, we'll develop faster," he said. Put the witches together, confine them, then ask them, "'Let's see, how do we get to the moon?' I believe they are capable of getting us to the moon!" His voice rose surprisingly high as he emphasized his point. It was as though even he was amazed by the strength of his argument.

We moved to the shade of a tree at his house while one of his wives set out plastic chairs and stools and distributed cold Cokes and bottled malt from a wicker picnic basket. The Mozio *rana*, unlike the *gambarana*, had traveled outside the northern region and spoke flawless English. "I would wish that instead of branding them that way, they would bring them together and give them the best of the best—the best of accommodation, the best of means—and they could come together and use their powers to help us be advanced," he said.

At one of Simon's anti-witchcraft meetings, the Mozio *rana* had presented a speech about the merits of witchcraft. Consider the powers witches profess to have, he told me. The ability to travel in the blink of an eye, to dart through the night air, to disappear for only a moment and claim to have traveled to the United Kingdom and back. The way they fly or transport themselves from one place to another, he said breathlessly. "Good-bye lorry fares! We could surprise the whole world. Ghana would invent something that had never been invented before."

The Mozio *rana* wore a white Muslim cap, a blue-and-white-striped boubou, and slim light-blue slacks. He cackled at some of the antics of the old women, their sass and gumption, and told me a witch had saved his brother and sister. The boy had been seriously injured in a car crash, so severely hurt that doctors thought he would not live through the night. He was resurrected from a coma by an auntie who traded his life for that of a bull. When the bull died she warned her family not to eat it, but to bury it instead. The Mozio *rana* clapped his hands and smiled. His brother went on to live another twenty-five years. The same auntie declared his sister possessed after she developed a stubborn illness. The old woman roasted a toad and rubbed some black substance into it. Toads are said to be poisonous and therefore taboo in the north, but she gave it to his sister and told her to eat it. He shook his head at the wonder of it; his sister is still alive today.

He remembered one of Gambaga's old *magazia*, a queen who died before Simon moved to the village. Legend had it that her sickly grandson accused her of stealing his medication. The drugs would be placed in his hand, then suddenly disappear on the way to his mouth. The old woman proudly produced the pills when she was accused, the Mozio *rana* claimed, then mimicked her trial. "I want that child to die because he doesn't respect me," he remembered her saying. "She wouldn't disturb you just to disturb," he laughed. There was a message behind her attacks. "People who didn't respect her were taught a lesson. She would let them suffer for a long period and finally die."

The written speech he delivered at Simon's anti-witchcraft meeting, mimeographed so its purple letters appeared on strong-smelling paper, made clear that he saw discrimination in the accusations that dogged vulnerable women. "The old, childless, poor and helpless women are the most affected," he read out to the gathering of traditional leaders. "The old lady who has no support but her old husband, the woman who is widowed, has no child at all or whose children do not make any impact [i.e., learned, rich] in the community are the 'witches' in our homes."

Rich women, "those whose children are well-to-do," were respected, but an outspoken woman became an easy target. "Because of our perception of womanhood, when a lady is outspoken, without further investigation, the conclusion is made that she is a witch," he told the anti-witchcraft meeting.

He was indignant at the way powerful people could claim to be witches—big men and big women, with good jobs, education, or salary—and no one would say anything, yet a vulnerable old lady without children or wealth could make people so furious they would beat her to death.

"Women whose children are all dead, or who are suffering from diseases like leprosy, epilepsy or rheumatism are associated with the craft by the public," he read out from the mimeographed sheet. "Women who lose their health and safety, who go about asking for alms to feed themselves, clothe themselves and secure treatment such as drugs or herbs for themselves are also branded witches. The question that comes to mind immediately is: is it a crime to beg?"

"Witchcraft exists all over the world," he explained to me. Witchcraft was God's way of differentiating between his people; it was a special power handed down from the divine. "Certainly God has not made a mistake by that. We humans have a number of ways of discriminating against what God himself put in place.

"It is not a coincidence that in Ghana, in Africa, here in the northern region, when a lady outlives her 'usefulness'—and I place that in quotes—when she can no longer give birth, she is seen as a burden to us and we send her away. That way we can marry a younger woman. We're looking for so many reasons to send her away," he said.

"I personally wish that the chiefs were empowered by the statute book of the nation to deal ruthlessly with people who believe these women are bad and must be ruthlessly killed," the Mozio *rana* told me as he drained a bottle of malt.

He believed witchcraft was an important element of rural African life. Punishments doled out by a witch were limited only by one's own imagination. Living with that threat became a form of social control. It was a deterrent from agitating one's neighbors, a prompt for showing respect and kindness and a way of promoting the neighborliness needed to maintain harmony and sustain interdependence in more remote villages. Because an accusation would be taken seriously only if the collective felt threatened, this created an arena to publicly air grievances and allowed each community to decide whether certain behavior fell within acceptable boundaries.

The problem, of course, was its abuse. When the fear of retribution became overwhelming or a woman had simply become a nuisance, she could find herself standing before a chief with nothing more than a chicken's death to decide her fate. Accusers might be expected to support their allegations with perceived threats or examples of suspicious behavior, but because the crimes were committed in an invisible, intangible universe there could never be hard evidence. Yet once the accusatory words were spoken there was little chance a woman could defend herself and no way of removing the dark mark of an accusation. A woman's life was literally destroyed, with only banishment at the witch camp or the promise of violent death to resolve the issue.

There was no question that people needed an outlet for their spiritual fears, but the government should demand proof of these allegations, the Mozio *rana* said. People would think twice before making an accusation if they knew they were going to have to back it up with hard physical evidence or face punishment themselves. "We are not needing any proof," he said. "Once we've made up our minds, if we say it is this, it is that."

The Mozio *rana*'s plan to harness the energy of Ghana's witches assumed they possessed magic, but many of the women and men who found themselves accused of sorcery were simply strong or smart. They were successful farmers whose ability to read weather patterns or properly apply fertilizers or pesticides had made their crops the envy of their neighbors. They were midwives whose ability to read a woman's body or save a difficult birth defied understanding. They were people who looked at the world differently, like the best scientists or theorists, and propelled discovery and innovation with their willingness to try something new. But their differences made them suspicious, and the north's deep-seeded mistrust made it hard to accept that success was owed to new methods, not old mysticism.

"It's very deep in the minds of our people," the Mozio *rana* said. "Day in and day out there are accusations. This thing is a kind of cancer in people's minds. Their minds are polluted."

It meant chiefs had to tread very carefully. In his own village, if the case was serious and could not be solved through conversation, the Mozio *rana* would send the woman to the *gambarana*, the only chief in the Mamprusi area with the spiritual power to deal with these women. It was telling that the *gambarana*'s power trumped the Mozio *rana*'s education. The Mozio *rana* could read and write, but the *gambarana* could "see." When it came to witches, the Mozio *rana* could offer his people nothing but mediation. Because a stay at the witch camp, with all its rituals and cleansing ceremonies, could not completely dispel a community's fear of a suspected witch, sometimes villagers took matters into their own hands. A woman from his own community had been beaten and had her skull cut apart with a knife when she returned to Mozio village. There were times when chiefs allowed the accused women back in their villages, he said, only to watch them quickly die mysterious deaths, leaving no trace of their killers.

"And once they're dead, who will you ask?"

CORPSES THEMSELVES WERE ONCE ASKED TO IDENTIFY THEIR ATtackers; in some places bodies are still wrapped in thick funeral mats and carried in circles atop the shoulders of strong young men while the village watches for unexpected movements, shifts or jolts pointing to a particular person. It's a ritual built on the idea that once a person is released from the bonds of a curse, the body's spirit moves its earthly appendages to out his or her tormentor and prevent further attacks.

Corpse carrying and poison oracles, tests that involved drinking noxious substances in the presence of a shrine to determine whether a woman harbored witchcraft, were outlawed by the British in 1874, after the colonial power declared southern Ghana under its control. While claiming to respect native customs, British administrators prohibited anything they considered to be against "natural justice and morality." That they banned witch finding was a clear sign of the division between the mind-set of colonial administrators and that of their new colony. For the British witchcraft did not exist, so it went against natural justice to punish people for a crime that, technically, they couldn't commit.

Shrines were not considered malevolent; in fact the spirits dwelling within the shrines were often looked at as protective guardians who, with the right sacrifices and maintenance, could bring great fortune. When I first arrived in the north I visited a small village celebrating its twice-yearly sacrifice to an earth shrine, an event that had taken on even greater significance since a village farther up the road had stolen the shrine's attention by stealthily offering sacrifices of their own. I was led to the chief's palace, where I asked to see the shrine. I'm not sure what I expected, perhaps something with an altar and an elaborate tableau of skulls and cowrie shells. Something exotic.

The old chief was surrounded by boys cracking peanut shells.

He had the impish face of a schoolboy prankster, but his smile revealed that his lower teeth were rotten; only gums remained on top.

"How is your husband?!" he shouted, by way of greeting.

He promised to lead me to the shrine if I gave him one goat and the equivalent of twenty dollars, a fee designed to be impossible. When a younger man came in to greet the chief he asked about my marital status and offered to make a bride price for me. When I began earnestly negotiating for a goat and twenty dollars, the chief laughed uproariously and pointed outside the hut's door. I'd actually passed the shrine on my way in but hadn't noticed it. It was nothing more than a clay pot, looped with dried blood, plastered with feathers, and protected by a circular half-wall and a gate of thorn bushes. It was shaded by a huge baobab, a spiritually significant tree in Africa, which was loaded with leaves at the end of the rainy season.

A shrine's humble appearance might offer no clue as to its power, but gifts of slaughtered goats or gallons of palm wine were offered to the fetish in an effort to entice its help in curing infertility or impotence, fattening profits, or guaranteeing a bumper crop. The shrine itself was merely a recognizable home for a specific spirit, a place to leave gifts and sacrifices. A shrine might have significance to only one man or one family, or its power might grow to be legendary, triggering pilgrimages from all over the country to consult a shrine known for its ability to resolve infertility or ferret out witches.

Meticulous records, reports, and correspondence penned by the British offer the first written accounts of the colony's approach to witchcraft; prior to that stories of the battles between strong witches and protective shrines floated from one village to another, carried along by the invisible grapevine. At the time of the British ban women confirmed as witches were either lynched, sold into slavery, or cleansed at an oracle. Rumors of a witch-finding cult called Domankana reached British administrators in 1879. Anyone could join the cult after paying a small fee to the fetish priest and pledging allegiance to the spirit. One received its protection in exchange for vowing to live according to the spirit's rules, which were initially viewed by the British as a useful means of fostering neighborliness.

Breaking the rules, by bewitching a neighbor, for example, meant a swift and brutal death at the hands of the spirit.

The British largely ignored witchcraft as a backward superstition until it grew tiresome or embarrassing, then witch-related activities were labeled "obnoxious customs" and outlawed. As Domankana's membership grew, colonial administrators began clamping down on the cult, fearing it had grown too large to control. By 1906 it was illegal to offer a cure for witchcraft or worship at a witch-hunting shrine or oracle. Two years later British administrators ordered the destruction of shrines related to two more witch-finding cults, after reports that fetish priests were mutilating bodies in an attempt to extract answers from the dead.

A new cult sprang up in the wake of the worldwide influenza outbreak of 1918. At the same time "satellite shrines" from the north's Tongo hills were being sold to charismatic young men for the princely sum of between fifty and four hundred pounds. Small clumps of dirt were scooped up from the initial shrine and carried away in the curve of a ram's horn by newly minted fetish priests who learned to honor and interpret for the shrine, revealing its wants and needs to those looking for spiritual favors. The satellite shrines were considered as powerful as the original, and the money paid for a sliver of a shrine showed both the confidence people placed in its power and the potential for profit that "ritual entrepreneurs" saw in its worship.

There were reports that the fetishes worked; in one area a curse that killed newborn babies seemed to lift, bringing life back to the village. But there was equal evidence of abuse. Brute force was often used to extract a witchcraft confession. One report, filed with colonial authorities in 1924 and detailed by Lawrence University researcher Natasha Grey, described a woman undergoing a witch-finding ceremony. It involved "thirteen good strong men" who "held her one on her neck, three men on her leg, three on her other leg, six men also hold her hands." The woman's vagina was then held open so any man could look inside, an attempt by witch hunters to locate powerful talismans they believed witches kept tucked up inside them.

Cult members were sentenced to hard labor for participating in ceremonies that the colonial courts considered torturous. One cult was banned for "terrorizing and tormenting weak and helpless persons." Courts fined priests for extortion, demanding that the spiritual men refund the money they had charged confessors and instead pay the courts five pounds. In one case the fines levied by a fetish priest against three accused witches amounted to more than a hundred pounds, more money than the average Ghanaian man made in a year. Despite vigorous complaints from missionaries in the country, the shrines themselves were allowed to remain open.

In 1913 British administrators formally instituted a policy of indirect rule, using traditional leaders and local bodies to enforce their policies and promote their interests. Although the British did not acknowledge the existence of witchcraft, the newly established Native Tribunal Councils instituted an ordinance in 1927 formally outlawing its practice in the colony. It was a difficult law to enforce. Because council members were not always gifted with the ability to "see" practicing witches, they began referring witchcraft cases to local shrines—the very places once outlawed by British colonialists—where the fetish priest could use his own methods to test accused witches.

Newspapers from the time show opinion about the shrines was split. Some saw fetish priests as no more than snake oil salesman, charlatans who churned up an all-consuming fear of vengeful spirits and dark-hearted witches, then took what little money their villages possessed to fight the very demons they had conjured. Others saw real benefit from the shrines and their caretakers, pointing to declining rates of illness or better crop yields as signs that the spirits had smiled upon them. Newly converted Christians complained it went against their faith to appear before a pagan shrine, but the councils could see no other way to settle the matter. When an accusation came there were few alternatives to clear one's name or seek spiritual reprieve.

The early days of British rule were filled with great change as dozens and dozens of tribes were bound together under the ban-

ner of the Gold Coast and subjected to unfamiliar laws and bureaucracy. That transition is usually offered as a reason for the
perceived increase in witchcraft. Ghanaians themselves seemed to
grow alarmed at the sheer number of shrines and the voracity of
their witch hunting. The colony's newspaper, the Gold Coast Times,
editorialized that the finding and curing of witches had become an
"industry," with the shrines acting as a "factory." They predicted that
witch-hunting fever would lead to riots and suicides as neighbors,
friends, and family traded damning accusations.

Fetish priests, however, proved to be shrewd businessmen. They
began forming associations, asking for licenses from traditional authorities that would allow them to continue to practice "traditional
medicine" free from persecution. The language of witch hunting
was changing, moving from destruction to healing, from "fetish" to
"medicine." Local authorities were only too happy to charge traditional healers one pound for a license each year, and it quickly became a moneymaker for both parties.

Squeezed between traditional authorities who saw witchcraft as
a reality and Christian missionaries who saw it as a hindrance to
spreading their message, British authorities began receiving more
and more reports from locals, British subjects, and missionaries
alike of abuse and inhumane treatment at shrines dotted throughout southern coastal communities and in the forests of the Ashante
lands. A British employee of the Akim Limited mining company,
for example, described a ceremony in which a young mother was
denounced as a witch. According to Grey, the miner saw the fetish
priest and his apprentices "dance up to the woman and drag her hair
with both hands, shaking her head from side to side, pulling her
cloth down, stripping her naked to the waist in the pouring rain.
Placing his muddy foot on her head, he would order her to confess."

In 1930, after investigating accusations of abuse and extortion
and receiving complaints from missionaries, the colonial government enacted a Native Customs (Witch Finding) Order that removed witchcraft from the law books and instead made witch
finding illegal, effectively shutting down what had become a mas-

sive industry. But what was written in the law books made no difference to what the people believed. Spirits didn't simply disappear with the stroke of a lawmaker's feathered pen; witches didn't give up their dark magic simply because it was illegal for the fetish priests to identify them. Ghanaians were left to struggle with curses and witchcraft with no legitimate way to seek reprieve. J. B. Danquah, a British-educated lawyer and philosopher, agreed to challenge the ban against witch finding, a legal contest that helped promote a national identity in the disjointed colony, as well as the idea that, when it came to issues like witchcraft, Ghanaians themselves could excel where the British had failed, by possessing the leadership needed to reconcile old traditions with modern times.

Danquah was born into one of Ghana's most powerful families: his brother was king of the Akyem Abuakwa, one of the country's largest and richest kingdoms. Born to a royal line but raised amid colonial politics, Danquah moved effortlessly between the two worlds. He served his brother as secretary before attending the University of London, where he earned a doctorate in law. Danquah argued that witchcraft was a very real presence in the lives of his countrymen and that this was well-known by both local and colonial authorities. He wasn't looking for the government to answer definitively whether witchcraft existed. He wasn't asking for reassurance that Ghanaians were right to feel threatened by witchcraft. Instead he expected the government to distinguish between those who were coerced into confession and those who appeared willingly before the shrines. Men and women who believed they were bewitched or believed they were practicing witchcraft needed an avenue to deal with their affliction, he argued, and this was something only a fetish priest could do. He compared the job of the fetish priest with that of a psychoanalyst, a very modern term to describe an ancient practice. People with problems went to the fetish priest seeking solutions. They talked about their problems and the fetish priest helped them pinpoint the cause, then helped them devise a strategy for coping with the problem. Compelling a confession of witchcraft was unfair, Danquah agreed, but to outlaw these witch finders was to leave people stranded with their belief, with nowhere to take their fears and anxieties. They needed people who could "see" to offer reassurance and solutions.

The courts agreed, setting aside the ban against witch finding so long as the shrine dealt only with people who willingly appeared at the oracle. The duties of the fetish priest were considered important local knowledge, and the Society of African Herbalists was established to help preserve traditional knowledge, improve the standard of local practices, and encourage scientific examination of traditional treatment. By 1940 virtually every district had made it mandatory for herbalists to operate with a license. In exchange for the license a traditional healer had to agree that his practice would avoid public nudity, coercive confessions, and body desecration or mutilation.

Since then Ghana's law books have seen little change in regard to witchcraft. Accusations are dealt with using more conventional codified laws: it is assault to harm a woman, even if she is suspected to be a witch, and murder to lynch her. Defamation could be used to defend one's reputation, but the few cases filed with the court hadn't reached their conclusion. Complaints could also be filed with the Commission for Human Rights and Administrative Justice, a government-funded watchdog group whose northern satellite offices were woefully underresourced.

NEARLY TWO HOURS NORTH OF GAMBAGA THE LANDSCAPE changed from flat, grassy savannah to a clustering of pink granite rocks. The Tongo hills, as they are known, are home to one of the country's most important shrines, a network of fetishes representing ancestral and earth spirits that embody the former colony's last frontier of resistance against British rule. Tongnaab, one of the land's most powerful witch-hunting spirits, lives in a natural hollow in these hills. Tongnaab could be called to attention by the clapping sound of its faithful; northerners and southerners alike seek its help. Napoa was so tormented by her witchcraft that she visited the sacred sinkhole, hoping its spirit could control her gift.

In April 2000 a local council made an application to UNESCO

to have the Tongo hills listed as a world heritage site. They argued that the area not only contains important and powerful religious shrines, but that its Tallensi architecture is unique and perfectly preserved. I rode there with Simon, who had never been to the site and was skeptical that Napoa had actually consulted the shrine. It was believed that pledging allegiance to Tongnaab and then failing to give up practicing witchcraft could have grave consequences. I didn't suggest taking Napoa with us. Neither did Simon.

After we turned off the country's main north-south highway Simon stopped several times to ask directions, studiously ignoring the plentiful signposts with arrows and mileage countdowns pointing the way. A Peace Corps volunteer had been sent to live in the Tongo hills in 2002 to help the community transform the network of sacred sites into an ecotourism project. Signboards, a visitors' center, and a gift shop had been constructed, accommodation was being built, footpaths had been cleared, and after intense debate a visitors' fee of one dollar for locals and $2.50 for foreigners had been set. A photocopied pamphlet briefly explained the history of the shrine, reaching back two centuries, and warned visitors that those expecting to visit the shrine could enter only if they were stripped to the waist. Clothing was considered taboo to the shrine; even the fetish priest had to enter topless.

The rolling hills framing the visitors' center were imbued with a sense of spirituality. When the Tallensi people discovered the hills they found smooth, dark rocks laid in natural formations as though they were the toys of God. Stone stacks still soar to six hundred feet in some places, with rocks balanced precariously on top of one another. Boulders spill down the sides of the hills as though they've escaped from a giant's bag of marbles. Nestled in the dark green of the surrounding forests and shrouded by mist from the morning's rain, the whole place has a magical feel.

It's hard to imagine how the Tallensi people first found the Tongnaab shrine, buried under a ledge of thick, flat rocks in a dry plain dotted with dark trees. The area was covered in forest when the Tallensi first arrived, the fetish priest told us. The land was loaded

with lions and leopards and hyena, animals no longer seen in West
Africa. He offered no clues as to what made a man first crawl into
the shrine's natural opening, nor what might have possessed him to
clap. There seemed to be no story describing the first time someone
stood in the shrine's presence and heard words where others heard
only noise. The historians Jean Allman and John Parker, who spent
four years researching the Tongnaab shrine and its place in Ghana's
ritual history, were told the spirit predated the Tallensi people, that
it called the people to it. The shrine had always shone on them, the
fetish priest said. It provided what the Tallensi asked for so long as
they met its demands.

Very little is known about the precolonial conditions of Ghana's
northernmost reaches. The combination of isolation and a lingering hostility toward strangers who might be involved in slave raiding protected the smaller northern tribes from French, German,
and British government explorers until the late nineteenth century.
British troops followed a route paved with treaties and peace agreements signed during an 1894 expedition that ended just north of
Gambaga and Nalerigu, at lands controlled by people they dubbed
Frafra, a smudging of words offered in greeting meaning *suffering, suffering*. According to Allman and Parker, a local government
agent born in a southern coastal community encountered people
who "move[d] about in perfect nudity" and decorated themselves
with pierced lips, noses, and ears. The only course to subjugation,
he reported to colonial administrators, was to take up arms against
people who carried poison-tipped spears and engaged in banditry,
earning them the reputation of being fierce and lawless.

The Tallensi people led a life of subsistence farming, cultivating
the fertile fields around the gallery of rocks, building their homes
within its protective embrace, and honoring its networks of spirits
and shrines. Twice a year the tribe performed elaborate festivals to
thank the ancestral and earth shrines for their blessings and to seek
out their continued help with plentiful rains and bountiful yields.
When necessary they fought off marauding tribes and repelled slave
raiders. They treated the pale-skinned British agents no differently.

It rankled the British that the Tallensi would take direction from an unseen deity but refuse to follow their rules. When in 1899 northerners continued to ignore British direction, the colonial power employed a scorched-earth policy, periodically moving through the region seizing cattle and razing crops.

Still, the British ban against worship at the shrine was largely ignored. Allman and Parker detail in their book, *Tongnaab: The History of a West African God*, how an armed formation of soldiers carrying two maxim guns and 27-pound field guns marched into the hills in March 1911, only to be held off by a hail of poison-tipped arrows. After five days of sporadic fighting between troops and tribe, the British carried out an artillery barrage, firing thirty-two shells before setting fire to the hills. Descendants of the defeated Tallensi warriors told Allman and Parker that their people lost the battle not because they'd been overpowered but because they'd defied the wishes of the ancestors. The attack coincided with an important festival, one that required fasting and forbade violence or hostility. After long deliberation the elders decided to break the taboo and retaliate. Already weakened with hunger, their defense was doomed by the broken taboo.

The British set out to demolish the shrine, then they forcibly removed and relocated the people living within and around the rocks. A fence was erected around the hills, and it was forbidden—to anyone—to enter or live within its borders. Pilgrimages were banned. Four years later an administrator riding through the area on horseback saw signs that the local population had been surreptitiously visiting and honoring the shrines. It seemed Tongnaab had been rebuilt and repaired. Small gifts and sacrifices were placed at the base of various shrines, hidden in the crevices of the rocks where passersby would be unlikely to see them. The discovery triggered a second campaign to destroy the shrine, this time using local people armed with machetes and matches. Experts were dispatched to lay dynamite, but they found their drill bits could barely make a dent in the hard rocks. Explosives nestled in the grooves of the granite produced only dust, leaving the boulders intact.

There was no point in continuing the ban against visits to the shrine: it was already mobile. Those wishing to consult the deity more frequently had only to purchase a bit of sacred soil, train as an apprentice, pledge their allegiance, and carry home their piece of the spirit. In the south a progeny of the Tongo hills became known as Nana Tongo. It was a shrine defended by J. B. Danquah that was indelibly linked with Ghana's quest for independence.

When the British anthropologist R. S. Rattray visited the shrine in 1928 he promised the spirit a cow if it aided his research. Rattray had done extensive studies of the customs and culture of the Asante and was considered Britain's greatest authority on the Gold Coast's southern tribes. He was drawn to the primitive north, however, to the kinds of people who were rumored to live traditionally, unconcerned with British or missionary morals. According to Allman and Parker, Rattray's journals suggest he was expecting to see "pagan gods and naked humanity" gathered before the Tongo shrines, but instead he met "well-dressed Africans who . . . had motored hundreds of miles from Kumasi, Kwahu and Mampon": "Among these were several of my Asante friends of old days, and I shall never forget the look of amazement on their faces at meeting me in such a place."

His fellow supplicants asked Tongnaab for help with their businesses, to allow their wives to successfully carry children, or to restore their health. One man complained of pains in his belly and asked the spirit to look at the illness, discover who was causing it, and kill the person so the man might finally recover his strength. When Rattray crawled out of the shrine to retrieve his clothes, he watched as the pilgrims were "painted with lines of red clay on their cheeks, arms and legs, their back and between their breasts.

"When I state that these supplicants were educated men and women, some of whom owned large businesses, well-furnished European houses, and not a few of them their own cars, in which they had come hundreds of miles to visit this pagan god, the power and influence of the old beliefs may readily be imagined," Rattray wrote.

The hills' most famous shrine is less commonly known as *ba'ar*

Tonna'ab ya'nee. It was cared for by a young man with a broad nose, wide eyes, and a healthy beard of long, dark whiskers. He wore a green towel around his neck and an apronlike cloth of woven purple thread that came to his ankles in a point. Atop his head he wore a red fez with a small mending scar. As we approached he fiddled with a bright orange mobile phone case and a tiny green flashlight. On his feet were blue plastic shower shoes with glaring yellow thongs.

He sat beneath a neem tree whose thin leaves created a gentle rustle in the breeze. Ducks waddled by. Nearby, one of dozens of small shrines was marked with the long-snouted skull of a donkey. It dangled from a braided rope threaded through the intersection of two raised arms of a weather-beaten tree trunk. A large, perfectly round grave marker rose two feet from the ground, as carefully coated with concrete as one would swirl icing around a baked cake. A finger drawn through the wet concrete left a curt epitaph: a name and the date of death. No slogans, no attempts to sum up a man's life with a short phrase.

Tallensi people who first found the shrine felt compelled to serve it, the fetish priest explained. Even today, when witches arrive at the shrine, they feel compelled to confess what they have done. If they deny, they're told to drink "bad water" that will cause them to die if they practice again. He invited us to see the shrine for ourselves, promising we would see signs of the god's power. Not a god, he corrected. The voice of God.

Our climb began at a tangle of smooth stones studded with donkey skulls, the first testament to the power of the spirit. The skulls represented the sacrifices made in thanks for gifts received. The teeth of the donkeys' clenched jaws, monstrous and perfectly square, formed a zipper to the back of the jawbone. The skulls had been squeezed between the rocks, arranged so their empty eye sockets stared out at passersby.

From its base trees, scrub, and stacked rocks hid the switchbacks of the path, making it difficult to get a sense of scale to the summit. In places the rocks made a natural staircase, but the distance between "steps" was sometimes so large it was easier to back up, sit, and swing up one's legs. Our guide was a small boy with bulging calf muscles and the "African sandal" of heavily calloused bare feet. I soon shucked my own flimsy flip-flops; it was easier to get a grip on the granite with toes that were free to curl.

I sweated in the sticky humidity. Simon began huffing and puffing long before we reached the top. I was a little unsure about going topless; we had passed plenty of people on the path returning from the shrine and I felt vaguely uncomfortable about parading around half-naked in front of strangers, or worse, Simon. He thought I should stay outside the shrine while he went in to investigate but changed his mind after struggling to the top. He sat heavily on a stone, sweat pouring down his neck, as our child guide looked at us with impatience. Simon couldn't imagine climbing any further. He deliberated aloud. After a few minutes sitting in a gentle breeze that wicked away the sweat, Simon finally decided that since he'd come all this way and I should not go in—it went from a choice to the unthinkable—he would continue alone.

I turned away from the rocks to catch my breath and realized we'd been so focused on the climb that we'd nearly missed the view. The rocky floor of the hills gave way to a green carpet, the deep green of mango trees, stretching on to the edge of the earth. It seemed unbearably empty; the small mud villages disappeared in their insignificance, their clever design erasing them from the landscape.

I could hear Simon talking to the child as they climbed, pumping him—"Truthfully now"—for a bit of raw honesty on how much farther it would be. I trailed behind, figuring I could at least sit fully clothed just outside the shrine and have Simon describe it to me. At the entrance was a strange bush covered in rags, the second sign of the shrine's power. There was a pink-and-black-striped blouse, a purple housedress, a faded lime green wrap, a rolled-up blue and yellow prayer mat, and a pair of men's navy work trousers. These were the clothes of the witches who'd ignored their pledge to the spirit, the child explained. A snarl of vines grew around the clothes, as though the shrine itself had wrapped its spindly arms around the rags. Women killed by the shrine were said to spend their final minutes shrieking confessions. They were warned when they swallowed the concoction that they'd be killed by the spirit if they practiced witchcraft again, and their families were honor-bound to return the women's possessions to the shrine if the spirit came hunting.

Inside the shrine the floor dropped away, forming a sinkhole where sound bounced off the walls. Hundreds of calabashes, carried up by people making sacrifices over the years, were stacked inside. One side of the dark hollow was covered in piles of orange pottery—more gifts offered to the shrine. A couple already inside clapped loudly, producing a melody of echoes ricocheting off the stone walls. Simon placed a twenty-thousand-cedi note atop a small basket—"So it won't seem as though I was just touring," he said—then crawled out like a crab.

We asked the fetish priest about Napoa, but he didn't seem to know her, or if he did he didn't let on. We described her: her lost teeth, her mannish face and reputation for powerful witchcraft, her desperation to atone for the death of her cowife's daughter. The details meant nothing to him. Many women came to the shrine seeking a cure for witchcraft, he said, but some were not willing to drink the bad water that would compel them to give up their witchcraft or face the wrath of Tongnaab. Those women were sent away, he said. The others drank and made their pledge.

The idea of a witch camp was foreign to the Tallensi. The women were allowed back to their villages because no one could deny the shrine's proven ability to enforce a woman's pledge to give up witchcraft. A village could feel safe in the knowledge that Tongnaab was protecting them. It was the country's most powerful witch-hunting shrine, a reputation earned over decades of identifying and controlling women practicing witchcraft. No one could dispute the shrine's decisions nor escape its punishment. No one needed to stay, unless the shrine was specifically asked to protect the woman from a threat or unless it perceived the woman was in danger. In those cases, if the woman agreed she was a witch she could end up at Gambaga, the

fetish priest said, although from his tone it seemed he was skeptical
of the *gambarana's* ability to control the women.

The priest pointed to the termite hills and fetishes behind him.
Tongnaab was not like those shrines, he said. It was not a god. It
was God. That's what made it infinitely more powerful than the
gambarana. "He is a human being. This is God," he said.

Simon decided there was no way Napoa had actually gone and
pledged her allegiance to the Tongnaab shrine. If she had she would
be dead, he said, killed by the spirit for her stubborn refusal to give
up her gift.

CHAPTER SEVEN

SUCCESSION TO THE ROYAL SKINS, A COLLECTION OF BRISTLED goat hides passed down through the generations to symbolize the collected wisdom and power of the ancestral chiefs, was based on the orderly rotation of branches of the royal family tree, known as "gates." When a vacancy arose, the area's ultimate tribal leader, the *nayiri*, as well as a council of elders and chiefs known as the kingmakers of Nalerigu spent a couple of weeks consulting their gods and ancestors, divining the choice for chief in a frenzy of prayer and sacrifice.

A chief did not have to be educated, rich, or even particularly skilled at leadership to be selected. The process was steeped in rituals meant to be guided by the spirits, but it quietly conformed to a power-rotation schedule that staved off deadly chieftaincy disputes. A chief had to die of natural causes before succession would move on to the next gate, a rule designed to keep saboteurs from spiking food or drink with poison in the hopes of speeding the wheel of succession back to their gate.

David Kansuk, the ninth of his father's eleven sons, was headed for university when his family nominated him to become chief of Nakpanduri village. He had already trained as a nurse and worked at a health and family planning outpost in Kpatinga, Hawa's home village, about an hour's drive from Nakpanduri. Kansuk admitted he was an unusual choice for Nakpanduri's chief, not only because he didn't actually live there, but also because his Christian faith went against the village's animist majority.

"You have to know how to handle the two things together," he said. "If I came out clearly as a Christian, a principled Christian, the chances of my missing the boat would have been very high. I said my brothers, who were pagan, they should do whatever they think they can do for me to succeed. But for me, I'll use the church and the pastors." Selecting a chief required traditional sacrifices, which Kansuk left to his brothers. "I told them whatever sacrifices, whatever divinations, they should do it. I will give the money to do it. But I was also praying with the pastors. The Nalerigu pastor, we were praying each night. For the fourteen days we were at Nalerigu, we were praying each night."

More disturbing to his competitors than his faith was his age. He was only forty-two. Since the average life expectancy in Ghana is fifty-nine, the longevity of a man who had lived into his sixties or seventies was often enough to qualify him for the job of village chief. But a chief's advanced age not only assumed he'd amassed wisdom and experience; it also ensured that each gate would have a relatively short reign.

The other families competing for Nakpanduri's chieftaincy immediately protested Kansuk's selection as his gate's representative since they felt it gave his family an unfair advantage: the man could live and rule for decades. Years and years and years could pass before power moved into the hands of another branch of the family.

"It was a hectic time," Kansuk said of his election. In fact it was violent and unpredictable. "Before I got to Nakpanduri, because of my age advantage, all the other four gates said no, they cannot sit down and see this 'small boy' rule them. So they organized themselves into a formidable opposition. They came together and they called on their supporters. They came out with guns and they blocked the road." In the chaos Kansuk's supporters managed to get him safely to his home, which they barricaded and guarded for three days before the new chief decided it was creating unnecessary tension.

"I was sure the [rival gates] wouldn't do anything. My father had served previous chiefs until he became chief. And my brothers had served previous chiefs. So there is no point for them to deny me," he said. "The tradition is, once a chief, you are chief until you die. So let's bury the hatchet."

The competition for chieftaincy stems from the potential for profit and power. Traditional leaders are often privileged, receiving gifts from their villagers as a sign of respect, levying fines or penalties as part of their judgments, and collecting taxes and "tributes" from farmers using their lands. A traditional chief might be most readily compared with a town mayor, a politician of sorts who sits at the head of the village and represents the town's interests, but he is so much more than that. Part priest, part judge, part marriage counselor, a chief can spend much of his time on the skins resolving disputes. Ghana's thousands of chiefs have been banned from politics since the 1960s, ostensibly because lawmakers want traditional leaders to maintain the appearance of neutrality, but they have always operated in the shadow of the national political system, often running parallel to courts and administrative councils, sometimes doing their work where more formal institutions are found lacking.

Campaigning for the chieftaincy was confined to the short window between the harvest and the next planting, producing something of a chieftaincy season, akin to the run-up to an election. It was a frenzied period of a few weeks when dozens of "enskinment" ceremonies took place across the northern region, culminating in loud celebrations where the *pito* flowed and the drums banged well into the night. A village's faith in their chief's leadership wasn't merely a product of strict African hierarchy, nor was it a mindless sort of blind respect attached more to the office than the individual. It was born of belief, a belief in the power and benevolence of the guiding ancestors.

"Once you are a chief, if you didn't come there by any other means, but you came there because you are from the royal line, when you sit on the skin you will just have the feeling you are with all of them," Kansuk said. "You have the feeling. You are in full control. That's the way you feel. And when you are talking, [the village's people] will not look straight into your eyes. You will see them bowing. It means they are taking it. And the fact they know your father was on that skin, your grandfather was on that skin, your great-grandfather was on that skin, because of our belief in ancestral power, that's the general belief, they know that you, the occupant of the skin now, it's not only you but all those who sat as chiefs, they are behind you. You, yourself, you have that feeling and the same people around you have that feeling. 'He has the backing of all the former chiefs. So whatever he is saying, we'll either take it or face the wrath of the ancestors.'"

Kansuk epitomized the struggle faced by modern chiefs. Some, like the *gambarana*, tasted the bitterness of poverty before ascending to the throne. Others, like Kansuk and the Mozio *rana*, were headed for middle-class lives. They had the security of a relatively stable government job to provide a steady income when the ancestors chose them to ascend to the goatskins. Their education, their experience, or their religion sometimes ran counter to some of the more traditional customs.

While the *gambarana* was willing to see witchcraft everywhere and the Mozio *rana* wanted to use whatever power witches possessed for development and innovation, Kansuk seemed caught in the chasm between traditional and modern. He threatened to use the courts to decide a witchcraft case after a man from his village, who had watched his neighbors torch his house and burn all of his food stores, had swallowed DDT to escape facing allegations of witchcraft. The man fell to the ground, foaming at the mouth, as his horrified accusers looked on. They raced him to the hospital, but he died before they got much farther than the outskirts of the village.

"I was prepared to prosecute them so it would serve as a deterrent," Kansuk said. It was unprecedented for the village to take a case of witchcraft to the courts. The man's grieving family talked him out of it; they were distant kin to the accusers and thought an arrest would only bring more trouble. "But I told the people that henceforth, my patience has been taken to the limit. Next time, I'm not going to listen to anybody."

What Kansuk knew of leading a small rural village had been gleaned from his father and his brothers, his grandfather and his uncles. He took his role seriously, viewing himself as a kind of mediator rather than a prince. He didn't settle disputes by siding with the highest bidder. Men seeking the chief's judgment would enter the courtyard of Kansuk's sprawling mud palace and place themselves at the base of the platform where he sat on a large pillow, surrounded by his council of elders.

"First you allow them to come with the story," Kansuk said. "Then you allow them to talk out. And after the end, they will now look at the chief. Then the old people will say, 'In the olden days, this is what we are doing.' They are guiding you as chief as to what was normal practice in the olden days. But it's left to the chief to use his discretion and then settle the case so there will be peace."

Kansuk couldn't handle witchcraft cases: he had no ancestral powers to do so. "The other chiefs, no, we don't handle this. We don't do it. The Gambaga *rana* is the only chief recognized the whole of our side to handle witchcraft cases. So if I sit in my palace to do it, it won't be effective," he said.

He regularly heard allegations of witchcraft in his position as a nurse at the health clinic. Families would often whisper their fears of witchcraft when they brought their sick relatives to him for treatment, and he would gently dissuade them from looking for spiritual reasons for the illness. He remembered a young girl, maybe fourteen, who died at the clinic from an attempted home abortion. He found stinking, rotted herbs pushed up inside her, likely purchased in secret on the advice of a traditional healer. Her family, oblivious to the pregnancy, was certain someone had used witchcraft to harass the girl and spent her final hours trying to coax a list of suspects out of her. The girl took the secret of her pregnancy to the grave. To hide the embarrassing truth she allowed her family to believe the lie of witchcraft, even though it carried with it the virtual certainty that an innocent woman would be destroyed by the accusation. Kansuk felt there was nothing he could say about the herbs or the botched abortion; he didn't want to betray the girl's confidence or her memory.

"It's ignorance," Kansuk said. "In an African setting, any mishap—anything that happens—should have a cause. Every death has a cause. So if somebody dies, the soothsayer says it's because of this, this, and this that he died. Every death has a cause. And if you are rich, sometimes they believe your riches is due to some other thing, like witchcraft. Maybe you are a witch. You are selling people's souls to the big markets. That is why you are rich. Even if you are rich, they can accuse you for being a witch."

PANDEMONIUM BROKE OUT WHEN THE REIGNING *gambarana* WAS chosen as Gambaga's tribal leader nearly two decades ago. Police shot three people in the melee, as drunken supporters of rival candidates for the chieftaincy squared off. The cycle of gates had placed the competition between Yahaya Wuni, as he was known then, and a man nicknamed "Wobgu," Mampruli for *elephant* and the symbol of Ghana's New Patriotic Party. Wobgu paraded his party colors, something widely considered unwise for a traditional leader, and acted as though he had already been chosen chief.

Yahaya Wuni, by contrast, was a farmer. Sometimes he filled in for his brother at his night watchman's job. Occasionally he earned a little money as a stone-cracker, banging apart thick rocks with a homemade hammer and selling the resulting pebbles. He had never been to school and could neither read nor write. The ancestors chose Wuni, but when he was enskinned as the *gambarana* more than fifteen years ago "he was wild," a local teacher told me. People thought he was power-hungry, desperate to prove that he had the gifts of a great *gambarana* by exaggerating his wizardly skills and making wild pronouncements.

"He was so hostile," Simon said, shaking his head. "That was the time when I would have preferred anyone be here doing this work but me." In the early days of his reign the *gambarana* refused to allow the women to leave the camp. Rumors of mistreatment made headlines in the local papers in the late 1990s. The "inmates," as the newspapers called them, were hired out to local farmers and put to work planting, weeding, and harvesting crops. A few newspapers went so far as to suggest that the chief was traveling to small villages and accusing women so he could add them to his army of cheap workers, although I never saw evidence of that, nor did I hear any reports of it from people living in Gambaga.

There was no denying the women were vulnerable. Alone and without financial support, they were susceptible to exploitation and rumored to be trading sex with Gambaga's men for meals, clothes, or a bit of cash. The older women were in pathetic shape, emaciated, without regular access to food or water and crowded two or three to a tiny compound. There were no medical services, either because the clinic didn't want to treat the accused women or because the women were too afraid or too poor to seek treatment. Simon buried four or five in his first year at the camp.

An association of women lawyers and a handful of female politicians began campaigning for the camp's closure. They traveled to Gambaga to stage a news conference, arguing that it was against human rights to keep these women in decrepit camps. The women were being unfairly targeted for baseless accusations, unfairly banished without trial, and denied the right to live where they chose, free from slanderous accusations. Unless the chief could prove his effectiveness, or the women themselves could prove they were indeed witches and therefore deserved banishment, the lawyers and politicians reasoned that the so-called witches should be sent home to their families and left alone.

"They just picked up on the wrong information," said Simon, who knew that women facing witchcraft accusations faced either banishment or death. At the camp the women could receive food rations from Catholic Relief Services and money for health care from the Presbyterian church. Closing the camps would leave them with nowhere to go and no way to survive. Simon agreed with the politicians' message, but he knew that mob justice would find the camp's women if they returned home without first seeking permission from their village chief or adequately preparing their family or accusers. He pleaded with the lawyers and politicians to listen to the facts: the accused women had nowhere to go and no one to care for them.

"Nobody went and brought them, they were lynching them then," Simon remembered telling them. "You say they should go: Go where? Where should they go? Have you gone to their villages to make sure there is a place for them and people to care for them? Have you investigated what will happen to them when they return? You are here twenty minutes and already you are solving this problem. In twenty years we're not going to understand it."

Simon recognized then that things couldn't go on the way they were. With the women unable to leave, the camp had become overcrowded, making it hard to argue against reports that they were being mistreated. Simon began praising the *gambarana*'s generosity and commending him for providing the women with an alternative to certain death within their communities. It was laudable that he took in the banished when no one else would have them. Through careful negotiation Simon eventually convinced the *gambarana* that the women should not be kept as though in prison. Instead he suggested the *gambarana* run the camp like a hospital. He could "treat" the women, curing their witchcraft. As word spread, Simon promised him, more women would come to replace those who had gone home.

"He was gaining from it, and he wouldn't like the thing to die off immediately. We had to work with him tactfully and diplomatically," Simon said. "He feared they would come and demolish it. That put the fear into him."

The problem inherent in placing the power over suspected witches into the hands of one man who profited from the discovery of more witches was obvious. A man who had known the depths of poverty—and the hunger and want that came with it—could hardly be motivated to reject the very thing that gave him his power and respect. His livelihood was tied to witchcraft; he could hardly be expected to use his authority to deaden belief in it. Even Simon was growing less convinced of his magic and more convinced of his corruption.

"The chief is always on the side of the sick person, the accuser, because he knows the woman will have to stay and there will be a bill to pay," Simon groused. The chief collected a fee for sacrificing the chicken. He expected the family to pay for the cost of a woman's stay. When they finally came to collect their mothers, sisters, or wives the *gambarana* collected a further payment for performing the final leaving ceremony. Altogether it could quickly add up to more than two hundred dollars—almost as much as the average family spent in an entire year.

Two women and a man had appeared at the *gambarana's* palace a few days earlier and the chief had convicted all three. Simon hadn't found the time to interview all of them, but he understood that one woman had been accused after a man came back from his farm claiming to have seen her in a dream. Simon poked holes in the story, found it wanting. Why was the man sleeping at his farm? How did he manage to have a dream in the daylight? It was anyone's guess.

Simon had once seen an illusionist perform magic and knew that he used hand signals, verbal clues, and other tricks to fool the audience into believing he could make things disappear and reappear. He was certain the assistants were in on the tricks, even if they'd just been pulled from the audience. He saw illusions in the *gambarana's* ceremonies too. The chief would lecture over the bird, sermonizing about the ancestors and the nature of witchcraft. This was a trick, Simon said, like the illusionist would use, because it gave time for the life to drain out of the bird so the *gambarana* could throw it in a way that would allow him to control how it landed. Simon believed the best strategy was to slit the bird's throat and cast it into the air immediately. That way it would struggle more and have a better chance of landing in your favor. "The chicken can be killed and you can talk and talk and it will be dead before he throws it," he said.

I WAS EXPECTED TO PRESENT MYSELF AT THE MUD PALACE EVERY few days and reiterate my gratitude for being allowed access to the women, but I'd learned not to go empty-handed. I sensed that the *gambarana* had only begun to plumb his position's potential for profit. The amount collected for *kola* climbed and climbed. A reporter from Reuters was charged fifteen dollars; a Dutch writer who stayed in the room next to mine at the guesthouse confessed she paid thirty dollars; two European tourists handed over nearly forty dollars each. The *gambarana*'s greed didn't seem to trouble the people he ruled. They felt that if visitors were willing to pay that much the *gambarana* couldn't be blamed for asking. The chief could not "chop" stones, I was told. He too needed to eat.

By the time I left the village *kola* paid to the *gambarana* had cost me about fifty dollars. I was conscious of setting an expensive precedent for the visitors who came after me and tried giving gifts instead of cash, presenting the chief at various times with photos of himself and some of his younger children, a jar of strawberry jam, a vial of the antibiotic ciprofloxin, a canister of multivitamins, a map of Africa, and three glossy commemorative posters of Ghana's leaders, printed for the country's fiftieth Independence Day celebration. I often wondered if he remembered me from one visit to the next. During each visit he inquired about my marital status and offered to take me as a bride. It wasn't flattery or love at first sight: he did the same with every white woman who visited him.

One of the town's teachers suggested with a mischievous grin that I take a few bottles of cheap liquor the next time I went to greet the *gambarana*. I never followed his advice; even I had heard that the chief had a serious drinking problem and had had to be ferried to the hospital on a few occasions to dry out. Over the years, as his drinking had worsened, his temper became the stuff of legend. He'd once ordered the demolition of a guesthouse belonging to a Canadian woman after she mocked his interest in one of the town's beauties. He'd also challenged the aging pastor of the Assemblies of God church to a fistfight after the man suggested that some of the accused women should be reunited with their families.

The *gambarana* never denied me access to the accused women, but despite the routine donation of gifts and cash he still refused all requests for another interview and grumbled to Simon that he saw no benefit from "all these whites." When I went to pay *kola* with Kizito near the end of my stay the *gambarana* stated plainly that he needed me to do something for him so he would always remember me. Whites were always coming to him, and people were always seeing the whites coming to him, he complained, but he had nothing to show for it. His family were farmers and there were many children to feed, clothe, and educate. He wanted me to do something sustainable, Kizito told me, helpfully suggesting that I could buy him a tractor.

Simon bristled at the *gambarana*'s greed in demanding *kola* from people wanting to visit the banished women. "They are not people put in a zoo where you come and pay and see them. We don't like that idea. If that is to happen, they should give [the money] to the women or to the home," he said, meaning his church project.

Simon told me it was common knowledge that fetish priests, who cared for and interpreted for the shrines, could not make money off the spirit's work. The spirits couldn't be owned, only appeased, and they did not tolerate greed. "That thing shouldn't be a money-making venture," the Mozio *rana* said. "It is to save a life and let the woman go back to her community." He shook his head, dismayed to learn the *gambarana* was collecting as much as two hundred dollars to perform ceremonies for the accused women. "The traditional way, cash is not part of it," he said. "The cash is too much. What do people have? How will they come by that? Why is he collecting this money, why should they bring it here and go back with nothing? It should be used to assist them in resettling properly."

Simon had begun secretly subsidizing the *gambarana*'s extortion after a man came to him saying he couldn't pay the twenty dollars the *gambarana* was demanding in exchange for his wife's release. Simon figured he'd spent the equivalent of two thousand dollars over the years. He'd done it by fudging his expense reports, never letting on to donors or his supervisors that the chief was demanding money. As Simon's budget dwindled, the *gambarana*'s fees only grew. Now the old chief routinely demanded upwards of fifty dollars for a woman's freedom. In a place where most families spent coins if they spent anything at all, fifty dollars was a king's ransom, a sum too vast to spend on the release of a suspicious woman.

Ayishetu Bugre was working with a local construction crew in order to save enough money to buy her freedom. The chief had already collected seventy-five dollars from her husband. Now he was demanding an additional seventy dollars for her release. The family's home had been burned to the ground; their livestock were released or slaughtered; their crops were razed. They had nothing, so Ayishetu found a job helping to build a house for the district chief executive. Six days a week she carried heavy pots of cement on her head for a house being built for the political appointee, a man in his twenties who had been picked by the ruling government in Accra to hand out government construction projects in the region. Ayishetu had been promised fifty dollars a month for her work, but confided she still hadn't been paid after two months on the job.

Simon believed his hands were tied. He couldn't confront the chief or make accusations, fearing the *gambarana* would toss him out or refuse to work with him. He also couldn't leave the women to find their own way home. "It's not a matter of an instant or immediate solution," he said. "We'll have to gradually and secretly discuss it with the Tamale people. It shouldn't be a one-person affair."

He envisioned the Commission for Human Rights and Administrative Justice—"the Tamale people"—or some other powerful group hosting a large witchcraft-themed workshop with all of the chiefs and all of the leaders from the other camps. They would explain for everyone to hear how the various shrines protected the village and the women. The other leaders would be asked to explain their fees, whether they charged anything for a woman's release. Everyone would then hear that women living at other witch camps were free to leave without paying. The accused women would know the *gambarana* was swindling them.

"Then maybe one of the women will have courage . . ." Simon began.

I felt a flash of hot anger. "'Have courage,' Simon? You expect these women to have courage? These women, who are vulnerable and old and who live at this man's mercy?"

Maybe a woman who is brave, like Ayishetu, he suggested. She could say to the chief, "But we heard at the workshop that the others are not charging."

"And so what?" I asked. "So what?"

We sat in silence, Simon staring at the floor. I knew I should apologize, but weeks of frustration had built up. Women here had such unbelievably difficult lives. One old woman, whose face was so lined it mimicked the weft and weave of cloth, also had the bulging biceps of an amateur body builder, a legacy of a lifetime of manual labor, of mornings and afternoons spent pounding mortar against pestle. On the road I had watched little girls silently trailing their mothers. They should have been in the classroom, but instead their necks strained under the weight of a bundle of sticks three times their size. They knew the drudgery of chores, not the play of child-hood. How could my life as a Western woman be so different from the lives of these women? Why couldn't they catch a break?

I knew there was no chance Ayishetu would fight this battle. Simon and I had met her husband, Harouna, on the road one night as he was cycling home from visiting her at the witch camp. He had looked deflated, almost forlorn. He desperately wanted to bring his wife home, but couldn't afford to pay the chief for her release. He didn't know what to do. Seventy-five dollars was too much money, he said, but what could he do but collect some cash and beg for his wife?

"They have nothing," Simon sympathized. "Their home has been destroyed. All of their animals gone. They have no money to pay and he doesn't know how he will ever raise such a sum."

Harouna told Simon that he didn't want his wife to be the start of any trouble. He was afraid of the chief's temper. He preferred Simon wait to make a stand until it involved another woman. Simon and I went around and around the issue. It wasn't realistic to expect the women to be brave, he allowed, but CHRAJ should host a workshop anyway. I didn't believe the chief would own up to what he charged the women. And how would CHRAJ ever host such a thing when they didn't have enough money to even visit this camp?

Simon hit on a new strategy: perhaps he could tell the chief that "international people" had noticed he was charging the women for their release, that in fact the women themselves had complained. I pictured myself pulling my wheeled suitcase down the dirt road leading away from Gambaga, having been ordered out of the village by the furious chief. The chief could limit access to the women, and if he felt threatened by the watchful eyes of "international people" he could end visits by aid agencies altogether, leaving the women even more vulnerable.

It should be an authority who talks to the chief, Simon decided, but he hadn't worked out who that authority should be. The other chiefs trusted the *gambarana* and sent their people to him. They wouldn't want to upset him. Simon obviously didn't want to talk to him either.

"Let's wait," he said. "I see the issue to be unpleasant now and the issue may deter our people from going," he added, meaning the fees charged by the chief could stop some families from coming to collect their mother, sister, or wife. "Imagine you come to collect your poor mother or wife and you have to pay a certain amount, and if you don't have it you can't afford to take her," he said.

"It's a sad issue," Simon continued. "A sad and delicate issue."

CHAPTER EIGHT

JAMES NEAL ARRIVED IN GHANA IN 1953, IN THE TWILIGHT YEARS of the British colonial hold over the country, to act as Accra's chief investigative officer. It was his job to ferret out corruption and theft in some of the country's biggest development projects. Working alongside local police officers, the British agent tracked stolen building materials and arrested civil servants accused of demanding bribes. His job was based on hard evidence, painstakingly gathered from stakeouts and stings, interviews and witnesses, until the case against a suspect could support an arrest and conviction. Neal held the typical foreigner's view toward witchcraft: it didn't exist.

"If anyone had told me then that Black Magic or Ju-ju, would endanger my life almost continuously, and eventually force me to choose between giving up my high-ranking position and accepting certain death, I would have laughed outright," he wrote in his 1968 memoir *Jungle Magic*. "I hadn't spent half a lifetime in overseas government services without developing a hard streak of skepticism where superstition and the like were concerned."

In Neal's mind, some African women used witchcraft to lure unsuspecting white men into marriage. He knew locals blamed a certain black powder for causing accidents and illness. He dismissed it all as "utter hogwash."

His first brush with the spirits came while investigating a theft at the colossal construction site of the Tema port, after an English engineer complained to him about a lonely tree standing in the path of the project. They'd tried everything short of dynamiting the tree to remove it, but it wouldn't budge. Finally a local worker suggested calling in a fetish priest. He believed a spirit was anchoring the tree's roots and needed to be coaxed into relocating somewhere better. Neal watched as a stooped old man poured three bottles of gin at the tree's base, then begged in the local language for the spirit to take flight, assuring it that the development of the port would be good for its people. With the ceremony over, the engineer called for his strongest cables and bulldozers, but the witchdoctor assured him it would take nothing more than a strong breeze to topple the tree. Once a rope was settled around its trunk a single, cautious tug up-ended it. The wizened fetish priest collected one hundred pounds and Neal began to wonder.

His job as Accra's chief investigative officer brought constant threats. Suspects made vows of revenge as they were led away in handcuffs. One promised to kill anyone who testified against him; the case was adjourned after two witnesses dropped dead and the judge fell ill. Neal's car suffered constant damage as suspects and their families vented their rage. Twice he found a dusting of black powder on the driver's seat; twice his Ghanaian police colleagues swept out the car and urinated on the detritus; twice Neal was persuaded to follow local customs to break the curse, which included tossing an egg over his shoulder. When he fell perilously ill and saw visions of strange attackers from his hospital bed, he finally succumbed to his colleagues' advice that he invest in protective *juju*. For fifty pounds a *juju*-man made him a kind of bitter medicine; for another fifty pounds he made Neal an amulet out of "a piece of lion, an elephant, a hyena, a wild dog, and some medicine." Neal carried it every day in his pocket and kept it under his pillow while he slept at night.

Virtually every investigation seemed to bring him into contact with witchcraft or *juju*. He learned that witchdoctors used "vibrations" belonging to a person's spirit to attack. As he traveled the country solving crimes he saw anti-witchcraft symbols smeared on fence posts and doorways, even on children. When he dreamed he saw young boys choking, being pierced with arrows. "Juju was everywhere around us," he wrote.

One night, while conducting a fraud investigation in the seaside border town of Keta, he woke to a blinding white light rising over the horizon as though it came from the sea. Dogs barked and howled, birds screamed, and insects shrieked as the huge ball of brilliant light rose to the height of the palm trees, appearing to Neal to be three times the size of the moon. Three nights in a row the ball of light appeared, and the town was abuzz with talk of the *juju* required to bring such a sight. Neal wrote that he couldn't accept that the light had been conjured by magic—but he also couldn't find a more plausible explanation.

It wasn't Neal's only brush with the inexplicable. He woke the morning of September 8, 1962, to discover that his alarm hadn't gone off. It was the day he and five local officers were set to conduct a major sting at the track, and he left the house feeling harried and rushed, cursing his faulty alarm. As the sting got under way he climbed to the empty top level of the racetrack's spectator seats to watch his men round up the jockeys, trainers, and owners who fixed races. He was standing at the top of the stairs when he felt someone or something push him from behind. In the split second before he bounced off the steps he glanced back and saw no one. He awoke in the hospital with multiple fractures to his left arm and leg, injuries so severe that he walked with a cane for months afterward. He realized that he'd been in such a rush to leave his home that he'd forgotten his amulet under his pillow, leaving him vulnerable to *juju* attack. When a witchdoctor came to warn him that his enemies hadn't given up their quest for revenge, he begrudgingly took the next boat back to Britain, convinced he'd only narrowly escaped the wrath of witchcraft.

The policeman may simply have fallen under witchcraft's spell, caught up in a web of whispers about dark powers. His conversion might be blamed on the power of persuasion. But there was something about a hard-boiled 1950s cop, a man whose mind was wired to think in terms of facts, verification, and substantiation, who'd come to accept the existence of witchcraft. He'd seen things, experienced things, and survived things that made him a believer. It made me think that the evidence was out there. If I could find it, I could be a believer too.

I desperately wanted to believe in witchcraft, if for no other reason than it was unseemly to question another's belief, the very definition of politically incorrect. Witchcraft was filled with contradictions, enough to painfully bend the mind of a nonbeliever. In their daily lives northern women held no power; they fell somewhere below teenage boys in the village's hierarchy. They were treated little better than servants, yet people claimed to fear them as witches. If women were really so dangerous, why not treat them a little better and reduce the likelihood of attack?

Outwardly these supposedly powerful witches lived, for the most part, pitiful lives full of drudgery and hardship. If they were really witches, why didn't they use their power to bring the kind of wealth that could buy an easier, more comfortable life? In the face of an accusation a powerful witch suddenly lost all her power. Why couldn't she simply strike down an accuser, turn him into a sheep before he made a damning accusation? Why didn't the fear of a witch's reprisal stop victims from making accusations? Witchcraft was so malleable it could be twisted to provide any kind of answer to any kind of situation, even where a more logical explanation existed. I was troubled by the ingenuous assertions my otherwise rational, hardworking Ghanaian neighbors made about witchcraft's powers. Sometimes they were like children who blamed the bump in the night on a monster under the bed when the more likely culprit was a branch knocking against the window.

As I grew accustomed to witchcraft's constant, hazy presence I found I was less likely to offer an argument when people blamed it for things like the deadly rollover of a *tro-tro*. I was less likely to suggest the problem lay with the condition of the road or the imbalance of the crates, tractor tires, plow discs, baskets, and goats piled atop it. My desire not to offend deepened as my mind opened, but I couldn't shake my Western roots. Because so much of witchcraft is unseen and so little is understood, it's easy to see only coincidence where others see calamity. In the absence of actual proof I remained skeptical. I wanted irrefutable evidence, something concrete that would make this belief make sense to me, not intangible dreams, unexplained coincidences, or invisible spiritual realms. Like Neal, the personal experience of a brilliant flash of light in an inky black sky would convince me that my neighbors were right to believe in the supernatural.

I needed to see to believe.

WE WERE PASSING THROUGH THE MARKET TOWN AND TRANS-portation hub of Langbinsi, en route to a small town called Janga, when thick black smoke laced with the choking smell of burned rubber began filling the truck. Wires beneath the steering column had worn down and sparked against one another, so Simon pulled over on the busy main street, drawing crowds of children who peered in the open window of the stalled truck with a mixture of excitement and fear. "*Salaminga!*" they whispered, curious but wary of my white skin. As a mechanic wrapped the wires in electrical tape it became a game for the children to tentatively shuffle in close to my window, only to peel away, giggling and giddy, safe from the pos-sibility that my jaw might suddenly spring open and finally reveal my jagged fangs.

I was on a fool's errand. I was going to sleep—or rather, not sleep—in the village of Janga because it was said to have plenty of proud witches who flew brazenly through the night sky disguised as fireballs. Since I'd decided that seeing a fireball would convince me that my neighbors were right to believe in witchcraft, Carlos had taken to calling me from his dorm room at the teacher's col-lege at two in the morning, jolting me awake so I could sit in the quiet outside my room at the guesthouse and scan the skies. Years before, when he was still a teenager, Carlos had seen a fireball sit-ting in a tree not far from the guesthouse. He'd been terrified and had taken off running. He believed there was something about the relative isolation of the guesthouse—it was perhaps five minutes from town—that made it attractive to witches. I hadn't seen any suspicious lights, despite the late-night wake-up calls. I thought my chances were best in Janga; it was said that the witches there didn't wait more than an hour after the sun had set to start their nighttime pyrotechnics.

Proof of witchcraft was a relative thing. At another witch camp, called Kukuo, I'd been told by an elder with teeth dyed orange by the juice of kola nuts that whites have even more powerful witchcraft than blacks. The man with the orange smile looked at me squarely and said, "You have a great deal of powers and what you do is push them into technology. You don't use it to destroy, you use it to develop human beings." So many conversations about witchcraft included this lament: that whites had learned to use their witchcraft for good, while blacks could use their witchcraft only to destroy.

The old man spoke of a visitor from California who came to the camp and refused all offers of accommodation. He eventually found a spot on the edge of town, in a clearing near the bush, and set up a tent. His desire to be alone, the villagers decided, to be outside the protection of town, was proof that he was filled with powerful spirits. (The more they talked about it, however, the more they talked themselves out of it, eventually deciding the man may just have been looking for peace and quiet. "The whites don't like noise," one man surmised.)

The man with the orange teeth claimed that whites made poisonous substances whose discovery could have been guided only by an evil spirit, offering battery acid as an example. The mobile phone was the most vivid form of witchcraft he'd seen come from the hands of whites. "Somebody can be here and communicate with a fellow somewhere out in the world," the old man said, pointing at me. "How else to explain how you can be here talking to us and then go outside and talk to your people?"

"It's a more powerful witchcraft," Simon agreed. "What is more powerful than that?"

Simon could duck direct questions about whether he believed in witchcraft, but the more time we spent together the more obvious it became that he too believed. As we drove away from Kukuo he spoke about a woman living there who identified herself as a powerful witch, a woman who traveled with the chief to keep him safe from the "spiritual missiles" his enemies threw at him. Simon declared her powerful indeed, although there was no tangible proof of witchcraft, other than the fact that the old chief continued to live. Simon was one of the most progressive men I met in the north; he taught his wife to drive and encouraged her to set up a business. But his comments made clear how deeply witchcraft was entrenched in the culture, suffusing even a man whose job was to lessen accusations of its practice. When I asked how he really viewed witchcraft, he told me it didn't matter what he thought. "The belief is ages old, it's a delicate issue," he said. "You can't say there's no witchcraft at all or even that you're against it."

AL-HASSAN LANGBONG SPREAD OUT THREE BOOKS AND A CRUMpled orange-and-brown school uniform. The cover of a mint green book, titled *General Sciences 1, 2, 3*, was intact, but there were only a couple of thin pages left inside, each outlined with brown ash. Soot was embedded in the spine of the book. The inner pages of a lime green mathematics book were also burned. Black splotches covered a Fonmatics writing tablet; it was inside a black plastic bag when it started to burn, and the melting polyethylene dripped onto the book.

The books belonged to Mercy Moferi, Al-Hassan's cousin. The first book, the Fonmatics, spontaneously burned while she was away at school. Al-Hassan told me the girl's sister was sleeping in the same room, got up to use the toilet, and when she came back into the room she saw smoke coming from the plastic bag. Another time Mercy drifted off to sleep wearing a bolt of African fabric as a wrap. She fell asleep lying on her green *General Sciences* book, only to be woken by her mother, who saw smoke coming from beneath her daughter. After they'd put out the fire, Mercy's cloth was ruined and her mother's fingers were blistered and burned, but the girl's skin was untouched.

The girl is cursed, Al-Hassan said. Anything she reads turns to ash.

"The Bible doesn't burn-o, but as for academic materials, it will burn," he said. I flipped open the burned pages of the *General Sciences* book to a lesson about the difference between a calabash and a gourd and another about the proper handling of sharp knives.

We stood outside Al-Hassan's brother's compound, where a Massey Ferguson tractor sat on soft tires in the shade of an almond tree. I was with Simon in Nakpanduri, a B'mobah village perched on the edge of northern Ghana's sweeping escarpment. It was so isolated that anyone wishing to speak on a mobile phone had to stand beneath a giant mango tree on the western edge of town; it was the only place in the village with any reception. Nakpanduri had leafy, pristine dirt streets and neat little mud homes lavishly decorated with thumb-pressed designs, but the picturesque little town had erupted in violent accusations enough times that its chief threatened to send to court anyone using suspicions of witchcraft as an excuse to take revenge against enemies.

By then I'd gotten used to finding myself in conversations that involved wild improbabilities. My disbelief had softened. At least three people I'd spoken with told the same tale of having their eyesight stolen by a classmate. All described their symptoms the same way: their textbooks suddenly filled with swimming squiggles where there had once been words. In each case their sight was restored by magical kohl ringed around their eyes for a week. I was unsettled by the sameness of the stories. I was also so surrounded by talk of witchcraft that the implausible edge of the stories had been ground down until they didn't seem so jarring or strange.

Al-Hassan invited us to his brother's compound. "The exhibits are there," he said.

Mercy was known as a typical secondary school student, a quiet, simple girl who didn't cause quarrels or hurl insults or rub people the wrong way. She was outside the village when we visited, gone to the farm to work while she was on involuntary hiatus from school. She enjoyed school, her cousin said, and asked for more books to replace the ones that burned. When the strange, unexplained book burnings continued to happen, Al-Hassan told us her mother suggested she go to sewing school, but the girl said she'd prefer to continue her education. Attending boarding school is the only option for many of the north's children because their own villages are too small and often too isolated to draw teachers or warrant schools of their own. The family pulled Mercy from school after her uniform, once packed amid her clothes in her trunk ready to return to school, was found pulled from the suitcase and burned on the floor. Its plastic zippers had melted and some of the polyester fabric had dissolved in the fire's heat. The family was too afraid of the curse, said her father, Jamong Swuuk.

The spontaneous fires were like something out of a Stephen King novel, but they were hardly conclusive. When it was suggested that this was the girl's doing, that it was a sign she didn't like school and didn't want to go back, her father and cousin just laughed. She couldn't have done it, they pointed out. "At times when it happens, she is asleep!" Everyone was around, they reminded me, and why would she burn her books, then ask for more? What if she didn't want to disappoint you, I asked. She was given alternatives, they said, like transferring into sewing school. It was suggested that when no one was looking, the girl burned the books herself, covertly lighting a fire without burning the book's covers by holding out the pages. But the men just shook their heads: it wasn't possible. They were convinced it was witchcraft.

The day the girl's cloth burned, her cousin said, she saw "them"—her attackers—coming to her and she began to wail and jump, saying they wanted to burn her. She couldn't see their faces, so she hasn't been able to identify them. Simon asked whether the family had gone to the soothsayer or diviner to find the answer, and the cousin answered, "Not yet." They were only praying to God.

The spontaneous book burnings weren't enough to convince

me, but after months living in a place immersed in witchcraft I really couldn't decide: Was it coincidence, a deliberate arson, or something supernatural? There were no clear answers as to why only the
inside pages of the books burned, no physical reason why a piece of
cloth should burn but leave the girl's body unscarred.

Those niggling doubts left just enough room for witchcraft.

I ARRIVED IN JANGA WITH KIZITO IN THE MORNING, LEAVING
hours to fill before the sky would surely darken and fill with the
fiery flashes of passing witches. We decided to pay our respects to
Janga's chief, a little speck of a man who wore huge, thick glasses
that bugged out his eyes with their Coke bottle magnification. He
was wrapped in a brilliant purple boubou and a black-and-white-
striped cap. A turquoise and red mask that once decorated the
snout of a horse hung from his palace's central support beam, and
a horse blanket was wrapped up and hanging over the door. The
horse died, he told me as he reached for the bit of its tail, bone still
attached, that was hanging above him. An outdated calendar set
to a month showing fighting elephants was the only other decora-
tion. Two objects that looked like baby mobiles of strange dirigibles
dangled above the doorway. They were *juju*.

The chief, Saaka Sumani, hadn't sent any women to the Gambaga camp in the five years he'd been chief. His village, about ninety
minutes from Gambaga, was his domain, and although he didn't
have the same spiritual might as the *gambarana*, Sumani decided
who was guilty and then sent the accused woman out into the
bush with his army of seven warriors, men steeped with spiritual
power, to find the herbs that would restore the victim's soul. The
bewitched bathed in the herbs; some recovered and some didn't, he
shrugged. Those who were found to be witches were also sent to a
shrine, where they pledged never to practice again, on pain of death.
Sumani also fined the woman the equivalent of about six dollars for
each of her surviving children; the money was meant as a deterrent
from practicing witchcraft. If she couldn't pay, he took the woman's
unmarried daughters as wives and sent her unmarried boys to act as

stable hands for his horse. He had so far collected ten wives, he said, then remembered one had died, so he was down to nine.

Witches are wicked, Sumani told me, and the ones in this town were particularly strong. It became obvious that because witchcraft is invisible every woman in the village held the potential for harm, could acquire or drop witchcraft at any moment and was therefore not to be trusted. Every woman was seen as subversive, apt to be planning and plotting a man's demise. "They have it in them and they share it among themselves," the old chief said, adding that the women don't need cash money to buy their spiritual gifts. They make payments in the spiritual world, where money is useless.

"Some who are fed up with it can transfer it to you and you won't even know," he said. "Someone can wipe their sweat and put it on you and it will be transferred. Even women who have it, when you tell them they have it, they will deny it from head to toe—but they have it."

I asked whether being a chief makes him more prone to witch attacks.

"They can't even do it!" replied an English-speaking assemblyman who had joined us. The chief protected himself with enough *juju* to render him immune to witches. "He has so many things in him they can't even attack him. He has some powerful things in and on his body, so they can't attempt."

The chief pointed to the assemblyman, then Kizito. They too look for protection, he said, declaring that each of them had obtained something to keep them safe. One's enemies never rested, though, so they were forced to seek out more and more powerful protective *juju* to keep themselves safe from harm. "As we are Africans, we all have it," the assemblyman said, speaking for the chief. "He was a small boy when they started their attempts on his life. Even he can't sleep. He went to get protection even before he became chief."

We were interrupted by the arrival of one of the chief's wives, an old woman who crawled to her husband and knelt by his side. After he'd fished in his pocket for a 5,000-cedi note, she skittered away on her hands and knees, effusive in her gratitude for the equivalent of fifty cents. From within the chief's palace there was an absolute cacophony of noise: babies shrieking, goats bleating, and pots banging. It became difficult to hear the old man's rasping voice as talk turned to whether whites have witchcraft. The Janga chief believed witchcraft couldn't cross racial boundaries. As a white, I couldn't harm a black, and as a black, he couldn't harm a white. Still, he wanted to be rid of witchcraft. On this point he was rigorous. Witchcraft was hindering Africa.

"It can destroy a whole town or a village," he said. "They will move a whole village, get up and move away." For the first time he looked directly at me. "If you have any means of getting rid of it, you should do it."

WHEN THE WORST OF THE DAY'S HEAT SUBSIDED WE WENT TO see a diviner, a young-looking man with thin clothes on his thin frame. He was rolling straw when we arrived, but looked up and smiled, showing off a beautiful set of gleaming white teeth and unusual eyes. They were greenish brown and ringed with kohl.

He sent a small boy to get some *akpateshie*, the fiery local moonshine, in a white pill bottle. While we waited in a small, stuffy room, the man told us he got his gift after the sudden death of his wife. She fell sick on a Thursday and died on Friday, leaving him alone with three very young children. He was so shocked by her death that he couldn't eat. He'd been living off *akpateshie* and cigarettes when he spilled some of the alcohol on the floor. He watched in amazement as the puddle reflected scenes of the village, pictures flashing by as though on a television screen. He saw someone in the village dying, so he ran to tell the family. When the man eventually died as predicted, Pumuga Dahamani's reputation as a diviner was sealed.

A diviner is a mystic who can see into the spiritual realm, identifying witches and reading the past or predicting the future using spiritually significant objects, such as cowrie shells or, in this case, streaks of spilled alcohol. Diviners are indelibly linked with witchcraft, as their visions can confirm the identity of a suspected witch. Pumuga sat on the floor, taking a capful of *akpateshie* in a pink shot glass. He harrumphed as he swallowed, the fire of the grain alcohol burning the length of his throat. His fingers slid across the floor as he moved the shot glass around. Then he spilled a splash on the floor and studied it quietly. We were transfixed. Kizito asked him whether he would go to school to study agriculture in the fall.

Pumuga sighed, moved the shot glass around, and stared deep into the spatter of *akpateshie*. His voice, when he spoke, was hypnotic and soothing. I don't know what Kizito learned; the future came in a language I couldn't understand, and Kizito was so enraptured he broke his concentration only to ask for some paper. He wanted to take down the instructions for the sacrifices that would help make the predictions come true.

As the day ran out we returned to the house to sit with our hosts. An ancient man in grubby clothes, one of the chief's special spiritual warriors, sat outside making gunpowder with sugar and charcoal. He brushed off my questions, muttering that he knew nothing of witchcraft, had only inherited the position on the chief's private army from his late father. He ignited the mix to show me its bright flare. It lit up the dusky pink sky with a white flash, like the flash pan of an antique camera, and quickly died away. This was for funerals and hunting, he said. I wondered whether its intense light looked anything like a witch's disguise.

When night fell and the power cut out, the village itself seemed to retreat. There were no loud cars, no deafening sports matches, no boisterous drinking spots. Even the insects went silent. Kerosene lamps lit the market, casting deep shadows over the remains of a pyramid of tomatoes and pots of bubbling stew. We bought bowls of stodgy beans and rice and ate quietly by the bright light of my flashlight. At bedtime my hosts pushed me inside, worried that I, like most whites, was as fragile as an egg and would be bitten by a mosquito and die of malaria. They shooed their sons and Kizito outside, promising that the men would wake me if they spied a fireball. We compromised, and I ended up sleeping in my clothes on a thin mattress laid across the doorway, shielded by a mosquito net. There was no moon and the sky had clouded over, leaving the night very, very dark.

Earlier in the day a high school graduate and proud "provisions shop" owner named Garafu told me that the village's status as the home of fierce witches was no longer true. The lingering reputation was akin to being convicted of theft, he said. You might go to jail and be released, but if anything is stolen again you will always be the first suspect. In the old days, he allowed, in the days when his grandfather was a child, they used to take the witches to the nearby stream. There was a heavy stone that they would tie around a woman's neck and toss into the water. The witch would be dragged in afterward and held under by the stone's weight. Now, with the Constitution, he said, they are not allowed to do that anymore.

"It was serious!" he said, emphasizing the shamelessness of the witches' work. "They were saying that even during the day they did their operations!" It used to be you would see the old ladies shuffling to the palace at least two or three times a week to answer to allegations of witchcraft, but now barely anyone went to the chief's palace with an accusation. Since the village got electricity in September 2006 not a single fireball had lit up the sky. In fact Garafu had never seen one in his twenty-three years.

When I rose in the morning I had a headache and my neck hurt. I wheezed my morning greetings. My spine felt fused. I had lain awake for hours in the heavy night air, but the dark sky stayed still and black.

CHAPTER NINE

ASARA AZINDU'S CURVES TOLD THE STORY OF HER SUCCESS. A huge woman with a slightly lazy right eye and knees weakened by her appetite, there was no greater symbol of her wealth than her prized figure. She looked like a well-fed letter Z, with generous breasts, a jutting stomach, and a big behind.

Living on her own in Gushiegu had come gradually. Her seven children had grown, married, and moved away by the time word came that her mother had fallen ill. At first Asara spent only a few weeks at a time caring for her mother, but the time away from her husband slowly grew permanent. To support herself she took on her grandmother's trade, cooking and selling rice in cauldrons so big they could be transported only by truck. She would fry the rice with a few finely chopped vegetables, then sell it in plastic bowls amid the crowded row of food stalls offering stew or hard-cooked eggs near the dusty square that hosted the weekly Gushiegu market.

The earnings weren't much, but Asara had a head for business. She plowed her rice profits into the mango trade, encouraging buyers to go to the smaller villages and collect the vivid orange fruit, which Asara would then resell in the north's bigger markets. She built extra rooms on her brother's house, where she cared for her mother for a decade until the old woman died, and welcomed tenants and their rent payments. She ran yet another business selling

firewood, the main source of cooking fuel in town. Asara hired a
tractor to drive to the more remote villages, where the driver would
collect huge bundles of heavy wood and bring them into the town
to be resold at a markup.

As her profits grew, so did her waistline. She answered to no
one, a lone woman living well without a husband, making her own
decisions about her business, her home, and her life. There was no
one to interfere, no one to challenge her decisions. Neighbors called
Asara an NGO, a sly comparison to the nongovernmental organizations, such as Save the Children and World Vision, that appeared
to have plenty of money and no one to tell them what to do with it.

Despite the nickname, Asara's undoing was offering what she
considered aid, in the form of loans and credit. As she sought out
her debtors, threatening to take them to the village chief if they
didn't pay up, dark rumors began to circulate about her business
acumen. Where did a woman get such smarts? How could she
manage so well alone? How did she amass so many cedis while others carefully guarded every precious coin?

Asara's competitors, the other women who cooked and sold
fried rice, had never been kind to one another. They traded insults,
whispered behind one another's backs, and were generally quite un-
derhanded in their attempts to wipe out their rivals. They began
spreading ugly gossip about Asara, about the mysterious ingredients she used to flavor her food, about the talismans she might hold
to give her such business prowess. Men who were once her best
customers grabbed her rice bowls and banged nails through them.
They vowed never to eat at her business again, a promise of violence
that hinted at the fear they felt eating food prepared by a witch.

The timing of the rumors could not have been worse. Every
winter a trade wind sweeps over the fabled merciless sands of the
Sahara. Normally held aloft by cooler monsoon winds blowing
in from the Atlantic Ocean, in the winter months the clash of a
low-pressure center over the northern Gulf of Guinea coast and a
high-pressure center hovering over northwest Africa gives the wind
strength. The trade wind, called the Harmattan, pushes toward the

earth, licking the Sahara's ancient sands and picking up dust seven times finer than a strand of hair. The air current becomes so clotted with grit it can block out the sun. The wind's hot, dry breath fuels bush fires and blows in disease. Its fine particles scratch at the respiratory system, opening invisible entryways into the blood system for meningitis and other lethal infections. Some of the infected thrash with seizures; others complain of nothing more than the feeling of a twisted neck. Its most common legacy is hearing loss, but if left untreated meningitis can quickly turn fatal. The disease is so prevalent in parts of Africa that the swath from Senegal to Ethiopia is known as the "meningitis belt," where anywhere from 25,000 to 200,000 people can be infected in a given year. Every eight to twelve years, as natural immunity wanes, the Harmattan blows in an epidemic.

As the rumors swirled about Asara's entrepreneurial skills, nearly 15,000 Ghanaians died of meningitis. It was 1997, an epidemic year, and more than 20,000 people became infected. One-tenth lived in northern Ghana, where almost three hundred people died. As the neck-twisting disease raced through Asara's crowded town, panic set in. There seemed to be no prevention or cure, no way of slowing the speed at which it could cause disability or death. When a trio of mystic men saw a spiritual cause for the spread of the illness, they took their vision to the chief, who summoned Asara to his palace.

She had been having trouble with a particular debtor, who had walked off with a bag of millet and now refused to pay. They'd exchanged angry words and she'd threatened to enlist the chief's help if he didn't come up with the money he owed. She calmly walked to the chief's palace thinking the man had simply gone to the chief first. She was completely unprepared for what awaited her.

The chief's courtyard was crowded with livid people holding sticks and calling for blood. Their fury spoke of the double trouble of a successful woman and a little-understood health crisis. They angrily accused Asara, along with two other women, of causing the meningitis outbreak. The diviners described their vision: in the spiritual realm they'd witnessed Asara poison the town's main source of drinking water with some kind of bad medicine that was causing children and adults to suffer sore necks and drop dead. The chief hadn't called Asara to help settle her affairs. He'd called to ask her why she'd used witchcraft to destroy the town.

"She never thought anything of that nature could affect her," Carlos translated for her. "If she had thought of that, that something would have affected her of that nature, she would have run away before they could have attacked her."

The literal embodiment of success, Asara proved a lone woman could fend for herself, but in the face of accusations that she practiced witchcraft her business sense and wealth were held against her. She was aggressive, demanding, and ambitious. She stood in contradiction to everything women were supposed to be.

Asara insisted she was not a witch; it was her enemies who did evil deeds, not her. Even in the dangerous chaos, as her neighbors held sticks and made threats, she felt the calm assurance of the innocent.

"She had [a] clear conscience. She was confident in herself because she knew she hadn't done something of that nature. The two other colleagues, they were crying and wailing. But she was not afraid because she knew she had no part in that," Carlos translated.

"While they were standing, the people just wished that they would have released them so they would beat them to death," Carlos continued. "They were shouting that they should release them and they will kill them."

CHARITIES AND AID GROUPS WORKING IN NORTHERN GHANA spend millions helping women achieve the kind of financial independence Asara enjoyed. Rural women are organized into groups and cooperatives and targeted for skill-building workshops and "income-generating activities." Most experts agree the training and microcredit loans are incentives rather than handouts, but they can't transform social hierarchies overnight. Asara's success brought its own problems, proving that putting money in a woman's hands can't inoculate her against a witchcraft accusation. In Asara's case it made her a target, largely because a woman's fate is still tied to marriage and children.

There were serious social machinations behind the accusation. Blaming a woman like Asara for the spread of meningitis solved several problems: it put the feeling of control back in the hands of a scared and panicked population; it righted the town's fine balance, allowing men to reassert their dominance; and it gave the other women selling rice an outlet for their feelings of aggression or hostility, something they were otherwise denied.

"For all she was doing for the people, it was her enemies," Carlos translated as Asara defended her innocence. "She believes that they did not desire her to do well, that she was well-to-do, had nice things to put on. Even if she goes back to her place—the way she was, she will not be like that. Her enemies will be happy to see her being wretched, that is what they wanted and that is what they have put her in."

This was the devilish detail of witchcraft. It followed the "tall poppy" principle, cutting down anyone who dared rise above the rest. It was witchcraft's worst legacy, according to Ben Kunbuor, a politician from the Upper West. The challenge, for northern women in particular, is balancing the desire for industriousness with the envy and resentment it produces. The willingness to attribute success to witchcraft shackled the small villages. "It kills the process of making use of an individual's talents or qualities," Kunbuor said.

Asara's story made me think of a report I'd read by a Cambridge anthropologist who'd lived among the Mamprusi in the 1960s and revisited the area in the 1990s. Tales of witchcraft had morphed with the opening of Ghana's economy, Susan Drucker-Brown wrote. Where witches had once been blamed mostly for mischief and misfortune, new stories began to circulate of women who could bury their victims in the flesh of a fruit or transform them into livestock, to be sold at the infamous Techiman night market. Selling their victims to unsuspecting buyers made the witches rich. It gave those who could "see" witches a new trait to watch for: avarice. Witches weren't just hungry for "meat"; they were hunting for cash.

It was more likely that women simply had more opportunities to make money, not stronger *juju*. Ghana's busy port routinely receives ships from China, carrying crate upon crate of cheap goods, such as children's backpacks, mobile phone covers, and knockoff Hello Kitty plates and bowls. As the variety of goods available at the markets expands, so do women's fortunes. With more to sell, women are better able to make a little extra cash, but because proper women are expected to be demure and modest, those with the cunning to amass money, like Asara, are assumed to be witches.

Kunbuor saw the way it stifled Ghana, the way fear and paranoia froze innovation and development. "The problem is, fear of being labeled a witch means few people with exceptional abilities will come forward and explain their success," he said. "A farmer who clears his land quickly and gets a high yield from his crop will be secretive about it, worrying that if his neighbors see his success they'll look at their own crops and point the witchcraft finger at him."

"Some women are part of the problem," said Rahinatu Fuseini, a program officer at Action Aid. "They will never come near you, but they'll tell everybody you're a witch. If you're accused or even suspected, they'll begin to spread the message."

The women are as bloodthirsty for a witch's demise as the men, Rahinatu said, partly because it's been culturally ingrained in them that women seen as witches should be attacked and killed, ostracized, or banished. "It boils down to our culture and our traditions," she said. "In our cultural setting, men are above women. They are the head of the family, the head of the community, and whatever they say, women are not given a chance to make their input."

Rahinatu looked to be in her late twenties, but was probably in her forties. She wore blue jeans and form-fitting T-shirts, her hair bolstered by extensions that fell to her shoulders in tight braids. She campaigned against violence and hoped to build a database of the women living in Ghana's witch camps, a catalogue that would contain a photo of each woman and details on her accusation, her marital status, whether she had children, where she came from, and whether she was interested in being returned to her family and community. She hoped to use the database to put a human face on those most affected by witchcraft, the women accused of using it.

"Our culture has made it such that women are not confident to do certain things," she said. "The men are the head of the family, the women only take instruction. There is a need for women to be involved in all the decisions that affect them. We try to reduce some of the myths and perceptions about what the role of women actually is.

"It's not easy because even the women themselves think, 'Oh, when I was growing up this is how it was done.' We don't expect the culture to change in one day, but as we continue to educate them, they will come to understand the important role they can play."

Asara believed she was the victim of her own success.

"She personally thinks because she was well-to-do, that she was very active in her business, that anytime any new business venture crops up, she takes the opportunity," Carlos translated for her. "It may be because she is well-to-do that she was accused. She even cited an instance where people come to borrow money from her and that they were the very people who even accused her of being a witch. She still says most of those people have not paid that money back to her."

Robbing a community of a woman accused of witchcraft had obvious implications, Rahinatu said. The work of keeping a family fed and cared for often fell to the women; a man might plant his crops and reap the harvest, but it was the women who turned the maize or millet into meals. "All these people they're accusing are in camps, and if they were at home they would have produced things, be doing things for themselves," she said. "They're farmers, traders, herbalists. They were doing things before they came to these camps and now they're just sitting there, waiting for people to come along and give them aid. They're a burden rather than people who are contributing.

"If this belief was not there and they were at home doing what they always do, they'd be contributing. But they're isolated and they can't do anything."

SHORTLY AFTER ASARA ARRIVED TO LIVE AT GAMBAGA'S WITCH camp, the pain in her legs grew so great she could no longer walk. She couldn't work as the other women did, selling water or helping with harvests or collecting *dawadawa* pods. She relied instead on handouts from Catholic Relief Services, the generosity of her roommates, and the bit of food her children brought when they visited. Her son sent his daughter, a bubbly six-year-old named Kubra, to fetch water and firewood and generally act as her grandmother's servant. Dozens of girls lived at the camp to help their aunts, mothers, or grandmothers survive; it was part of Simon's job to pay their school fees and ensure that the girls got time away from their chores to get an education while they lived at the camp.

Asara needed the help because she could only crawl on knees so swollen and tough they resembled elephant hide. When visitors spilled off the *tro-tro* from Tamale or arrived in the white SUVs of their charity groups, she could be counted on to be around the camp, always willing to tell her story in exchange for a few dollars. She gave her account countless times to countless visitors; she even became the subject of a German-language book called *The Witch of Gushiegu*. Unfortunately not all of the details were accurate, whether because they were simply lost in translation, confused in the telling of a long story, or polished over time to draw a more sympathetic response. A British journalist wrote in a report from the early 1990s, for example, that Asara's brother delivered her to the camp, but her family told me they drove her in a truck, although they may have meant that they delivered some of her things. When we spoke Asara insisted that she ran empty-handed from town, following her two co-accused into the bush, where she managed to slip into a copse of trees and lose the villagers who called for her blood. She then managed to walk on weak knees nearly fifty miles to Nalerigu, along the way losing all her documents, the deed to her Gushiegu home and the papers that confirmed her identity. At Nalerigu, she remembered, a stranger paid for her to ride the last few miles to Gambaga in the back of a passing truck.

"She didn't even pick a single item from her room when she was being chased," Carlos translated. "The items she was using for her business, the tables, the chairs, and the saucepans, the pots—she didn't pick a single item. The people vandalized her house. And the structure she was sitting in while she did her business, they vandalized it. Most of the properties were being destroyed by the people. She took virtually nothing." Her only son came looking for her but found only level ground where his mother's house had been.

Simon helped Asara return home to her family in 2001, and she stayed for about nine months. He hoped to send her home again, so we drove to the tiny village where her brothers lived, to speak with them about the possibility of her returning home. Simon had been to the village once or twice before to speak with her family and knew the route there well. Her brothers lived in what was generously called a village but was actually nothing more than a few family homes grouped together beside a dirt road. There wasn't so much as a market or a store, just an official blue sign announcing the village of Zei.

Asara's brothers were hunters; animal skulls were piled up near the entrance to their compound, a few extra jawbones laced among them. There were a couple of bicycles and a box of corncobs and shea nut husks piled up around the room. A gaggle of knobby-kneed boys crowded around the middle of the room or huddled together on goatskins on the floor, drawn by the excitement of unexpected visitors. They stayed still and quiet as Simon translated the conversation, but midway through a long, rambling story a couple of boys began grimacing, tucking their faces in the elbows of their T-shirts. A boy with his T-shirt pulled up over his nose kicked at a bony dog, who got up without protest and limped away.

An old man identified as one of Asara's uncles told us that his niece had been successfully selling rice when there was "a little misunderstanding" involving the other rice sellers, who became angry and started circulating rumors that she was a witch. It was jealousy, the man said. One of her brothers complained that they'd had no peace when Asara was selling her rice, as there were always fights and quarrels and competitions. She was living in her own home when the first accusation happened. They tried to reason with the chief, making about ten trips to plead with him to leave Asara alone before she was ultimately banished.

The first time Asara returned from the witch camp, after five years of banishment, she lived with her brother and his wives, but they found it difficult to get along. Asara did not heed her brother. She was forceful and pestered him about money-making schemes. An accusation of witchcraft automatically robbed her of any entitlement to respect, but Asara bossed around her juniors and generally disrupted the accepted hierarchy. After nine months her brother decided he wanted her to leave.

It was around that time that a cooking pot overturned on one of Asara's nieces. The little girl had been playing near the bubbling pot when another adult walked by and brushed against it, upsetting the pot and spilling its boiling contents. Scalding soup washed over the girl, and the burns were so severe that the child died. Although Asara had not been directly involved she knew the little girl's death would trigger questions about what had set the chain of events in motion. Witchcraft was the obvious answer. Fearing she would be blamed, Asara voluntarily returned to Gambaga's witch camp.

It had been another five years since she'd returned to the witch camp, and her uncle was willing to come to Gambaga for her again, although he would still have to pay the fees requested by the *gambarana*. The chief of the village where Asara had sold rice had died, and a long-standing feud over his successor had left the position vacant. That meant no one could officially veto her return, and because two of her daughters were now living in Gushiegu there was a possibility that Asara could be quietly reunited with them and live in a part of the bustling trading town where she was unknown.

Privately Simon confessed that he was eager to see Asara resettled. I was surprised to hear the edge in his voice. He liked her, he shrugged, but had problems with her—harsh language for the eternally even-keeled Simon. He too had run into problems with Asara's scheming. As we got into the truck to leave her village he pointed to one of her sisters-in-law, a perfectly round woman whose legs looked cartoonishly spindly compared to the size of her gut. That was how big Asara was when she first arrived at the camp, he said. She had "reduced small" in the more than ten years that she had been exiled but remained quite fat, fatter than all the other women.

It was puzzling that a woman unable to walk managed to eat so well. She couldn't work like the other women did, but she was getting money somehow. The other women living at the camp were equally baffled by Asara's weight, but had decided that her witchcraft was "very, very strong," Simon said. Her brothers told us she traded the used clothing donated to the camp for food, but I wondered if she was also engaged in prostitution, perhaps exchanging sex for a few dollars, bags of grain, or cooking utensils. Her compound showed no other signs of any obvious trade. When I asked how she managed to survive, she insisted she relied on charity.

"If she doesn't cook, she doesn't eat," Carlos translated. "She'll be very happy to have the opportunity to live with her people again. If she doesn't have [food to eat at home], someone will cook and give it to her, but for here [in the witch camp], once the food that the charity organization gives them finishes, they will have nothing. So they are really toiling."

Asara could see business opportunities all around her, but no one trusted her after she was accused of witchcraft. "She has not had any means to start a business. She has no money with her," Carlos translated. In her old life she would have bought and resold the firewood her colleagues collected. She would have started a provisions shop catering to the accused women. "She has desire to do that, but she cannot even get to a place where she can start a business again."

During the ride back to Gambaga Simon confided that Asara's secret income came from selling the camp's water. It was against the rules, but she did it anyway. Simon had arranged to get Canadian funding to drill a borehole and install a tap, then inaugurated it with a small ceremony in which he and the *gambarana* explained that the tap was not to be used by anyone but the suspected witches, a delicate enough issue since the community was vehemently opposed to privileges for women accused of witchcraft. Both men emphasized that the water was a gift to make the lives of the old women easier. It was not meant as an "income-generating activity," and the women were forbidden from selling it.

He'd settled Asara at the compound closest to the tap because she was crippled, but she had taken advantage of her proximity to the precious resource. Simon suspected that while the other women were out working Asara took small bribes from the community's women and allowed them to fill their buckets at the pump, which rarely had a queue during the day. Simon shook his head. It seemed Asara's business instincts could not be silenced. He was furious about it, but had resisted revealing the source of her relative wealth to the other women. He preferred to send her home rather than confront her with his allegations, even if his silence allowed rumors of her powers to grow unchecked. He simply redoubled his efforts to get her out of the camp.

CHAPTER TEN

CARLOS WAS ABOUT TWELVE THE FIRST TIME HE WENT TO A witchdoctor in search of objects infused with supernatural powers, known as *juju*. He was looking for something to charm women, and he went with a fourteen-year-old friend who had already purchased a similar power. He laughed at the memory, at the thought of ever using *juju* to attract girls. The charm was a bracelet made of roots and a stalk woven together with ropes and cowries. A fowl was slaughtered and its feathers and blood were used in the *juju*.

Because he was polite, reliable, and spoke five languages, Simon had recommended Carlos as a translator, but it soon became clear that Carlos had a lot more to offer. He was familiar with witchcraft in a way few others would admit. He spoke about it candidly and honestly, something few others were willing to do.

How did you know where to go, what to ask for, I asked.

"Ah!" he laughed, raising his eyebrows suggestively. "It's like we already knew. There was *a need* for me to go."

"A need?" I teased.

"That was for women," he said with a shy smile. "Most of my age-mates—even now that's what they go for. Not serious *juju*."

He can't remember exactly how he paid for the bracelet, but remembers giving some cash, some kola nuts, and some Royal cigarettes. He claimed, in that time-honored way, that the bracelet wasn't for him but for a friend. His friend was interested in a certain girl, he explained, but they figured the girl was bluffing about how she felt about him and they wanted to charm her into showing her true feelings. He smiled, admitting that he later used the charm for himself. "By then my friends were having it and my friends were using it, so I thought, why not?" he laughed. "It was working, to be frank," he added, grinning. "I used it many times."

He can't remember the cash value, but "the amount was not small," and he remembered the ritual *kola* was precisely 6,600 cedis. He didn't wear the charm but held it or put it in his pocket. There were recitations to make, chants he can no longer remember, and then he was told to repeat the girl's name three times. His earliest *juju* required the girl to agree to the mild enchantment; the *juju* he got later could bewitch a girl whether or not she was interested.

His very first girlfriend was garnered this way, he told me sheepishly. I feigned shock, asking if the poor girl knew she was under a spell. "She did not know! How could she know?" he laughed, then he turned serious when he remembered that things ended badly. They went to separate high schools, and rumors reached him that she had many other "friends." "I was jealous," he said.

Carlos dabbled a little further into *juju* while still a secondary school student. "Childish things," he said. He bought a kind of charm that wrapped around his wrist and could make men more attractive to women. He claimed, again, that he never used it for himself, only for friends. He bought *juju* that could make a man's fist strong enough to crush a coconut. That one he did use for himself, in fights over women. "You might be at a funeral and you might see a woman and when you call her over and start talking to her, then her man will get jealous," he explained. He gave it up when he realized fighting wasn't really getting him any closer to women.

In the days before poisoned *pito* made witchcraft personal, Carlos had a dream in which he saw a big black dog trying to bite him and awoke to see bite marks between the thumb and index finger of his right hand. He traveled home from his boarding school to show his father, Stephen Anena. An animal leaving bite marks in your dreams meant you were the victim of a witch's attack, one that sucked your blood, but he had no idea who would do such a thing.

He was only playing around with *juju* that would make him strong—until his father died. Carlos and his brothers saw their father's sudden, suspicious death as the result of a witch's attack. Three of Stephen Anena's sons delved into witchcraft after his death in search of revenge. "Here, if you have it, it is prestigious," Carlos said. "We see it as being a man. After my father died, that's when I went really deep into it. I thought I should revenge it or arm myself or my family."

STEPHEN ANENA WAS HIS FAMILY'S FAVORED SON. EDUCATING A child is an expensive enterprise when there are fees, textbooks, transportation, uniforms, and shoes to consider. It is common in large, poverty-plagued families to pin the family's future on one son, to divert the money that would have gone to educating each child for a year or two and spend it instead on sending the favored son as far as high school or college. Investing in the future of one child could lift the whole family, since whatever material wealth he obtained was expected to be divvied up among his brothers left struggling on the farm, whose own futures had been sacrificed.

As the only educated child out of ten children born to village farmers, Stephen trained to become a teacher. Standing on the steps of the school where he taught in Gambaga, he announced one day to a friend that he'd seen the woman he wanted to marry. She sold little bags of peanuts on the school grounds. It was the 1970s, and Stephen looked like he would be comfortable in a smoky New York jazz club, wearing flared tight-fitting pants and an equally tight-fitting button-down shirt. The object of his affection, Comfort, was a handsome woman, with wide features and big eyes. Now she is a tall and sturdy woman with somewhat mannish features, prominent cheekbones, a gap-toothed smile, and slitted cat's eyes. Carlos is practically her spitting image.

The pair talked; Stephen told her he wanted to be "more than playmates," he wanted to make her his wife. They courted for a couple of months. Whenever she had time Comfort visited him at school. He would come to her house and take her for evening walks. Sometimes they went to an open-air spot for a drink, where they would talk and listen to music. They were in love, Comfort said, and although he was ethnically a Frafra, her parents approved of her choice.

They went through traditional rites. Stephen gathered together a goat, a sheep, a dog, a red cock, and a speckled black guinea fowl and paid a dowry of four cows. He was considered a catch. Comfort was twenty-one when they married; her husband was twenty-six. Within a year they had a baby boy named Kingsley. Another seven pregnancies would follow, including two sets of twins, but only six children survived. The couple's sole daughter died as an infant, unexplained and quick as a wink, the only symptom being vomiting that started after a day at the market. The little girl had been tied with a cloth to her mother's back. When Comfort bent forward to set down a bucket, trickles of vomit poured over her shoulder. She raced to the hospital, but the little girl was dead before they arrived.

It was one of the few dark days in a life of relative comfort. Back then the family lived in government housing on Gambaga's main road, in a concrete house with a metal roof. Comfort's business grew from selling peanuts to cooking and selling rice, beans, and Ga *kenkey*, a sour-tasting, starchy specialty from the south. They were devoted members of the Presbyterian church. Stephen became headmaster at the Gambaga Junior Secondary School, promoted to within sight of the top spot in the district. Their six boys were all sent to elementary school and secondary school, and each had dreams of higher education and well-paid jobs.

Then in April 2000, when Carlos was still a young teenager away at boarding school, a messenger came to the family's home looking for Stephen. It was about two in the morning, but Comfort's father was sick and the family wanted Stephen to judge his condition and advise them what to do. According to Comfort, Stephen threw on some clothes and jogged over to his in-laws. The old man was frail, but Stephen told Comfort he was confident her father would recover. At some point, as the rising sun was bleaching out the night, the family offered him a drink of *pito*, the yeasty brew made from fermented millet grain. Stephen told Comfort that her sister handed him a calabash and he drank.

When he got home he told Comfort he felt unwell and was certain her family had given him something "unwholesome" to drink. He meant poison. Comfort ran to her mother's house to confront them, warning that if they gave her husband something poisonous, they needed to confess and give him something to counteract its effects. She was hysterical with panic. Her mother scoffed, acted insulted, and told her to go away.

When Stephen began experiencing problems with his belly, Comfort ran to the *gambarana* and complained that her mother had poisoned her husband. The chief told her to go home, collect a chicken, and let her mother know she was to report to the palace, also with a fowl. It was highly unusual for a daughter to allege witchcraft against her own mother. Although witches are rumored to attack their own family, accusing one's mother would only cast suspicion on oneself, mostly because it's widely believed that witchcraft is hereditary. Such an accusation would only boomerang to implicate the daughter.

When the fowls were slaughtered Comfort thought hers landed in a way that confirmed her accusation. The *gambarana* agreed. Normally a woman found guilty of practicing witchcraft is ordered to go into the bush and collect herbs to counteract her curse, but Comfort's mother refused to provide any remedy. Comfort told me that her five brothers and sisters, enraged by the accusation, gathered at the *gambarana*'s palace and beat her for bringing such shame on the family. For her part, Comfort's mother denounced her daughter for standing firm in her suspicions.

To an outsider it made little sense to suspect Comfort's mother of attacking her son-in-law. He had grown into a prosperous man whose education ensured a government-paid position that allowed him to keep his wife and sons well cared for. Had he lived and the family been able to continue on their path, Comfort's mother might have had six well-educated grandsons, all with salaried jobs. It was a development worker's dream. But witches were believed to be jealous and vengeful; stories of witch attacks against those blessed by life's advantages were common. People believed they attacked their own family's brightest because it was the best way of proving their commitment to their coven. Witchcraft's protection and power came at a cost, and the hungry witches had no choice but to pay.

MEANWHILE STEPHEN SLOWLY, SLOWLY LOST HIS HEALTH, sliding into aches and pains and urinary problems that stole days from school and landed him at the clinic and finally at the hospital. He could eat and talk, but he was burning with fever. His whole body was hot. His sons felt helpless. Comfort took him to the white doctors, who treated the mysterious infection with antibiotics, giving him a week's course the first time, a two-week course the second. Finally, ten months after he drank the *pito*, the doctors suggested he go to Kumasi for surgery. Carlos claimed his father's films showed some kind of metal lining in his bladder.

When Stephen came home from the hospital he dreamed that someone was picking apart his stitches. In the morning they found that the surgical wound had opened and his bladder was draining urine into his body. They took him back to the hospital, where doctors said there was nothing more they could do for him and sent him home with his family. Three days later he was dead.

With Stephen gone, the grieving family was kicked out of their government housing. Hospital bills chewed through their savings until there was nothing left. As Comfort ran up debts, people chased her from the market. They came to her door, harassing her for money. "My mother couldn't shop at the market anymore—oh truly," Carlos whispered. "She had bought so much on credit."

Comfort moved to a shabby room in a compound where she could brew and serve *pito*, charging the equivalent of a few pennies for a smooth calabash bowl of the yeasty liquid. "If our father was living, this is not the way she would be living," Carlos said.

"Sometimes she can't pay the rent. It's difficult and the utility bills sometimes cannot be met." His youngest brother, Bright, shared a dingy mattress with their mother in a room lit by a single naked bulb. Furniture saved from the smart government house had been crammed into the single room. An ancient red TV sat in the corner, unplugged and unused, and thick plastic jerry cans and cooking items lined the walls. Clothes were piled up in plastic bags and slung across the exposed beams. Two chairs, their cushions covered in blue plastic, sat against the wall. Carlos confided that his mother could not sleep through the night and that talking about her husband's death would upset her too much. "She takes drugs to help her sleep," he said, pointing to a pill bottle on the bed frame. "Oh, seriously!" A photograph showed her late husband dressed in purple and red traditional dress, with a moustache and the beginning of a paunch. Comfort turned the picture to face the wall. It caused her too much grief to look at it.

"If he was to be alive, he would have aided her, taken care of her," Carlos said. "Because he's not alive, schooling has been seriously affected, even [delayed]. He would have helped with her business, offered her financial assistance to have a booming business."

Carlos had been conditioned since birth to see misfortune as a witch's handiwork, and he was convinced a witch had killed his father. He believed his father had died not because the *pito* had been improperly fermented, nor because his father had contracted a strange stomach ailment, but because his grandmother practiced witchcraft.

IT WASN'T THE ONLY TIME CARLOS'S GRANDMOTHER WAS ACcused of being a witch. The catechist at Gambaga's yellow Catholic church believed his wife had also died at the hands of the old woman. Raymond Manlokiya was a teacher at the Zobzia primary school and lived next to the Church of St. Theresa, where he performed the services and rites. When he suggested we go somewhere quiet, we ended up inside the church, sitting on its bare wooden benches, talking about what the Vatican might say about witchcraft and how Raymond counseled parishioners who came to him with problems they attributed to it.

This was before Pope Benedict XVI visited Luanda and urged faithful Catholics to give up their superstitious witchcraft beliefs: "In today's Angola, Catholics should offer the message of Christ to the many who live in fear of spirits, of evil powers by whom they feel threatened, disoriented, even reaching the point of condemning street children and even the most elderly because—they say—they are sorcerers." A Catholic News Service report on the pope's visit noted, "Church leaders throughout Africa say belief in witchcraft is . . . tearing villages and urban societies apart." In fact priests gathering for the Synod for Africa would study how to use missionary messages to break witchcraft's stranglehold.

Raymond felt that because witchcraft was mentioned in the Bible God-fearing Christians could not be blamed for believing in it. The thick walls of the empty church muffled the usual roar of passing motorbikes and the fuzzy screech of music blaring through the neighborhood. It was the most quiet I'd experienced in months. An electric candle gave off a red glow that lit up the exposed beams and zinc roof, highlighting the fourteen Stations of the Cross. Raymond explained that he never belittled a person's beliefs, but instead sympathized with them.

His wife, a woman in her thirties who bore him five children, began complaining of chronic malaria around the time she had a quarrel with Carlos's grandmother over the price of a grain bag that the older woman used to carry home her portion of food aid rations that had been delivered to the church. Embarrassed that the catechist's wife had pointed out her mistake about the price of the bag, Carlos's grandmother sputtered about revenge.

Within days Raymond's wife was at the Baptist Medical Center, the nearby hospital, complaining of headaches, body pain, and fatigue. They sent her home with drugs, which proved ineffective. A second and third trip to the hospital brought no relief. The doctors could find no medical reason for the stubborn persistence of her weakness, her lethargy. It was the kind of unexplained, seemingly incurable illness most often attributed to witchcraft. Humiliation over a grain bag hardly seemed to be enough to raise a witch's ire, but the old woman's threats rang in Raymond's ears.

Then his wife woke one night, terrified, crying, "Don't you see her? What is she doing here? What do you want?!" Raymond could see no one. "Don't you see her standing there?" she screamed, pointing to the foot of the bed. The woman she saw was Carlos's grandmother. While Raymond was teaching at school the next day his wife took her suspicions to the *gambarana*.

Convicted again by the birds, the elderly woman still refused to acknowledge her guilt. The *gambarana* responded by banishing her from town. If she wouldn't submit to the chief's power and pledge her allegiance to the witch-hunting shrine, she couldn't live in Gambaga. The next night Raymond's wife raved. He remembered her sobbing, "They're coming to kill me. They're trying to kill me! They'll kill me tonight! Tomorrow is far away!"

She was right; by morning she was dead.

After he buried his wife the doctors told Raymond that she had a problem with her heart, that part of it was rotted, but when I asked the catechist whether he believed his wife had been killed by witchcraft he replied, "Oh, absolutely, one hundred percent." He didn't call for Carlos's grandmother to be punished, saying that it was in God's hands. "God is in control and will deal with her wickedness accordingly."

The true cost of that dark belief was difficult to measure. Carlos's grandmother had been chased out of town. Comfort had been cut off from her siblings. Her boys, suddenly pushed into the position of men, watched their bright futures fade. Dreams of steady government jobs as engineers or administrators evaporated when they could no longer pay the tuition required for tertiary-level schooling. Without a family home Stephen's sons scattered. One left to find work in Accra, but no one had heard from him in months. Kingsley, the eldest, was forced to drop out of college in Tamale; suddenly, at the age of twenty-six, he was responsible for the family's expenses, and his five brothers needed to be fed, clothed, and educated.

The belief that Stephen had died at the hands of a witch continued to haunt his family. Carlos told me the story of his father's death while home from teacher's college for a weekend. He was determined to walk the path his father had laid out for him. No matter the short-term hardships, Carlos knew he would only continue to struggle if he didn't carry on with his education. He had been back at the teacher training college for only two weeks, but the school had already come looking for tuition; he was a full year behind in his payments and they threatened to send him packing. Over the course of the weekend he made the rounds to church members and family friends, collecting a dollar here, five dollars there, explaining his plight and begging for the money. He could not promise to repay the small loans.

ABOUT A MONTH AFTER CARLOS RETURNED TO HIS STUDIES IN Tamale I went there to visit him. I found him participating in a raucous, drum-filled Dagomba celebration in a sunny courtyard. The party was crammed with men dressed in northern finery. Their heads were topped with traditional hats loaded with talismans, some wrapped in leather, others in red fabric with small mirrors sewn into the middle. Like his fellow celebrants, Carlos wore a deep blue Dagomba-style tunic, a thick woven shirt designed to be so voluminous it swirled about the hips. It was a gesture of respect for his Dagomba classmates, who were selecting their class chief. As the dry speeches droned on, Carlos showed me pictures of himself standing at a podium delivering a speech during his campaign to be class secretary. He lost, but had been chosen as chief of the students like him, who were not ethnically Dagomba. I'd seen Carlos lead prayers on Sunday morning at the Presbyterian church. He was a natural speech maker, full of fire and passion, and although he wanted to be a pastor I thought he would make an excellent politician.

We wandered away from the drums and dancing to sit on a bench in a shady spot of grass outside his dormitory, an ugly gray block jammed with men in their late teens and early twenties. Bunk beds reached up to the ceilings, hidden behind windows covered with towels, bed sheets, and flags adorned with marijuana leaves and Bob Marley's mug. American rap music blasted from somewhere inside, even though it appeared the electricity was off. Carlos could have been inside studying sociology or general sciences, but instead he told me about how, in the wake of his father's death, he visited many *juju* men, sometimes obtaining the same *juju* from several different people. In case one failed, there would be another on backup to offer protection.

He was always hunting for protective charms and *juju* that would either keep bad people away or disarm their bad spirits. He wore talismans sewn as a belt, rings stitched with mysterious substances, and leather blocks on a string around his neck. There was a certain *juju*-man that he "worshipped" who was teaching him the ways of black magic, and he followed that man everywhere, begging him for stronger and stronger *juju*. For some of the *juju* he was asked to bring a cock or a fowl. For others he was asked to collect sticks or a specific bit of cow dung, such as the top tip of a cow patty. Carlos had his sights set on avenging his father's death, and finally he asked his mentor for the kind of *juju* that would allow him to kill his enemies with only a verbal threat. The old man refused, saying that Carlos was too young for the *juju* to be effective. But Carlos couldn't be dissuaded; he pestered the old man until he eventually relented and prepared an ingredient list, telling his young apprentice he would have to be coached in the ways of using this powerful *juju*.

Carlos was told to find a "bear paw." We could not decide what animal his mentor was talking about; some of the elders called it a small donkey, he said, but it resembled a bear. When I insisted that Ghana doesn't have bears, he assured me it does. No matter how many ways I asked, Carlos refused to tell me what power lay in the bear's paw. It made me wonder just how far he'd fallen into the world of *juju*.

"Do you see how hard it is for witches to confess, even though I wasn't practicing?" he said.

So it *was* for witchcraft, I exclaimed. It would have made you a witch!

No, he laughed, amused at my eagerness to label him. What he meant was that when confronted with the misdeeds of his past, it was hard to admit that he had ever strayed so far into the black depths of *juju*, that he had ever felt such an all-consuming need for revenge.

He was working at collecting the bear paw and the other ingredients required by his *juju* master, borrowing money from friends to pay for the rare items the old man had requested, when a divine revelation convinced him to give it up. It wasn't his education that persuaded Carlos to walk away from his search for witchcraft; it wasn't the lessons he was learning in his health or science classes. It was God. The epiphany came on a Sunday, perhaps sometime in 2004, maybe in May or June or even July. He was in Bolgatanga, Ghana's northernmost city, preparing to take private exams that would help him get into college, when he went to church with a friend.

"I attended a church service, and that was just the end," he said with a shrug. He remembered with a grin that the pastor was standing in the middle of the congregation, up on a plastic chair, hands raised in a V above him, inviting the Holy Spirit to come down and infect the faithful.

"In fact, I felt the touch," Carlos said, his smile spreading across his face. "And it was awesome."

He had always attended the Presbyterian church, but now he felt there was no turning back. "I personally believe I had an encounter with the Holy Spirit," he said. "Having *juju* became awkward: it would not tolerate the new life I was ushered into."

When he returned home to Gambaga in October after taking his exams he prayed over his talismans in hopes of breaking their power, then burned them. Now he lives by Exodus 20, the Bible verse outlining the Ten Commandments and the directive not to worship any gods but God.

The feeling of revenge simply went away. "It just disappeared. One shouldn't try to revenge, but should forgive," he said. Sometimes the chants pop into his head and bubble from his lips. It takes control to keep them locked away. "That thing manipulates so the ones you want to hurt are your own family," he said.

He planned to finish his three years of teacher training, then teach for a year or two, then open an evangelical Presbyterian church before branching out on his own. He intended to lace some of his sermons with an anti-witchcraft sentiment, to encourage his parishioners to protect themselves with Jesus' love, not with talismans and idols. He wouldn't hunt witches, he said, not like so many charismatic church leaders in the south did. But he would help the witches to find God and be delivered. "I think it is the root of Africa's problems," he said.

For Carlos witchcraft was about protection and revenge, but it was also about appearances. If you appeared to have strong witchcraft working in your favor, there was a chance enemies would leave you alone. Of course there was an equal chance that an enemy would simply seek out something even stronger, something that could trump the protective amulets. Carlos shrugged when I asked how much money he had spent acquiring *juju*. All he knew was that every cent he had went into witchcraft. His parents were giving him money to pay for school, but instead he bought talismans. His friends gave him money and he turned it into *juju*.

"Even if I were rich, witchcraft is intensive. The more you have *juju*, the more you have to sacrifice, and that involves money," he said. "You're always drained."

It was one of the saddest ironies of witchcraft: those most in need of its promises of power and prestige could least afford it. Ruled by superstition, bound by tradition, and caught up in appearances, too many people spent what little money they had on rituals and sacrifices to entice the supernatural to give them success. "You take it today and you think it's glamorous, but it will spoil your own life," Carlos said.

Life in the north was undeniably hard, and unrelentingly so. Rains disappeared without reason. Crops failed without explanation. Wives and fathers died and no one understood why. In desperation people with nothing to spare took what little money they had to the witchdoctor, hoping it would be enough to turn the capricious favor of fate. Witchcraft may have been nothing more than a convenient scapegoat when things when wrong, but hunting its practitioners and avenging their dark magic was a way to take charge when things seemed out of control. Carlos had learned that there was always something stronger, darker, more powerful. The greater fortunes it brought, the more power it bestowed. The more convinced one became of witchcraft's powers, the more one was willing to spend to maintain it. It was a spiral few northerners could afford.

CHAPTER ELEVEN

Simon and Evelyn's eldest daughter, Prinsilla, had life-saving surgery at the Baptist Medical Center when she was about ten years old. The hospital's sprawling stone buildings could seem like an oversized palliative ward crowded with sickly, skeletal malaria and tuberculosis patients, but Prinsilla's was a story of hope.

She'd been sick with what her parents thought was chronic malaria, battling fevers, diarrhea, and weakness, and for months they'd shuttled up and down the smooth two-mile stretch of pavement connecting Gambaga to the hospital in Nalerigu—"Until everyone was fed up with us," Evelyn said—but nothing seemed to work. Finally Simon insisted they admit Prinsilla so the doctors could see for themselves the little girl's torment. She would toss and turn in the night, moaning and crying. A German doctor said he would perform exploratory surgery to find the cause, assuring them he would make only a small incision. But when their daughter emerged from surgery three hours later, "she had been split from here to here," Evelyn said, pointing first at her crotch and then between her breasts.

The doctor told them he had never seen anything like it. At first he could see nothing unusual, but then he found two worms pinching Prinsilla's intestines closed. Evelyn mashed the tips of two fingers together to demonstrate. They were strangling the intestine, closing it off. The doctor talked about sending the worms to Germany for analysis, but the family never heard anything more about it. Evelyn had no idea where these worms might have come from. "Can food turn into worms?" she asked. She didn't call it witchcraft, but she also didn't understand how worms found their way into her daughter's gut.

Medical mysteries cluttered the wards and waiting rooms at the BMC, as the hospital was known. Treatment started at home with cheap Chinese-made drugs; when those failed, the sick went to an herbalist or a witchdoctor to find traditional remedies that might help symptoms subside. By the time patients came through the BMC's admitting doors, many were in the last stages of their illness. They'd unwittingly let the disease grow until it was masked by dozens of complications.

"Some people are sick and we don't know why, and they die and we still don't know why," said Dr. George Faile. "That's frustrating."

A bust of Faile's father, also Dr. George, sat in the grassy fore-court of the sprawling hospital campus, a floppy straw hat perched on its head. The bust hadn't seemed right without it, since the balding, pink-skinned doctor had never gone without one. Faile Sr. was one of the first doctors at the BMC and spent most of his life there, although he died back in the United States. The second Dr. George, slender with a head of thick dark hair and a matching thick dark moustache, was raised in the place where his dad tended to the sick. He returned to the States to study medicine and came back to Ghana in 1987 to volunteer for a while. He returned again in 1989 and has been at the hospital ever since. He didn't necessarily want to come to Ghana, he said, but the work was there and it was the kind of medicine he had always wanted to practice.

The one-story hospital was built in 1958 as an outpatient clinic and run and paid for by the International Southern Baptist Con-vention. Baptist missionaries stationed in nearby Nigeria had been sent to Ghana in the early 1950s to survey the region for the site of a new hospital. At the time there were no small clinics dotted around the countryside and the closest hospital was in Bawku, more than two hours northeast by car.

Like most hospitals, the BMC is a confusing maze of corridors. During the day dozens and dozens of patients sit in the shaded, open-air waiting rooms. Some spread a square of fabric on the ground and rest with their arms curled around their sleeping heads. A few women quietly nurse bright-eyed babies as they wait for their name to be called. Family members track back and forth carrying small parcels of food. Even a routine visit to the hospital is an all-day affair; delays are inevitable and, for the most part, patiently endured.

A row of consultation rooms leads to the metal doors of the operating room and its dated turquoise tiles. I spied a somewhat worrying poster on the swinging operating room doors, something about double-checking that it was the "right patient, right procedure, right site." Patient files were simply large flimsy flip cards, like the kind libraries used to use to keep track of borrowed books.

It was not an easy job, Faile admitted, sitting down to talk in his office after he'd treated the day's last patient, a young woman with disfiguring lesions on her face. The hospital was literally swamped with patients, many of whom had little understanding of what was happening to their body. The north plays host to a staggering list of potentially fatal pests and parasites, a few of them found in food but many of them waterborne. Ghana is also home to some of nature's cruelest and most monstrously disfiguring diseases. One could swell a man's legs or testicles until he resembled the elephant the illness was named for. Another, passed by the bite of a fly, gradually turned the eyelids inside out, until the eyelashes rubbed away at the eyeball, causing blindness. They were the kind of illnesses most Western doctors only read about, but they often popped up in the BMC's wards. Of course it was the more mundane respiratory infections, diarrheal diseases, skin lesions, burns, fractures, and generic illnesses that kept the BMC busy. The most common illness doctors saw was malaria—the mosquito-borne disease caused more admissions, more mortalities, and more treatments than any other—but the north's salt-heavy, starch-rich diet had created an epidemic of hypertension, a disease well-known in the West, with myriad silent and serious complications.

Faile's office looked like any medical office anywhere, painted a stark white and cluttered with the paraphernalia of a busy practice. Medical books were scattered around the room, manuals for the treatment of pediatric diseases, a basin for dirty scrubs, a pair of blue surgical clogs on the floor. A row of white coats lined one wall. The only difference, perhaps, was the electric fans turned up full-blast, providing a constant hum.

A posting on the hospital's website asks for donations of bed sheets, old church offering envelopes, and empty film canisters, hardly the kind of high-tech equipment more commonly associated with hospital care. The bed sheets are torn into three-inch strips and used as bandages; about five thousand envelopes are used each week to dispense prescription pills, and ointments and creams are sent home in the film canisters. It isn't fancy, but it gets the job done.

Hospitals with better equipment might be able to treat a lot of the advanced tumors they see at the BMC, Faile said, but there is little they can do when patients arrive at the hospital with cancers that have been allowed to progress to the terminal stage. "There's a lot of stuff we can't figure out," he said, "and it's a frustrating thing when you can't figure it out. There are a lot of lab tests we can't do. We don't have a lot of the investigative tools you'd have elsewhere." They didn't have the machines or the drugs to offer aggressive treatment. Even patients who responded well to chemo could receive only so much; there was not a lot of the toxic, cancer-fighting substance to go around. They couldn't do elective chest surgeries, such as angiograms or bypass surgeries, because the BMC doesn't have the equipment needed to thread balloons into arteries or reroute blood pathways. Many patients wait so long to seek treatment that their disease becomes too advanced anyway; they can't survive surgery and are simply sewn back up and sent home to die.

Tuesdays and Thursdays are surgery days. Each year the hospital sees about 60,000 to 70,000 outpatients at the thrice-weekly clinic, plus another 7,000 to 8,000 inpatients, who rotate through the hospital's 123 beds. In a year Faile, the sole surgeon, performs 1,000 to 1,200 major surgeries and about 3,000 minor procedures.

By July he had already performed 600 major surgeries that year, at a rate nearing seven per day.

The mind boggled.

He was quiet about this, stated it matter-of-factly and smiled humbly when it was pointed out that this was quite the workload. There was so much to do because there were so few qualified people left in Ghana to do it. The country produces about two hundred doctors each year at its three medical schools and sends a handful of students to be educated in Cuba, but once they have finished their training, which is entirely paid for by the Ghanaian government, many leave for Britain, South Africa, Canada, or the United States, lured by the promise of higher pay, lighter workloads, and better working conditions.

The shortage of doctors is bridged by the growing number of herbalists, often untrained men and women selling bottles of brown liquid and tins of white powders, whose offices are marked with large signs painted with cartoonish depictions of the symptoms they treat: drawings of a naked child squatting over a brown puddle or a wrinkled, white-haired man hunched over a walking stick. They don't always wait for patients to come to them; sometimes they climb onto the *tro-tros* to pitch their snake oils while passengers ride through the city streets. A vial of pills guaranteed to treat all of mankind's ills while simultaneously boosting one's energy, preventing the flu, increasing fertility, and thwarting kidney, heart, and liver troubles could be purchased for as little as a dollar.

Dr. Earl Hewitt, a balding family physician with twinkling eyes and pink skin, treated thousands of patients alongside Dr. Faile. The doctors lived in the bubble of the hospital campus, in housing behind the main clinic. They had few nonmedical interactions with the local population. Just being outside the hospital was difficult: they were instantly recognized as the "white doctors." Hewitt understood that the local people believed there were three kinds of illnesses. White illnesses could be treated anywhere, by the clinic or the witchdoctor or at home. Red illnesses were far more serious but should be treated spiritually at the herbalist or witchdoctor, always

locally. If the illness progressed it was considered black; a black illness could be treated only at the hospital after it was determined
that it could not be treated locally.

"They start in the red and they treat locally, and then when they
get to the point of death, then they come here. They die on the way
here, they die in the operating room, they die in the office, they die
waiting for their labs, they die in the wards. They come here to gasp
their last breath and die," he said, his Mississippi twang untouched
by a dozen years in Ghana.

WE'D COME TO ASK THE DOCTORS ABOUT A PERSISTENT RUMOR
that the hospital had evidence of witchcraft. It was a story I first
heard from Carlos, then from the Mozio *rana*, about a child whose
grandmother was spiritually stealing his medicines. Simon had a
slightly different version of the story, but the gist was the same:
technicians had somehow managed to capture irrefutable evidence
of the spiritual theft on the film of an X-ray. If there was any place
that was likely to see the mysterious consequences of witchcraft, the
kind of physical illnesses whose roots were planted in the spiritual
realm, it would be this crowded hospital.

There are few situations as likely to turn one into a believer as a
health scare. When faced with the fragility of one's own mortality
it's common to strike bargains with God, to plead for a return to
good health in exchange for some sort of sacrifice, whether a promise never to smoke again or a vow to rekindle a flatlined relationship.
It can also be a time of great open-mindedness, when no potential cure is discounted, no matter how outlandish. When modern
medicine fails, the desperately ill chase the promises of better health
held in healing waters, traditional remedies, chakra realignments, or
exotic ingredients. It's the feeling of helplessness that prompts the
search, and though the sick may say they're looking for a cure, what
they're really seeking is reassurance, relief, and reprieve. They want
to take back control, to take back a body betrayed by illness and
steer their life back to longevity.

It's a human impulse to ask why: Why me, why now, why this?

That compulsion to find an explanation has led to great scientific discoveries. Understanding what's happening in the body and what happens when disease causes normal functions to go awry has given doctors an arsenal of treatment options. Scientists know how blood moves, they know the effect a blockage can have, and they've devised ways of opening, repairing, and rebuilding pathways for the essential flow of blood. Researchers are motivated by a pressing need to understand—and thereby devise a means of controlling—the way an illness attacks.

It's been argued that science and witchcraft seek to answer essentially the same question. Asking a diviner to determine who is responsible for the tremor in a relative's handshake is no different from the frantic search for genetic abnormalities that lead to Parkinson's. They are both fueled by the same basic questions: Why this person, why now, what triggered the disease, what could have prevented the illness, how can it be treated, reversed, or even cured?

In a world where spiritual health is as important as diet, exercise, or genetics, it stands to reason that it too should be explored for the answers to the question of why. If one could pinpoint the cause of an illness in the spiritual realm, it too would offer prevention, treatment, and cure. If that cause turned out to be mortal, open to threat, intimidation, and negotiation, the sick could strike back or strike bargains and regain control.

WITCHCRAFT WAS NOT A DIAGNOSIS AT THE BMC, SO PATIENTS brave enough to speak to the white doctors about their fears of being bewitched were usually referred to Pastor Paul Musah and his cohort of hospital chaplains.

"We give the patient hope," said Musah, who wore heavy black bifocal glasses, like a 1950s television host, and a chaplain's uniform made of heavy green fabric. His tunic was styled after the kind Chairman Mao used to wear, and its breast pocket was filled with pens. He was missing his front right tooth. "We lead them to Christ and encourage them to give up their fears. The Devil has power, but God is more powerful."

Musah came to work as a chaplain at the BMC in 1980, after a falling out with his congregation over the issue of polygamous marriage. The Baptist Church was popular for its ceremonial baptisms and its idea of rebirth, but it was also strict. Musah was the only Baptist minister in Nalerigu at the time, but he refused to continue ministering to people who only nominally adopted the religion. The medical center is technically a missionary endeavor; the BMC's website notes that some forty churches have been seeded "as a result of ministries associated with BMC."

Musah shared Faile and Hewitt's frustration that so many patients appeared at the hospital in the last stage of their illness. Western medicine suffered from an image problem, he said, because it was expensive and unknown, so patients treated it as a last resort. They exhausted all other options before walking through the hospital's doors. Too many people died because they'd waited too long to come, which entrenched the perception that the white man's hospital was a place of death.

The reluctance to seek out medical care was mostly related to cost. A health insurance scheme introduced in 2004 had yet to be fully implemented in the more remote regions of the north, and even if the care was free there was still the cost of getting the patient to the hospital and feeding him while he was in the wards. The country was serious about improving its health care system, but was struggling when there were not enough doctors or nurses, when their equipment was inadequate and their access to the latest drugs insufficient. Traditional healers exploited its failings, Musah said, stepping in with herbal pain remedies and short-lived cures, lending credibility to the belief that the witchdoctor was stronger and more powerful than the white man's doctor.

"In Africa, in this area, in the north, if anything unusual happens like this, they will see the soothsayer to find out who is involved," he said. "He won't say he doesn't know, he will always provide an answer.

"If you are sick and not getting well, on and off for a year or so, you will think there is someone causing it. People will even consult their gods."

All the chaplains can offer the patients is the assurance that God is their ultimate protection against the devil's witchcraft, he said. Christians who believe in Jesus' power will not be affected. "The Devil has power and can kill—we're not denying it. But God created you and He can control things if you put them in His hands."

On a typical day Musah and his fellow chaplains visited ten to fifteen outpatients, plus five or six patients on the wards. They were most often referred to patients newly diagnosed with HIV, patients considered terminal, and those under stress or contemplating suicide. Musah hauled out a dog-eared school notebook, carefully delineated with ruled lines of blue and red ink, to show that in the first three months of 2007 forty-four people were tested for HIV at the BMC, with thirty tests coming up positive. Ghana's HIV rate is thought to be about 3 percent, the same as in the United States, perhaps protected from the epidemic ravaging eastern and southern Africa by the expanse of the Sahara and underdeveloped regional trade, a legacy of poor roads, and the hopscotch of English- and French-speaking countries. The north's isolation made the few hospitals difficult to reach, understaffed, and underfunded, yet Musah's notebook showed that HIV had still found its way into the community.

The chaplain's log also hinted at the coping mechanisms some northerners used to survive the harshness of their lives. Alcoholism was a serious problem, and the hospital's beds were frequently used as a place to dry out. Musah chuckled ruefully about the new headmaster at the local junior secondary school, a well-known "serious drunk" who was often brought into the BMC to have his stomach pumped. Even Gambaga's chief had spent time in the wards recovering from a binge of drinking. People drowned their hardships in fermented *pito*, a millet-based brew, and *akpateshie*, the fiery local moonshine. Particularly young women and men who were earning wages, Musah said with a disapproving shake of his head. They spent all they had on drink.

For each page in Musah's list of counseled patients there were at least two entries of suicide attempts nestled in the list of patients with cancer, terminal diseases. and heart problems. Suicide was a serious taboo, but in the first six months of the year the hospital had seen six patients who'd taken poison or DDT or mixed battery acid with water and swallowed it. Life in the north was Sisyphean, and Musah's book of patients was a sobering reminder that despite the remarkable resilience that propelled most people onward, there were some who simply couldn't take another day of struggle. There was a woman who'd come just the previous week, Musah said. She'd swallowed thirty pills meant to treat malaria. Her family didn't believe her when she said she needed to go to the hospital, and by the time they organized a vehicle it was already too late. She was dead by the time she arrived.

Musah was constantly called on to counsel women who found themselves competing against another woman for their husband's attention. Their stress took a physical form, presenting as inexplicable symptoms that didn't seem to have a physiological cause. Some fell mute, refused to eat, and couldn't sleep or bathe. Others complained of headaches and joint pain, phantom symptoms that could not be diagnosed using laboratory technology. These were the kinds of patients who stubbornly saw witchcraft as the true cause of their troubles, Musah said, and the simultaneous arrival of a new wife and the onset of symptoms did not go unnoticed.

"We pray with them and advise them to be patient with their husband. We tell them to try to continue to play their role as housewife. The new one gets more attention and the old one feels jealous. It's a serious problem, especially during the lean season when there's not much food," Musah said. That was partly why he lobbied against polygamy: he could see the toll it took on the family. With only one man responsible for earning enough money to support many women and children, nutrition often suffered, stressing the women and making the children more susceptible to disease.

THE LINK BETWEEN SPIRITUAL HEALTH AND PHYSICAL HEALTH IS not one that's well understood or appreciated by Western medicine, but cases where patients die because of physical symptoms triggered by mental stress are common enough to have earned a name: psychogenic death. For some, prisoners of war, for example, it's a matter of hope. As hope fades, so does the body's resolve to live. For others, such as the voodoun faithful in Haiti, a broken taboo is enough to set off a chain of symptoms resulting in death.

As the ethnobotanist Wade Davis explains in *The Rainbow and the Serpent*, his scientific exploration of zombie death in Haiti, a mind conditioned from birth to believe in curses will succumb to a "self-fulfilling prophesy" when a taboo or spiritual code is broken. It's the power of suggestion: tell someone he's cursed and he'll start seeing enough signs to believe it.

"According to this view," Wade writes, "the victim ... becomes caught in a vicious cycle of belief that indirectly kills him, perhaps, as some suggest, by making his body susceptible to pathogenic disease. His psychological state can be imagined. He is doomed to die by a malevolent curse that both he and all those around him deeply believe in. He becomes despondent, anxious and fearful. His resignation is both recognized and expected by other members of his society. They join him in speculating how long he may survive, or who is the source of the curse."

Where would otherwise educated people get the idea that their loved ones died of a metal lining in the bladder or a rotted heart? Faile admitted he put too much emphasis on treatment and not enough on communicating with patients, but he was so busy and they didn't really understand the mechanics of what he was saying. Sometimes, he said, he stood in the hospital hallways attempting to explain a diagnosis, but quickly found his explanation spiraling further and further away from the symptoms until he was giving a basic biology lesson. Patients placed their absolute faith and trust in the white doctors, but Faile would later hear the confusion of grieving family members telling other relatives that they did an operation and they didn't know why. Then the person died.

"I wish I knew more about local treatments," Faile said. He didn't discount the local medicines entirely; he'd seen dislocated shoulders that appeared to be expertly set and knew folk remedies, such as poultices, were common. "They must be doing some people some good sometimes," he said. "Otherwise they wouldn't do it. But I don't know what they are."

Ghana attempted to embrace its traditional healers by licensing them, but there were always charlatans setting up "prayer camps," where they promised to use God's healing power to cure physical ailments. In many cases the treatments were worse than the illness. A patient had recently come to Hewitt in agony. A year earlier he'd been left partially paralyzed by a stroke, and after growing tired of dragging his one side he decided to seek treatment from a local healer. The witchdoctor lined his paralyzed side with dozens and dozens of tiny razor nicks and poured boiling water over them. The wounds were severely infected by the time Hewitt saw him; the rotting tissue was rapidly eating away at the man's healthy tissue. The smell of the necrotic tissue was so clear in Hewitt's memory that he told the story with a faint look of disgust. They'd had to clean the wounds, drain the infection, and cut away the dead tissue, leaving the man worse off than when he sought the witchdoctor's help. The infection still wasn't responding to treatment, and there was little more they could do.

If the man had come to the hospital instead, Hewitt might have started him on a course of aspirin and drugs to reduce his high blood pressure and stave off another stroke. Hewitt believed the man might have seen some slight improvement, particularly if he was able to do simple physiotherapy exercises at home. But the patient wanted immediate results. He didn't want painful exercises and incremental improvements. He wanted to be able to walk normally again, and when the witchdoctor promised just that, the man was willing to pay any price.

One of Hewitt's tuberculosis patients, hunched with the devastating pain of TB of the spine, had come just the day before to tell him he was fed up with the pain of the backbone crushing his spinal cord and was ready to try traditional treatment. He mentioned boiling water and herbs and predicted they would pour the water on his legs. Hewitt strongly warned him against it, but to no avail. In the end all he could ask was that the man test the water temperature before the procedure to ensure he wouldn't be back at the hospital with scalding or burns.

"There's a lot of stuff they won't tell us," Faile said. "I think sometimes they take medicines or herbs or potions or even drugs they buy from the market and they won't tell us what they took." Sometimes they don't even know what they're buying, he said, so the doctors have no idea what kind of effect it might be having on their patients.

Neither doctor had seen anything at the hospital to convince them that witchcraft was real. Patients might come with vague complaints that don't really make sense, but Hewitt said his first priority was always to puzzle out a medical cause. He didn't have time to inquire about witchcraft or whether there were spiritual problems in the patient's life that might cause physical symptoms; psychotherapy wasn't a priority when there were literally hundreds of sick patients waiting.

"I believe in evil spirits," Faile allowed. "I think they exist and I think they can affect people." But in virtually an entire lifetime at the hospital he had never seen any physiological evidence of witchcraft causing an illness. What the local people saw as bewitchment he saw as mental stress. There was a woman on the ward as we spoke, he said, whose behavior was very bizarre. There was nothing wrong with her according to their tests, but she was having a sort of seizure, a kind of twitch of the mouth. He could get her to stop if he talked her out of it, making him think it was psychological.

As a Christian hospital, Faile said, God is the only thing they can offer to patients who believe they're suffering from witchcraft. They counsel patients to turn to God to release them from the bondage of evil. But it's not common for patients to complain to them of such things, he insisted. Mental problems are likely to be caused by witchcraft, he said, but mostly because patients believe in it, not necessarily because the person is bewitched. The stronger the belief, the more stress and strain it caused the mind and, subsequently, the body.

For all the doctors ignored or denied allegations of witchcraft, they unwittingly starred in legendary stories about great witches. Faile chuckled as he recounted the rumor of a patient whose X-ray film showed a hand dipping in front of his mouth, blocking his ability to swallow his medication. Simon and I exchanged a glance. This was the story we'd heard. Faile smiled. Sometimes patients like to have X-rays because they're looking for spiritual skeletons; they're certain that because the X-ray machine can see what's inside us, it can also see spirits. And sometimes the films really do show extra hands, he said, because a parent might be holding a child or because a technician hasn't moved his hands away quickly enough.

I asked if the hospital really had an X-ray showing the drug thief. Faile shook his head. It was just a story.

Feeling emboldened by the chance to finally set rumor against reality, Simon asked Faile whether he'd ever done surgery and found something strange in someone's body, like a talisman. Or a stone, I added, thinking about a story Simon told me about a woman from Burkina Faso who had a stone or an egg pulled out of her body. He'd heard she fashioned it into an amulet and wore it on her arm.

Faile reached behind him to a desk covered with drugs and specimen bottles, opened a drawer and pulled out a chalky white puck, about the diameter of a tennis ball. My eyes widened as he set it on the table before us.

"Wow," I said, "is it a kidney stone or a gallstone?"

"It's from the bladder," he answered.

Simon reached out to feel the stone in quiet awe. I asked him if he understood that it wasn't literally a stone, not like the stones by the river, and attempted to explain that it was a buildup of calcium. Faile sat quietly as I tried to remember why the body needs calcium, how it's used, what could cause it to accumulate and form a stone. I soon understood Faile's despondency when talking to patients: each sentence required further and further explanation, as though the stone had opened a Pandora's box of questions. I knew I should stop when I began babbling about the dangers of eating ice cream and drinking tea. Faile merely smiled, helping me here and there as I struggled to explain how this stone could find its way into the body naturally, not through witchcraft.

Simon set the stone back on Faile's desk and asked what the rock could do to the body. The doctor answered that it was painful and could block urination.

"No person would see this and think it was natural," Simon declared. "They would say it was witches who did this, who put it inside the body."

CHAPTER TWELVE

THE RAINS WERE UNDENIABLY LATE. THE DRY HEAT AND LACK OF rain had sapped any moisture from the dirt road leading away from Gambaga. A huge chunk of the road had crumbled away, tumbling down a ravine and leaving the road only wide enough to accommodate one vehicle. A thin stick adorned with the faded remains of a red T-shirt had been planted near the edge of the huge crater as a caution to drivers. Two other waving flags sprouted up on the road between Gambaga and the paved road at Walewale, warning drivers of potholes deep enough to bust an axle. Tire treads broke down the rough road, leaving a carpet of fine dust that rose up in huge, lingering clouds behind passing traffic.

The weather was making everyone irritable. Rumors swirled through Gambaga that a hunter had accidentally trapped a baby crocodile in the river, one that was said to contain a powerful water spirit. Its anger at the crocodile's death was to blame for the severity of the drought. There would have to be an elaborate burial for the crocodile in order to appease the spirit.

Simon heard that the *gambarana* had been sacrificing "all kinds of animals" in hope of bringing rain. The town's Muslims meanwhile sent a truck around town with a loudspeaker to warn women away from the bush, where the men were performing a rain-calling ceremony. I hung around the guesthouse, waiting to see what would happen, wondering if hanging out some laundry would help or hinder the cause. The blue sky gradually darkened, turning a bleak gray. Clouds gathered in the afternoon and a strong wind created whirling dirt devils. Only a few raindrops splashed on the parched ground before the skies cleared. Another rumor flashed through town. Apparently a man crossing through the bush where the rain-calling ceremony had taken place had been struck by lightning.

The ground should have been soggy with heavy rain, but the drought held firm, making the temperature unbearable. I slept under a thin sheet to save myself from mosquitoes, but usually woke with my scalp drenched in sweat. The drought had drained the man-made lake that powered Ghana's hydroelectric plant and the entire country was on enforced power rationing. A government schedule suggested the power would blink off for twelve hours every two days, but in Gambaga the lights would dim randomly, often at odd hours. The fans would slow to a soupy swirl, then stop completely, frozen for at least eighteen hours, usually several days in a row. It was maddening; there was something about the unpredictability of the power cuts that felt like psychological torture. The guesthouse had a noisy generator that could be switched on at sunset to power the lights and fans until midnight, but since the cost of fuel seemed to jump each week the manager eventually quit running it.

In a place where people kept their families alive on mere pennies, my money seemed to evaporate. Simon's silver truck had sat for several days outside the mechanic's garage, suffering from some kind of problem with the battery that caused it to dry out and overheat, sending thick gray bursts of smoke out from under the hood. (I was willing to pay whatever the mechanic asked; I didn't want to repeat the experience of being stranded on a little-traveled road, as we were one afternoon on our way back from visiting the family of one of the accused women. After dousing the engine fire with sand from the roadside, Simon took advantage of our unplanned stop to collect herbs growing in the ditch. Later he sheepishly admitted that he may have thwarted his own attempts to flag down a ride by

sturdy woman with curlers in her hair stopped me; she told me she
was not fine, she was hungry. "Give me your yam," she ordered. A
few steps later I passed a gaggle of boys sitting in the dry drain-
age ditch near the soccer field. They yelled their hellos, followed by
"Madam! Give me your yam!"

"No!" I called back, cradling the ugly tuber like a baby, prompt-
ing a chorus of giggles from the soccer field. "It's for me!"

I walked a few yards more, then heard a little voice pipe up. It
sounded as though this was the young boy's only chance to ask for
his heart's true desire. "Madam!" he squeaked. "Give me . . . a football!"

On the day the women planted Simon's fields the blue sky held
no hint of rain, and what could be seen through the dust clouds had
long ago turned a monotone shade of brown. The vividness of the
red soil had been bleached to a dirty tan and the deep green had
faded to a similar shade of parched yellow-brown.

The sunny sky heralded only suffering; mud villages already
grappling with hardship and prone to seeing the manipulative
hands of witches behind their misfortunes now had to contend
with a changing currency, rising fuel prices, frequent power outages,
a relentless drought, and empty markets.

Simon's corn died without sending up a single shoot.

I THOUGHT I UNDERSTOOD THE NORTH'S HARDSHIPS. I THOUGHT
I understood the desperation that came with the poverty, and the
tension that bubbled up around those forced to rely on others
to survive. I thought I understood the interlocking nature of the
north's problems, the way poverty fed into, and fed off of, the lack
of education, clean water, and health facilities. I thought I'd seen the
worst of the suffering that came when the safety net of one's family
and village was pulled away. Then I met the women of Gushiegu's
hidden witch camp.

Every week the banished women living in Gushiegu, where
Asara had once sold rice, waited at the edge of the market with
bits of cardboard folded into the shape of a dustpan. They carried

makeshift brooms fashioned from fistfuls of spiny dried grass. Once
a week they followed the cargo trucks and lingered where women
sold millet or rice measured out in tin cans. Lean teenage boys saun-
tered through the dusty clearing, their yellow plastic sandals leaving wide footprints as they threaded through the temporary rows
of tomatoes, onions, and yams. The boys carried small coolers and
sold icy plastic baggies filled with burgundy *bissap* juice, the frozen nectar of the hibiscus flower. There wasn't an inch of shade in
Gushiegu's open-air market, but the women traders looked as cool
and comfortable as they would sitting in front of a fan. They lov-
ingly rearranged impossible pyramids of tomatoes with the finesse
of food stylists. Scarves in an eye-popping array of colors were effortlessly wrapped around their heads, the placement and tension of
each knot lending uniqueness to the headwear. Around them girls
with the shorn heads of students clacked together coins, their baskets of cool water sachets forgotten at their feet as they flirted with
the *bissap* sellers with the well-placed punches and mock pouting
that makes up the universal language of teenage love.

At the end of the trading day, as the sun slipped behind the
town's low buildings and the vendors refilled their woven sacks and
set off for home, the waiting women descended, using their ersatz
brooms and pans to sweep up any spilled grains. Their only competition for the remains of the market, for the produce too ripe to
fetch a price, were the scraggly chickens furiously pecking at what
would otherwise be the women's meal.

I'd learned of Gushiegu's hidden settlement of banished
women from another Canadian journalist living in the north; even
Simon knew nothing about it. We arrived in Gushiegu just as the
sun slipped beyond the horizon. Despite its reputation as a bustling market town there were few places to stay. One guesthouse
was full of construction crews working on a new hospital at the
far end of town and the other was still a concrete skeleton. Simon
slowed alongside a man wearing a button-down shirt made of fabric
stamped with the Presbyterian Church logo and they discussed our
options. Emmanuel Sasu offered us shelter at the local School for

Life office, where I slept on a cot and Simon and Kizito unrolled mats and slept on the floor. Sasu reappeared early the next morning, offering to help find the women and translate. As we sat under a willow tree eating piping hot doughnuts for breakfast, Sasu pointed to a woman walking toward us under the weight of a heavy tin jerry can. She was a witch, he said, calling out greetings as she turned into the crumbling compound next door.

Within minutes a half-dozen women had gathered. When we asked about scrounging at the market, a tall, thin woman disappeared inside a hut on the verge of collapse. Its surrounding wall had broken away in chunks. Damu Dagon returned carrying a metal bowl with tiny holes nailed through the bottom. Into the bowl she dumped millet swept up from the market and began shaking it. Interspersed with the bead-sized grains were bits of downy white feathers, some plastic string, dried blades of grass, rough rocks, and small pebbles. The seeds were sieved three times before they were soaked in water and sieved again. It was meant to feed more than seventy women, but there were only enough grains to fill up a small salad bowl.

"We'll eat anything but shit," Damu joked. She looked like Olive Oyl, the beanpole love interest of Popeye. She was rail-thin, dressed in head-to-toe black, with small red chickens printed across her long skirt and a yellow and green headscarf tied pirate-style around her head. Her cursing was meant to be funny, but considering the truth of the joke I couldn't bring myself to laugh.

Her hunger wasn't the product of famine, drought, or war. It was her everyday existence, the sad consequence of an old woman exiled in a place where survival depended on a web of able-bodied family members. "They find themselves struggling to fend for themselves," Sasu said. "They sweep the market to get grain, they help people on their farms, they plaster rooms. Those whose children are well-to-do give them food."

There was no shrine at this camp, no traditional authority slitting the throat of sacrificial chickens. There was only sanctuary. It was considered the country's only urban camp and signaled a shift in the way—and why—women were banished. Four of Ghana's witch camps had sprung up around a powerful spirit and were tucked away in remote villages. Nyani was essentially the only witch camp where men accused of witchcraft lived, largely because its isolation ensured that new arrivals could find untended farming plots nearby. Kukuo's camp had formed first, near a potent shrine, then a village grew up around it. Nabole camp, at John's remote village in the far reaches of northeastern Ghana, was only for women of the Konkomba tribe. The Christian charity World Vision had adopted Kpatinga camp, building octagonal concrete huts with corrugated metal roofs for the accused women, which quickly became the focus of bitter envy in neighboring communities. Only Gambaga had a dedicated social worker and a chief whose ancestors gave him the power to find and control witches.

Gushiegu's camp started with a single woman, who staggered into the chief's palace covered in bruises and begged him to allow her to stay. She had been labeled a witch and banished from her village with nowhere to go. The chief allowed her to sleep in one of the abandoned huts on the edge of town. As word of the chief's clemency spread, more women began arriving, until there were seventy-eight banished women living in the camp. Most were elderly, but one woman carried an infant and walked with a young daughter hanging onto her skirt. Her husband visited just long enough to make her pregnant, Damu joked.

The women weren't really witches, she told us, they just weren't wanted. It was telling that the absence of a shrine to control the women's witchcraft did not seem to bother their accusers. It suggested they weren't really afraid of a witch's attacks. There was no pretense of ominous dreams or unfortunate coincidences, there was only the success of their sons and the jealousy of their neighbors. Their banishment was the product of intense rivalries. Damu's definition of prosperity hinted at the sliver of fortune that separated success from struggle in her village. A woman might get enough to eat, maybe even enough to send a child to school, and that was enough for her neighbors to accuse her of practicing witchcraft. If there was a co-wife—and virtually all of the women had been in polygamous marriages—she would orchestrate the woman's demise by manipulating her husband into making an accusation.

Most had been chased from their villages amid violence. They'd been hit with stones, whipped by chains, or beaten with sticks. All had been left to their fate. The Konkomba people "don't mind" if their mother is at a witch camp, Sasu told us, meaning they don't bring gifts of food or charcoal or sleeping mats. If family members came to Gushiegu on market days the women tried to keep up appearances, scraping together what they could to cook for their children, even if they had nothing to spare.

Sasu led us around the camp. The community had accepted the women, he said, seeing them as outcasts rather than witches. The village was mostly Dagomba, while the women were Konkomba, and because they believed witchcraft couldn't cross ethnic boundaries the community didn't worry about witch attacks. "They don't fear them," Sasu said. "They rather feel pity for them. They help them and even give them clothes."

We sat in Damu's shared compound as she sieved millet and cracked jokes, making the men chuckle. In each of the villages we had visited, we'd been offered small stools or plastic chairs. In this place I sat on an overturned metal bowl while Simon and Kizito squatted or sat on the ground. There were no cooking pots in the yard and no food drying in the sun. Damu's wrists, collarbones, and cheeks stood out, knobby and sharp, her skin stretched tight. I felt a faint sense of panic at the idea that we would just drive away, leaving the women to their misery.

"She's eating here, but when she's at her house, the children provide for her. When they return from the riverside, they bring her water," Sasu translated. "Here if she gets to eat, she has to suffer before she eats."

Damu came from a tiny community called Busum, a place so small it wasn't on the map. Three of her neighbors lived at the Gushiegu camp, a testament to the hostility and paranoia of their village. Damu was one in a long list of women married to a man who had already grown old by the time they wed. He died while she was pregnant with their youngest son, who had long since grown old enough to have children of his own. She had four sons, and they each had two wives who, as custom demanded, had doted on Damu. Her sons were considered rich farmers in her small part of the world, a place where the young men "were always accusing the old ladies," Damu said. They'd get drunk on *akpateshie*, "blow fumes on everyone," get worked up about something, and then make threats and accusations. The men turned their quarrels to their enemy's mother. "If you have a child and they don't like the child, if something happens in the village, they will get at the child through making an accusation."

She still feared for her children, worrying someone might poison them because others saw her as a witch. She remained at Gushiegu's witch settlement because she worried that returning home would bring blame for even the smallest of her neighbors' misfortunes.

"Here is better than her own place," Sasu translated for her. "If someone dies, they will say you are the person. Even if she died and was sent to her village and buried, they would say her ghost comes out and bewitches them."

WE LEFT THE WOMEN WITH A BIT OF MONEY FROM A BRICK OF cash I'd hidden in my backpack to cover the cost of repairing unexpected breakdowns. Divided eighty ways, it was barely enough for each woman to buy a handful of chilies at the market. Simon drove away in silence, lost in what we'd seen. He'd found Damu charming and funny. She reminded him of one of his old favorites at the Gambaga camp; they even shared the same name. That woman was also a joker and she too vowed never to return home, but Simon had reunited her with her family several years ago. He was shaken by the experience of meeting Gushiegu's collection of outcasts, deciding that this was the place most in need of his help.

"These camps need a permanent [charity], not just NGOs that come and go," he said. The women remembered "whites" occasionally coming through the Gushiegu camp, asking questions and offering "small money" for food. Two white women had come to register the women for the National Health Insurance Scheme, but no one could remember the name of their charity. The banished women needed better housing and an advocate to work with their families, Simon declared. They needed someone to convince them that women should not be sent away on flimsy accusations or used as pawns in the quarrels of a town's young men. They needed access to medicines and proper food.

It's difficult to know how to help women accused of witchcraft when their hardships stem from a belief system that most charities and aid groups don't recognize as real. For most development agencies witchcraft represents an impossible conundrum. Few want to be seen as furthering the belief in witchcraft, but none is willing to openly denounce it. They may want to make the women's lives easier, but they're reluctant to just give them the things they really need, fearing it will create dependency or, worse, unintentionally encourage desperate families to dump their wives, mothers, or sisters at a camp.

Survival in northern Ghana requires a wide net of support: someone to carry water, build fires, undertake laborious food preparation, wash clothes, care for children, sweep, plant, weed, and harvest. It's too much for one person alone, particularly someone who doesn't see or walk well and can't lift heavy loads. The chasm between what aid groups think they can provide and what the women think they really need is littered with wasted money and useless gifts. In one camp ostentatious yellow latrines built by a Danish charity sit unused and abandoned as the women make their way to the privacy of the bush. Visiting family quickly appropriate the bicycles and donkey carts donated by another charity. The gifts were meant to make collecting water and firewood easier on the old women, but it was hard to blame their impoverished families for helping themselves. Besides, communities surrounding the witch camps slipped easily into jealous resentment if they saw the women receiving favors or privileges. Their banishment, after all, was meant to be a punishment.

In the absence of actual help the old women desperately searched for the money they needed to feed and clothe themselves. They sold water alongside the much younger schoolgirls, helped with harvests, or hired themselves out as farm hands to plant or weed growing crops. Timari Tama, meaning "There is hope," was formed in 1996 to help the women living at Gambaga organize themselves into money-making cooperatives. Solomon Bukari, a laboratory technician at the Baptist Medical Center, helped run the group with his aunt.

"Our aim was just to get some income-generating ventures for the women to be working on," he said late one afternoon as we sat on an empty bench in the shade of one of the hospital's waiting areas. "The work is going round, helping people to get something to feed on."

Amina Adam, his aunt, came up with the idea for a shea butter processing plant. Shea trees, with their long, low-slung branches, are plentiful throughout the continent's hotter, drier areas, growing in a belt that stretches through nineteen countries, from the dry Guinea grasses of northern Ghana all the way to the savannah of Sudan. Liquid extracted from the tree's nuts has long been used in West Africa as a cooking oil and a kind of pomade for dry, brittle hair. Carvers and hunters work it into wood and hides and drum skins to make them more malleable. Fat from the nuts is also prized for its properties as an emollient and moisturizer. It's found in high-end body creams and lotions and is sometimes substituted for cocoa butter in chocolate. Rubbed into the skin it can treat anything from acne to psoriasis and is used to reduce the redness and irritation of rashes, to fade scars, reduce wrinkles and stretch marks, and treat eczema and arthritis.

Like so many African staples its production is incredibly arduous, and almost exclusively done by women. To extract the oil, shea nuts are boiled, dried, pulverized, fried, kneaded, and boiled again in a process that can take more than a week. But it's big business. A single ton of creamy white shea butter can fetch four hundred dollars on the export market. The U.S. Agency for International Development has spent millions fostering the shea nut industry and connecting producers and manufacturers with buyers. It estimates that 4,000 tons of shea butter were sold from West African markets in 2007, earning nearly one hundred million dollars. Involving the banished women in the industry should have been easy, considering that fluctuating supply is responsible for the butter's price, but Solomon couldn't find a buyer.

"In fact, we don't have a ready market, so it makes our productivity very low," he said. "There's a stigma to it: no one will buy something to eat if it's made by a witch, so very few people will buy oil to cook with or something for your body if it's come from the women."

Solomon and his aunt were not deterred. Amina was interested in the welfare of the women because she too was a northerner. She had married a "big man" in Accra and lived comfortably in the capital, where her husband worked as a manager with the Electrical Company of Ghana and sat on the board of directors at the Volta River Authority, the two bodies directly responsible for the country's faltering electrical supply. Amina hoped to return to the north one day and didn't want to find herself banished to the camp, denied her human rights. Solomon's aunts—"Several," he said—had already been sent to the camp.

Despite their disastrous first attempt at marketing shea butter, aid groups lined up to provide Timari Tama with the money they needed to keep the cooperative going. Action Aid gave money for a small, low-rise concrete building to act as a processing plant, which was erected at the southwestern edge of town. The Canadian International Development Agency gave money for processing machines and dug a borehole to provide the operation with a steady water supply. The African Women's Development Fund, run through Ghana's Ministry of Women and Children's Affairs, set up a side project, buying sheep for the women to raise and building a paddock for them near the shea processing plant. Then Timari Tama switched gears, announcing they would outfit the plant for *dawadawa* processing instead.

Dawadawa is considered a spice rich in protein that's often used by West African families in place of meat. It's made from brilliant yellow African locust beans, which hang in pods looking not unlike vanilla beans from trees with fan-shaped leaves. Again it's a grueling process transforming the beans into the pungent, dark paste that's sold in golf ball–size mounds in most markets. Collecting the seeds requires knocking them from the tree branches. The seeds are boiled for up to a day to soften their seed coat, which is removed by smashing them in a wooden mortar with a pestle. The thick yellow pulp surrounding the seeds, thought to be a good source of fat, protein, and lysine, an amino acid, is added to meat, stews, soups, or cereals as it's also rich in a sweet carbohydrate. Once the seeds are separated from the chaff, they are reboiled, then drained, cooled, and packed in leaves in order to ferment. A bacterium more commonly associated with spoiled milk, another linked to "hot tub rash," and a staph bacterium that causes urinary tract infections work together to break down the beans into the foul-smelling paste. The *dawadawa*'s awful scent is so strong, Simon told me, that some women keep it in their rooms to dissuade their husbands from visiting them at night.

Gambaga's accused women were encouraged to gather up enough seeds and firewood to make an industrial-size batch of *dawadawa* paste. Solomon rented a truck and drove the paste to the market in Bawku, but came back with only 140,000 cedis, the equivalent of about fourteen dollars. There were no sales, he said, and he couldn't hide the source of his *dawadawa*. People just wouldn't buy food prepared by witches.

A woman living at the witch camp, who was identified as the leader of the *dawadawa* producers, claimed that they didn't want anything to do with the project. They knew it was bound to fail, and for women bent on survival all that collecting, shelling, boiling, mashing, sieving, and fermenting would never earn them as much as simply collecting firewood or selling water. It would only eat up their time.

"When they came to open it, we were not in agreement," the woman said. "They went and saw the chief," Kizito translated, "but the chief said they should just do it. He told them that in all towns they have opened a shea butter project there. They only accepted it because of the chief's advice."

Each of the cooperative's one hundred women was expecting to receive at least twenty dollars from sales. In the end Solomon sold the *dawadawa* at a cut rate just to get rid of it. He resold the remainder of the seeds and closed down the project, using their savings to give each woman the equivalent of about twenty dollars for her trouble. Solomon admitted that the project hadn't really achieved its goal, but he spoke as though he considered its shutdown to be temporary. Processing equipment, purchased with thousands of donor dollars, is still in place, sitting idle at the locked plant. "If there's no market, there's no selling, so there's no money," Solomon said. "We don't provide enough as of now because any time we get money for them we want to work with them and get profit and recycle the money. But mostly when we get money there's no profit and it ends like that. But we still try to get them money."

By the late 1990s Timari Tama had run its course, attempting shea butter and *dawadawa* processing and sheep rearing as income-generating projects, without success. In 2001 the charity helped link the accused witches with the Ministry of Women and Children's Affairs, which sent staff up to the camp to distribute blankets, mattresses, and secondhand clothing. In 2004 Solomon's aunt Amina tried raising more money for the project, asking for eight thousand dollars through Global Giving, a website devoted to improving the lot of African women. The money was meant to be divided up among the project's members and handed out in hundred-dollar increments over three years, with the remainder staying as seed money for future projects. Donors had pledged only $2,077 before the posting expired.

With the project all but closed, Amina traveled to Canada on a three-week course through the Montreal-based Canadian Human Rights Foundation. She filled out an application for her nephew, who went in June 2005 and stayed for three weeks. He loved Montreal, he told me, smiling. The people were amazingly friendly, even though he didn't speak any French. Solomon said he still sometimes visited Gambaga's witch camp and occasionally dropped off donated used clothing, but his trip to Montreal hadn't ignited any fervor to attempt another money-making project. In fact Solomon's enduring memory of the experience wasn't the human rights course, but the city itself—its smokers, in fact. They were so plentiful, he laughed, he even considered taking up the habit, just to fit in.

ANN THOMPSON HAD FIRST ARRIVED IN GHANA AS A NEWLYWED. In the decades that followed she and her husband moved their three children from their native Canada to Sierra Leone, Liberia, Malawi, Zimbabwe, Botswana, Lesotho, and Swaziland. They'd lived all over Asia, with the exception of China. Ann looked like a typical suburban mom, with short dark hair and stylish clothes, not like a woman who had spent the greater part of her professional life bouncing down rough roads through remote locales in an effort to reduce hunger and poverty.

Ann had returned to Ghana as a widow, and she lived in a small house on the edge of Tamale with a sweet-natured German shepherd named Felix. The dog was so huge the neighborhood children considered him a rare breed of cow. Ann had come to set up a food security project that put hungry communities in charge of the grain-grinding mills and sheep-rearing projects that would give them enough to eat. She heard about the women living as exiles in Gushiegu from a colleague. When she went to investigate she found what her Ghanaian coworkers called "disorganized witches," a reference to the fact there was no traditional male leader looking out for them.

"They were living in really dire circumstances, in abandoned houses, and their main source of food was going to the market to sweep up grains," Ann said. "I had worked in Bangladesh, which is about as bad as you can get—and Ethiopia—and thought, this is a terrible story."

Her project declared the disorganized witches a vulnerable group and bought the women a grain-grinding mill, hoping that the fees collected from its use would help them buy food. Her employer, AgriTeam, donated about two thousand dollars to buy bags of rice and maize, enough to last until the mill turned a profit. Meanwhile Ann decided to raise some money to buy land for housing and farms for the women. She wanted to put up some huts and buy some seeds to plant and some chickens and goats for the women to raise. She put a note up on Give Meaning, a fund-raising website, urging friends to help pay for her project.

Donations came slowly. Ann was hoping to gather twenty thousand dollars but in the first few months raised only three thousand, hardly enough to keep the Gushiegu women fed through one rainy season, let alone buy land or build houses. "I was disappointed," she said. "I have a lot of friends with a lot of money but fell far short of what I was hoping to raise. I thought if each of them gave a hundred dollars, that would do it." She looked off from her porch. "It's always unexpected who gives and who doesn't," she said diplomatically. When we spoke she was unsure what would happen with the women. Gushiegu's regent had promised to give her twenty acres, but she received less than six, meaning there was no room to farm and limited room to build huts. Out of her own pocket Ann paid about two thousand dollars for the land; her employer paid for its survey and registration. "We're at an impasse," she told me, making no secret of her frustration. Permission to build the much-needed shelters had become tangled in village bureaucracy. They'd decided to build traditional mud block houses with thatched roofs. She had a budget for only thirty, about half as many as the camp needed, but she wouldn't see construction, even if it happened. Her contract was up, and after three years spent establishing the food security project she was due to leave Tamale the next day. She was heading back to Canada, where she would focus on a new granddaughter and consultation work with projects in Cambodia.

Ann's husband had been fascinated by *juju* when they first lived in Ghana, but she shook her head. "I cannot believe in witchcraft in any form," she said. "If you believe in it, it can really affect you." She paused. "But I mean, let's get real."

For Ann, Gushiegu's sad collection of outcasts demolished any romantic notions about the power or wonder of witchcraft. Branding a woman as a witch had become too easy, and the consequences too great. The women were starving. Most were grandmothers and great-grandmothers whose shame and humiliation would echo through their descendants, making them even more vulnerable to banishment. "To me, it's such a complex situation," she said. "It's such a terrible infringement of human rights, but such a complex social situation. You have this culture—and it's not just Ghana, it goes on elsewhere—that has such a strong belief in the supernatural."

She remembered listening to a preacher with a regular radio show who talked about how everything in Africa is spiritual. "He was talking about witchcraft," she said, "[saying that] because we don't understand, we blame witchcraft. That's the problem. People are not educated. They don't know that the unexplained death of a child could be, well, what could it be?" she said, resignedly, with a shake of her head. "Anything.

"Where you have this belief system, everything is caused by God, or caused by spirits, or caused by witchcraft or caused by whatever—nothing just happens. What can you do?

"That's what's so terrifying here," she said, dropping her voice. "Even people who are highly educated, when you really get into it, they believe certain aspects of the supernatural. It's just too, too ingrained.

"It's an incredibly cruel and unfair situation."

Witchcraft, and its accompanying belief in the power of the supernatural, contributed to the pervasive sense of lethargy and fatalism, the longtime enemies of people like Ann, who were committed to development in the north. If the fates and spirits decided a man's future, it took away his drive, his ambition, his fire.

I asked whether she saw witchcraft as having an impact on development.

"It's a circular issue," she answered. "If there was less poverty, if there was more development, there wouldn't be accusations. This is a poverty issue. It's poverty, it's jealousy, it's the supernatural. If something goes wrong, then you finger somebody and a life is ruined." She'd never discussed it with Gushiegu's accused women, but figured the lives of their families were likely ruined too.

"There are physical hardships, but they live such hard lives in the village anyway," she said. They had survived a lifetime of living within the straitjacket of rural African society, endured childbirth, disease, poverty, and hunger, only to end up alone and starving. It was heartbreaking.

"What strikes me, over and over, is the social hardships. They're old women. They should be sitting under a mango tree playing with their grandchildren and chatting with their friends, not wandering and going to the market and sweeping grains off the floor to eat," she said. "It's just really unjust."

Months after leaving Ghana Ann found funding for twenty-four small square huts for Gushiegu's banished women. The huts were built in a long row and inaugurated with a small ceremony, which she did not attend. The Lesothan wife of her Canadian successor at the food security project continues to raise funds for the Gushiegu women.

It was the first time Ann had gotten personally involved in a project. In all her years of living and working in the world's poorest and hungriest places nothing had ever presented itself in quite the same way, she said. She could identify with these women and the uncontrollable circumstances that led to their banishment.

"I'm older, I'm a widow, my kids are grown, I've got the resources, I can think about it," she said. "But really, what touched me this time is that this is a woman's issue and a poverty issue and these women, by and large, are the same age I am.

"I'm educated, I have power and money—I'm not rich, but I have money. As an older single woman I still have some power. I'm still a credible professional. And I just looked at these women and I thought: That could be me."

CHAPTER THIRTEEN

My translator Kizito's father, an elder at the Assemblies of God church, had forbidden his son from performing animal sacrifices or buying talismans and fetishes, but when I asked to visit someone who could "see" witches, Kizito quickly agreed, borrowing some bicycles so we could ride to Nanoori, home of a diviner who was said to be one of the best in the region. Kizito wanted his fortune read.

We pedaled past the patients waiting outside Gambaga's low-slung health clinic, past the painted metal sign pointing to the Outcast Home, past the abandoned sheep barn and a borehole locked with a bicycle chain that were remnants of Solomon Bukari's ill-fated Timari Tama project. We turned off the gravel road onto a little footpath that took us past a dry streambed filled with rocks, then walked up a hill, climbed onto our bikes again, and cut through a tiny path in someone's maize field. The diviner's house was the first we came across after leaving the outskirts of Gambaga.

A few old men were stretched out sleeping under the thatched awnings at Atia Timpani's mud hut. There was often a line at his door: people waiting for treatment for anything from fever to stomach ailments; people looking for answers from their past for questions about their future; people who suspected witchcraft was causing an illness they could not quite kick.

Kizito and I were ushered into a square, windowless room made of mud at the front of the compound and asked to wait for the witchdoctor's son. Three little children, all in various states of undress, played with puppies in the courtyard. We sat on a bright orange prayer mat before an altar covered with black chicken feathers in the corner. The diviner's son came in from the fields wearing two pairs of shredded pants and a windbreaker open to the waist; as we sat in the stuffy room we could see beads of sweat form all over his body. As the diviner settled onto the mat, his son explained that he spoke some English, which he later explained was because he'd been sent to school, but he was called home when his father became too old to farm.

His father told us that witchcraft is real, and he has the gift to see it. People sought witchcraft because they needed protection for their families, his son explained. Everyone has their personal god who watches over them like a "guardian angel" and follows them like a shadow. Occasionally this god needs to be appeased or maintained through sacrifices. If a person dabbles in *juju* and the god does not agree, "the god will leave the person," effectively ending the person's physical life.

His father could help a person interpret the needs of his personal god and guide the sacrifices made in its honor. He was so popular because for years he had roamed this country and two others seeking herbal remedies and *juju*. He told us his father was 120 years old and had the identity card to prove it, although it wasn't produced. The diviner wore a puffy, African-patterned cloth cap on his head, a plain black T-shirt, and graying blue slacks. He had barely a crease on his face. He remembered the first time he saw white men, who came riding on horses. He remembered captured boys and girls for sale at the market, for amounts that no longer meant anything in today's economy.

People came to him most often for his ability to read the future, he said. If he saw danger in his mind's eye, for example, he warned them to reschedule a planned trip. He could also see witches. Usually they were chasing a person, disguised as a fireball or carrying a fireball. He never made an accusation, only confirmed that the person was under attack and formed a counterplan to make the person impervious to the witch's powers.

He got his gift at birth, he said, but it didn't express itself until he was a young man. While he was sleeping the voice of God came to him in a dream. It told him to take care of a minor god, honor it with sheep and fowls and cattle and cats, then he could seek his farm, his fortune, and his family. He married and had a son, and then his visions began. Soon he was "roaming" to learn more about ways to heal people using *juju* and spiritual powers. He could also help with stomach ailments and aches and pains.

Women identified as witches shouldn't be killed, he cautioned, because some of them could still give birth, and their children might grow up to become very powerful men. If they weren't given the chance to live, they couldn't be given the chance to lead.

I was told to take a cowrie, a smooth, milk-colored shell, hold it in my hand, and place money on top of it, then think of a question I wanted the diviner to answer. I placed a 20,000-cedi note on it, worth about two dollars, and tried to focus on what adventure would come next in life. Instead I found myself thinking about marriage and babies. I did not consider myself superstitious, but I avoided walking under ladders, sometimes tossed spilled salt over my left shoulder, and could admit to reading horoscopes. I found the monthly forecasts strangely reassuring. In the same way witchcraft holds sway over those who put stock in it, the idea that the stars spelled out the future to those able to decipher it appealed to me. I was willing to believe in it.

The old man reached into a corner and produced a little leather pouch covered in feathers. He took out a handful of little curios and shook them around in his hand, then spread them on the floor, mixing the money with them. He carefully watched their placement, then scooped them up, laid the money aside on the pouch, and shook and spread the baubles again. There were eleven cowrie shells, some with little holes in them, some with big holes, as well as a white button, a washer, and an industrial nut. Three brownish seeds and one black one landed near something yellowed that looked like an animal's tooth. There was a slim, curved piece of bone, a shiny black rock with flecks of silver and gold, a thin, tarnished silver loop, and something that looked like an almond-shaped peach pit. A cloudy pink stone, a crumpled piece of metal, a putty-colored stone, and a white bean rounded out the diviner's tools.

A Canadian priest who held a doctorate in anthropology and had lived in northern Ghana for more than thirty-five years had once trained to become a diviner and had later written a paper parsing the diviner's techniques for reading the shells and baubles. Jon P. Kirby wrote that the placement of the objects triggered leading questions that could focus the conversation on something troubling a client, from a recent quarrel to an age-old vendetta. Diviners also "read" their patients, the way a palm reader looks for calluses as a sign of manual labor, or the faint tan line of a wedding band as proof of recent marital troubles.

The old man picked out various pieces, moving them to the side in a series of rhythmic movements that became almost hypnotic in the stuffy heat of the windowless room. "There is hope and opportunity," he announced. There were twins at my mother's house, and I should present them with a black and red fowl for slaughter. This meant nothing to me; there are no twins in my family, not even reaching back a generation or two on my mother's side. He later told me I should also take them a sheep, "but for rearing, not for slaughter."

I was going on a journey but I would not stay long, he said. Someone had done *juju* for me, but I was ignoring it. The only *juju* I'd knowingly had performed for me was a disappointingly commercial episode a few years earlier at the Fetish Market in Lome, the capital of Togo, where I'd bought protection for travel. In a poorly lit room surrounded by tables of dried lizards, rats, and bats, whale bones, miniature owls, and snarling dog heads, a *juju*-man had offered me his business card and the choice of six amulets: a matchbook-size square of wood for love, a blob of clay to protect one's home, a necklace stuffed with forty-one herbs for good luck, an ebony seed pod for improved memory, or a simple stick of ebony, sharpened, blessed, and used to stir the drink of a man looking for "buffalo power," as the guide put it, doing a little pantomime of a man pushing with his crotch.

For five dollars I bought a travel fetish, a small red talisman made of roughly whittled wood and entwined with thick string that would ensure safe voyage. I was supposed to whisper my destination into the hole at one end, then my wish—"safe arrival" being the most obvious—before sealing it shut with the stopper held on by the string. Considering the state of the continent's roads and the frequency of road accidents, I diligently carried it everywhere, figuring I could use whatever help I could get.

"You will have riches," the diviner said. He scooped and shook the cowries and buttons and seeds dozens of times, each time telling me something new. There will be rain, he announced suddenly. There will be a fatal accident on the road. He pointed to the direction of the predicted crash with a wave of his hand. A woman from Gambaga will die, although not necessarily in the accident.

My firstborn will be a boy, he said as he set aside a cowrie shell with a hole on one side. It reminded me of a one-eyed cartoon face, the seam between the two sides of the shell making a perfect grimace. "That is your husband," his son said. He will be white and will have a car.

You will have a long life, the diviner concluded.

I smiled.

Days later, when I joined Simon and Evelyn for dinner, I teased Evelyn about my future husband and our apparent son. "Oh, thank God! Wonderful God," she shouted, laughing and clapping her hands. As we sat in the inky night she told me there would be a funeral in the morning for an old woman from the village who had died that day. Simon piped up with the rest of the gossip: a car had overturned on the road to Gambaga and a teenage boy was crushed.

SIMON CASUALLY ASKED WHETHER I WANTED TO MEET ANOTHER powerful witchdoctor, a man he knew from his ancestral village, who was living just up the road in Langbinsi. We climbed into the truck with Evelyn sandwiched on the bench seat between us. Simon told me that she wanted to do some shopping at the market. He also said she'd been having back pain, and thought the witchdoctor might be able to help, but I suspected it was something other than back pain.

We pulled up next to a fallen baobab at the edge of the village and emerged from the truck to find Kodigah Laan Bimobah, an energetic little elf of a man with twinkling eyes and a mischievous smile. Entering the mud walls of his compound required stepping over a wobbly stone set over a calabash, the same sort of *juju* Napoa's husband used to disarm evil spirits. Crossing the threshold of Bimobah's compound, however, was akin to marching up to the demented curve of a carnival mirror, losing one's balance, and falling headlong through the looking glass.

The round room was dark and choked with sweet-smelling smoke. Its walls had been painted black by the smoldering fire. It was hard to take in, a visual feast of sticks and calabashes, rags and cowries and paint. Clay pots were piled up by the door. Gnarled walking sticks rested next to metal bowls and mysterious, small square objects wrapped in dark leather. Feathers stuck out of a multipronged stick wrapped with gauze. There was a tin teapot, a blue thermos, and a blue pitcher, and I could see an ancient hunting rifle leaning against the wall, but otherwise it seemed that everything was made of natural materials, such as wood or the faint yellow-orange of dried gourds. There was a stalk of something green growing from the base of one of the calabashes; it looked like the tender shoot of a new corn stalk. A little stand near the doorway was covered with an overturned calabash plastered in chicken feathers.

Barry White's sexy baritone sang out from a black battery-operated radio suspended from the thatched ceiling. The lyrics to "Just the Way You Are" floated into the pungent smoke to ensure a smooth transition to a trance-like state.

Before we'd even settled on a mat and let our eyes adjust to the dim light, the barefoot witchdoctor was up and retrieving what looked like a papier-mâché stuffed goose. It was yellow in color and coated with feathers, with some cowrie shells and a plug of silver at the end where the goose's head would be. The whole thing was splattered with what I assumed was red paint but was probably chicken blood.

Bimobah pulled out a long tube-shaped object wrapped in layers of red rags and wound with string. It too was covered in bits of feather and string. The dried head of a baby crocodile glared out from one end. These were his spiritual guns, he announced, and he never traveled without them or attempted any treatment without them. The first acted as a trap, catching the witches who were attempting to harm him or his patients. Simon jokingly called it his AK-47, and the witchdoctor laughed with delight.

"A soldier without a gun—who fears him?" he shouted.

Bimobah opened a calabash to show us he'd been making fetishes for people, including what looked like little kites covered in rags. They were stitched shut and wrapped with multicolored string. They were used to "tie up" a place, he explained. If you were traveling, the amulet allowed you to "tie up" the armed robbers and the bad drivers you would otherwise meet along the way. When you're a stranger in a place, you might "tie up" the police or the bankers or the government people—anyone who might otherwise cause you trouble.

Bimobah told us he was guided by dwarves. There were two types of dwarves, he said, pointing at my pinkish skin covered by my typical black T-shirt. "One is the color you are, the other is the color of your shirt. They are the ones that if you don't take time, you won't get anything." Some don't talk, and some live underwater. They whispered to him all the time, it seemed, as he consulted them while divining and murmured things like "My people are saying . . ."

The tip of Bimobah's left index finger was missing to the first knuckle. He wore a thick, studded circle of silver around his left ankle, dark shorts, and a filmy white button-down dress shirt that reached to his knees. He sat cross-legged, his head covered in white bristles. His teeth were rimmed in brown; the front ones seemed to be worn shorter than the rest, producing a Barcelona-style lisp.

He treated virtually any ailment that came to him because there were no illnesses that did not have witchcraft at their root, he declared. Infertility, for example; that was always the work of witches. He couldn't bear to hear that some women believed they couldn't have children, because it was all a matter of removing the spiritual obstacle or retrieving the woman's womb from the spiritual realm. He performed operations to cure infertility; when we asked him to explain he refused to be more specific.

Witches take possession of a person's soul, he said. They might harass you every night, or they might suck your blood to sell at the infamous night market in Techiman. It's very expensive, what they do. "The women are very, very bad. Because they want money. They want to kill you and sell you at Techiman. Or suck your blood."

He could provide medicine for people to "chop" that would give them protection, he said, wringing his hands. "Without this one, they can't last for five or two months," he said. When witches see him coming—and they can see him approaching in the spiritual world—they don't arm themselves. "They rather fear me."

Using a mixture of English and Kusar, Simon's first language, Bimobah told us he can "see" witches, that there were two sicknesses that proved their existence and that he treated both: one was AIDS and the other was madness. He treated madness, which is in the blood, using "operations," slowly replacing the old blood with a blood tonic. He sucked out the bad blood, a small bit at a time. Although I asked dozens of questions about this, he merely giggled at my obvious interest.

With AIDS, he said, the body feels as though it has just come from a fridge. Normally when witches are working their dark curses, the whole body feels feverish. He wouldn't tell us how he treated AIDS, but said that after about two years there was nothing more he could do for the person. All of their cells were gone and they couldn't be helped, he shrugged. He offered us plenty in the way of divination, but he wasn't exactly forthcoming about how he worked his particular witchcraft.

Simon told him that Evelyn had been having health problems,

so he pulled out his divination shells and they chatted for a few minutes in the local language before he declared that he would bring herbs to treat her on Sunday. Evelyn seemed relieved. The witch-doctor spilled out his divining bag, revealing a few of the country's old coins—cedis and pesawas pressed back in the 1980s—a couple plastic rings from bottle tops, a red nut, a black bead, a chicken foot, a bird's leg bone, a knuckle from a chicken leg, a yellowed tooth, a broken key, the ring of a keychain, a white button, a piece of metal that looked like a belt buckle, two bullet-shaped plugs of silver, a triangle-shaped stone, two milky white rocks, a tiny jawbone, and a heavy metal washer.

He picked out four cowries. He whispered to them, chanted to them, threw them, picked them up again, placed them square, ran his fingers over the spill of divination tools, and then threw the four cowries again.

He turned his attention to Simon. "You yourself are not well. The thing is within you and you don't know it," he said in English. "You are not well."

He told Simon that someone from his mother's house was working against him. Simon was meant to be a very important person, but they were robbing him. "Even if they give you plenty money, you won't know what you've done and the money will be finished immediately."

He advised Simon to make an apology: he must buy a sheep and give it to his father's father's mother, to the twins. "That's where the witches began," he said. (Simon said afterward that he had been told before that his problems originated in his mother's house, but when I asked whether he would try to resolve the problem by doing all the rituals and sacrifices, he dismissed it. Even if he wanted to, he couldn't remember the diviner's instructions, he shrugged, as he hadn't written them down.)

The diviner asked me to put out my hands. I cupped them and he put all the divining objects into my palms and asked me to spread them on the floor. I did so, and he intently studied the pattern I had made. He removed about half of them and had me spread the remainder again. Then he picked out the four cowries, whispered to them, and had me spread those. We did this a couple of times. He picked up the shells and had me pick up the shells, and this exchange—me, then him, then back to me—went on for so long that I got lost in the heat of the room, the smokiness of the air, the monotony. I was drawn into a dreamy trance; no one was saying anything.

He told me various things: that I would not be staying long in Ghana, that I was struggling on my own and was not rich.

Then Bimobah went still and said to me in perfect English, "You've already met a man who is interested in you, is that not so?" I snapped back to attention, turning bright red. I'd met someone while on holiday in Sierra Leone, and after a lengthy, long-distance courtship of emails and international phone calls we were considering our next steps. He was preparing to move back to his native Australia, then to East Timor, a half-island nation still healing from a brutal separation from Indonesia. The witchdoctor peered over his reading glasses. "He requires you to make a journey." I nodded. "You will have to make a journey to be with this man. He is serious, but you are not. If you make this journey and you are with this man, you will be very happy. And everything will be in good working order," he said, illustrating exactly what he meant by "good working order" with a lewd motion. I could only smile at the gesture, masking how shaken I felt at the accuracy of his words.

"Hallelujah, praise the Lord!" he giggled.

As we got up to leave, stumbling from the dark, fantastical hut into the blindingly bright sunlight, Bimobah complained that his business had dwindled largely because of electricity. Workers had installed poles and strung electrical wires in Langbinsi two years ago. Ever since the power was switched on "the witches don't do nearly as much," he grumbled.

"Evil fears the light," Simon said to me.

THE FOLLOWING SUNDAY MORNING SIMON CALLED TO TELL ME to come over: the Langbinsi witchdoctor had arrived with his

AK-47 to treat Evelyn. It was chaos when I arrived. None of the animals required for the ceremony had been gathered, so each of the younger children was sent out to round up a chicken. They needed a total of six, at least one red, one white, and one black. The older boys were ordered to find a sheep. Simon had promised to pay Bimobah fifty dollars and a pig, which also needed to be corralled.

The witchdoctor sat on a plastic chair with his AK-47 at his feet. Simon directed the search for the animals while eating the remains of the previous night's TZ, a white porridge-y substance made from maize flour. Evelyn buzzed around wearing a brilliant sky blue one-piece dress. An African print cloth was tied around her waist, but there were sequins at her throat. Simon and the witchdoctor stepped outside to sacrifice a chick, pouring libations from a bottle of clear alcohol and calling incantations to wake up the ancestors and request their help with clearing Evelyn's spiritual block. It was the first time I'd ever been invited inside the Ngota home; we always sat in the screened-in porch, where Evelyn did all the family's cooking over charcoal briquettes. We moved to the back, to a small, hot, and dark sort of storage room, where I sat on the floor. Evelyn knelt next to me. The witchdoctor sat before us on a small stool.

He was carrying a woman's purse and a large black plastic bag filled with wood and herbs. He placed the wood and herbs inside a clay pot that Evelyn had brought him, then poured in a bucket of water. The herbs smelled of peppermint. He filled a calabash with water while three live fowls, barely a few months old, were brought in squawking. The children had managed to find a black one, a red one, and a white one. Evelyn held the black one while Simon, still eating his breakfast, held the other two. The spiritual AK-47 was placed at the base of the clay pot.

The witchdoctor added some red liquid from a white jerry can and a few green leaves to the clay pot. He recited over everything— "Excuse me," he said in English, an apology for carrying out the ceremony in a dialect I couldn't understand—and then directed Evelyn to give the fowl to me. I held the struggling bird in my hand before he reached for it and plucked out a few feathers, mumbling his recitation the whole time. Evelyn had already whispered to it. Simon mumbled something that sounded like a prayer, then the witchdoctor asked Evelyn a question. Simon held the bird, its head in one hand and its body in the other, offering clear access to its throat. The witchdoctor made a quick incision with a razor blade.

He threw the pullet toward the door, where it flapped frantically, working its way with one mighty heave to our side of the room and bouncing off my shins before coming to a rest on Evelyn's lap, its beak to the ceiling. "Praise God!" the witchdoctor shouted. "Our God and creator, who gives us life and answers our prayers!"

The same was repeated with the red fowl: Evelyn passing the bird to me, my offering it to the witchdoctor, Simon holding it while its throat was slit. This one didn't die so dramatically, but also produced a "Praise God!" from Bimobah.

"He doesn't want these sacrifices and you are calling his name," Simon muttered.

"What?" the witchdoctor said.

"I'm joking," he answered.

I couldn't seem to process what I was seeing. Simon was a man employed by the church, a man who identified himself as a social worker. What was he doing hiring a witchdoctor to cure his wife's condition? His wife, a devout Muslim-turned-Christian, was kneeling before a witchdoctor in a room speckled with the blood spatter of dying chickens. Africa's animist traditions were alive indeed.

The last fowl also died well, with its beak to the heavens. The witchdoctor called for a frog. I shrank back against the wall, sending up a small prayer that I would not be included in this portion of the ceremony. I've had an irrational fear of frogs since I was a child; I didn't think I could bring myself to willingly touch one. The witchdoctor confirmed with Simon that a sheep would be produced. There was no point in continuing without a sheep; a sheep was integral. "They are there," Simon promised. The Ngotas' sheep, like all the animals in the village, was free range and hadn't yet been found.

The frog came pinched between Simon's fingers. "I'm going to make an operation," the witchdoctor said to me, drawing a fresh razor blade from his purse. Evelyn hiked up her dress, up past her waist all the way to her neck, exposing her left breast. The witchdoctor made six incisions beside her nipple, quickly drawing the razor straight down, three swipes on top and three on the bottom. Then he rubbed the frog against the fresh cuts, all while praising God.

"Don't shame me," he added.

After a minute he removed the frog and searched through his handbag for a small plastic bag of black powder—burnt herbs, I was told later—which he rubbed on Evelyn's wound before returning the animal to her breast. Is it paining you, he asked. Evelyn closed her eyes, held her breath, and grimaced.

I sat stunned.

"It will die," the witchdoctor said, mistaking my expression for one of concern for the frog. After a few minutes he casually tossed it out the door.

As the sprightly witchdoctor carefully repacked his purse, he instructed Evelyn to suck charcoal, bathe using the herbs mixed in the clay pot every fourth day, and drink malt for at least three months. The family was rushing to change into their Sunday best for services at the Presbyterian church when the sheep wandered into the yard, producing a mad scene as the children, in polished shoes, frilly socks, and carefully pressed shirts and dresses, encircled it to push it closer to the house. Evelyn enticed it within reach with a plateful of corn and some clucking noises. With a rope around its neck it was led into the house, where the witchdoctor cut off a lock of its hair.

Another chick was captured. Its throat was slit and the blood drained over the hair and the sheep, which stood placidly chewing, its lower jaw moving sideways as the chick died with its beak on the floor.

"They don't want the things to go away!" the witchdoctor remarked, a reference to whatever spiritual blocks had been placed within Evelyn.

Simon walked with him to the main road, where he could flag

down a passing car. He was irritated by the witchdoctor's fee and
hoped to use the stroll to renegotiate. I walked out with Evelyn
and the children. I stepped delicately, worried that an angry, blood-
covered frog waited in the weeds. Evelyn had shucked her blue
dress, hiding her fresh wounds under a white undershirt and a wrap
skirt made of yellow fabric stamped with the Presbyterian Church
logo. She hurried down the lane, the children boisterous behind her.
They were headed for church.

LATER THAT NIGHT, WE WERE GATHERED AS USUAL AROUND A
plastic table in the courtyard at the guesthouse, the stars like spilled
salt in the sky above us. Guinea fowl squawked from the trees,
their metallic call sounding like a rusty wheel in need of oil. Evelyn
looked calm and happy, setting out a squat Thermos of white rice
and a bowl of spicy peanut-flavored sauce laced with cooking oil. I
could picture her face, serene and trusting, as she underwent that
morning's ceremony. There was no hesitation in the way she pulled
up her dress, no fear as the witchdoctor cut into her breast with a
razorblade. Frogs are taboo in most of the north; most people are
forbidden from eating them. But Evelyn's doe eyes had closed in
complacency as the witchdoctor pressed one into her fresh cuts.

That beatific expression stays with me still, proof that witchcraft's power is strongest for those who believe in it. Evelyn prayed
to Jesus with her whole body, her eyes closed, her lips moving, her
hands closed into fists, her arms raised for emphasis. She also placed
herself wholly in the healing power of the witchdoctor's magic, believing it would chase whatever spirits were causing her problems.
For her there was no contradiction. How could she live in a place
populated by witches and crowded with spirits and fail to consider
that witchcraft was responsible for her problems?

Simon, however, clearly saw the paradox. It went against his
training, his experience, the years he'd poured into caring for the
women, the time he'd bounced down rutted back roads, the hours
he'd spent persuading remote village leaders that the women posed
no danger. Maybe he'd only agreed to the ceremony to appease

Evelyn, but Simon was equally confounded by Evelyn's condition. There was no obvious answer, and they were desperate for some kind of explanation.

Witchcraft was an explanation where none existed, a convenient cause where no other could be found. It was strange comfort in times of distress. It was a means of predicting the unpredictable and controlling the uncontrollable. For women like Winangi, who bought witchcraft to protect herself and her children from their alcoholic father, it gave power to an otherwise powerless life. For Carlos it was a means of making sense of his father's death and an outlet for his grief and anger. For Kizito, forbidden by his father from seeking out witchdoctors or diviners, it was a fascination, the diviner's oracle a source of reassurance in uncertain times.

The increase in allegations of witchcraft was a sign of a culture under stress, hurtling toward an uncertain future. Ghana's northern men moved about in flowing traditional tunics, but they carried mobile phones in their pockets. Like their women, they were impossibly stretched trying to bridge both the traditions they valued and the modernity they craved. Even in my short stay there was plenty to bring worry: the introduction of a new currency, a serious drought, crop failure, an unreliable power supply. There was more to want and less to go around. Rural villages already strained by jealousy and paranoia were too fragile to withstand much more. Tension bubbled over, spilling into accusation. When times were tough, even the most educated, the most devout, fell back on tradition.

Inundated by stories of strange coincidences, it took impossible strength to resist witchcraft's lure. I still can't say I believe, but I don't disbelieve either. I went to the north believing that women accused of practicing witchcraft were simply victims of human rights violations, that calling a woman a witch was a cheap way of dealing with the difficult women who demand their due. But living in Gambaga had convinced me that there are people who are more in tune to the vibrations of the natural world, who interpret what the rest of us cannot hear. For a time I too fell under witchcraft's spell.

CHAPTER FOURTEEN

THE SKY BLUSHED PINK WITH DAWN LIGHT AS SIMON AND I LEFT for one last interview in Tamale. I needed to visit the office of the Commission for Human Rights and Administrative Justice, the government watchdog group that Simon hoped would host a conference on witchcraft and put an end to the *gambarana*'s extortion. CHRAJ's investigators were responsible for looking into complaints of corruption, abuse of power, or dereliction of duty, a catchall term for a man's responsibilities to his family. They probed complaints of illegal termination and nonpayment of social security and were supposed to hold workshops on rights and freedoms to help change some of the "obnoxious customs" that no longer fit the country's Constitution. They were also meant to monitor the overall human rights situation and write a report for Parliament that painted a picture of progress or lack thereof. If anyone was tasked with keeping northern women safe from witchcraft allegations, or ensuring their survival once accused, it was CHRAJ.

I encouraged Simon to drive faster, faster, to finally push the needle above 40 miles an hour. I was desperate for a few days in town. The power in Gambaga had dwindled to a couple of hours a few times a week and my notes piled up, scrawled on the back of photocopied foolscap by the light of a flashlight. I couldn't sleep for the oppressive heat. My diet consisted mostly of fried yam and white rice; I longed for protein and dreamed of Caesar salad. I planned to splurge on a room with air conditioning and a ten-dollar steak dinner slathered in mushroom sauce.

I was growing depressed at how little will there was to actually do anything about the sheer number of women living at Ghana's witch camps. "Solving" witchcraft seemed a hopeless task. It would require an entire cultural shift, which in itself seemed impossible. At a gender activist workshop at the Gambaga administrative building I had sat in relief under fans that whirred with a generator's power as Enoch Cudjoe, executive director of a local aid group called Songtaba, opened the meeting with a question. He was looking for other organizations to join his umbrella group; their membership fees would help fund his campaigns on women's rights. He asked the eleven women and twenty-three men in the room to come up with a list of human rights, and they answered with food, shelter, decision making, education, life, and health before Enoch brought the exercise to a halt. "Not all of us, even in this room, have the right to the things mentioned here," he said. "We see women relegated to the background. We don't consider them."

Enoch, so slim in his crisp gray slacks that his belt looped nearly double around him, was like an earnest teacher on his first day in front of a class. He meant well, but there was little appetite for his message. The participants were soon running roughshod over him, proving the term *gender activist* was a misnomer. A man sitting in the back row piped up with a bullying question that suggested women were either happy to be dominated or too lazy to make change. Who gave men the right to be the decision makers, he asked rhetorically. If women have their rights, why don't they use them? "Nobody's depriving them from their rights. Why can't they pick up their rights?" he asked.

He found like-minded men in the crowd. A man in a white cap who sat with his arms folded defensively across his chest jumped up to declare that he didn't want to talk about women's rights. He didn't want to hear about anything being taken from men. A man in the front row rallied behind him, providing a provocative theory on the gender divide. "God created man first and from man, God created woman. So what does that show?"

The meeting was brought back under control by a female police officer whose white bobby socks peeked out above her no-nonsense shoes. "Men are the head of the family," she began. "It says so in the Bible. But men have come to abuse this by making we women a slave. We cannot say [anything], because he will say 'I am the head of the family,' and it extends down to the children and the youth. They know they are not to speak because men are the head. This has led to the oppression by men."

A young man stood, adjusted his ball cap, and offered a glimmer of hope for those worried that the north's machismo would continue to pass from generation to generation unabated. It's not a matter of religion, he said softly; it's biology. Men and women are the same, except for their sex parts. It is only culture and tradition that keeps Ghanaian women down, and that is largely because of ignorance and poverty.

There was a question from an old chief, who suggested that maybe the camps should be wiped out and instead the law should be allowed to take its course. Why are only women in these camps, he asked rhetorically. Simon took up the question anyway. It's because women marry and move with their husbands; they are strangers in their village and no one will speak for them, he answered. Men have their brothers and fathers and uncles, but women have no one. They cannot withstand a beating and don't know about taking people to court. Plus, if a man is accused, he can pick up everything and move and start over. "A woman cannot easily do that."

"Witchcraft is not something we can prove scientifically," he added. "If we go to the police to report it, they will not know how to handle it. Because it is a traditional issue, they say go back to your traditions.

"It's a gradual procedure. Maybe one day, one day it will come."

Days later, a UN special rapporteur on violence against women arrived at the government building to find it all but deserted. It would be only one in a series of delays and disappointments for Dr.

Yakin Erturk, a sociology professor at a university in Turkey and a board member at the UN Research Institute for Social Development. The Tamale police detachment forgot she was arriving, then insisted she wait more than an hour while they organized a purely ceremonial police escort. The district's gender coordinator, having waited patiently for Erturk for most of the morning, wandered off in search of something to eat only moments before her motorcade arrived. Some of the district's dignitaries, who should have been on hand to greet Erturk, were out attending workshops. The aid groups sponsoring the workshops paid them a per diem for their attendance and for many it was a way to supplement their government salaries. The rapporteur had to settle for interviewing a lonely clerk, the sole occupant of the sprawling offices, who claimed to know virtually nothing about the witch camp.

I couldn't see how Erturk's visit would help; it would only produce another report lamenting the treatment of the north's women without actually tackling the hardships they faced. While there seemed to be no shortage of ideas on how best to reduce the number of women accused of practicing witchcraft, nearly three thousand women and men lived in Ghana's six camps. Action Aid wanted to build a database that would show that witchcraft was usually blamed on old, defenseless women. Help Age, a charity devoted to elder issues, wanted to create a calendar to highlight the connection between accusations and times of hardship, figuring that once the link was made, communities would be more likely to recognize drought or food shortages as the cause of their problems, not witchcraft. A northern radio station was making plans to record progressive village leaders and elders speaking out about women and witchcraft; they hoped to turn the recordings into radio programs that would help shape opinions on the issue. Then there was the help offered by the witch camps themselves, the sanctuary found in Gushiegu's crumbling ghetto, the latrines, the donkey carts, the *dawadawa* and shea butter cooperatives. Despite it all, accusations kept happening.

There was still no way to punish an accuser, nothing to act as a deterrent from making a phony accusation, no way for a woman to restore her reputation, nothing to keep her safe when her community turned on her with sticks and stones. Despite the thousands of women living in Ghana's six witch camps CHRAJ investigators had received only one formal complaint involving witchcraft. It had come from a man related to one of eighteen women accused by a professional witch hunter, who had ordered the women to be stripped naked and beaten. "It must be very terrible [before a woman complains] because the woman will not see peace," said Al-Hassan Seidu, the acting director of CHRAJ's northern office.

He worked in a large building tucked away on a residential street. A paralegal by training, Seidu had been with CHRAJ since its inception in 1993, a time when prisoners waited years for bail hearings. His bare office consisted of a glass-fronted bookcase and "in" and "out" trays stacked with colored paper. In the office next door the walls were papered in anti-witchcraft posters. One showed a squinty-eyed woman with one tooth alongside an older woman carrying a baby on her back and an old man holding a walking stick while sitting in a chair. Its message was unclear, but it turned out to have been sponsored by the Embassy of Finland in Kenya, with Kenyan contact information printed in tiny script at the bottom. Another featured a man with long, sharp fingernails holding a cauldron of fire while glaring out with evil-seeming eyes and a scene of old people being beaten with sticks or stones. Each picture was crossed out with the slash of a diagonal red line.

Seidu was a slim man with a quiet voice and a wide smile. He wore a heavy business jacket and a skinny tie, despite the sweltering heat. "The position of women in Africa, especially Ghana, the woman has no voice. It is not easy for her to report a man," he said to explain the lack of investigations. Sending a family member to court wouldn't cross their minds. Besides, courts could hardly award damages or restore a woman's reputation. Accused women took their demolished reputations and hid themselves at the witch camps, since they knew no other remedy for the anger and violence that came with an accusation.

"Your entire life is destroyed. This cannot be described in monetary terms. How do you redeem your image?" he asked. "In just one day, somebody dreams he saw you holding his neck. Don't forget that the symptoms of a high fever can make a person talk strangely. But people will not think scientifically; they will see it as witchcraft."

Seidu had been tasked with the impossible: to shift society away from witchcraft using virtually no resources. He couldn't entirely rely on the police; they were underpaid and lacked even rudimentary investigative tools such as telephones and vehicles, and besides people didn't trust them. The courts were also considered both slow and mismanaged. Seidu's territory was the size of the Republic of Ireland and his handful of investigators had only one vehicle, a battered truck they often loaned to police so they could investigate cases serious enough to warrant criminal charges. The office's entire fleet of motorcycles had been grounded as they waited for the money to pay for repairs.

"We want to pursue things, but we don't have the logistics," Seidu said. "The police officer is there with his bare hands. The state mechanisms are not strong enough, so we would rather focus on the social attitude." They'd put together a package with the help of aid groups to educate people on the severity of accusing a woman or beating her, but it had been years since they'd had the money to produce or distribute them.

"It's embarrassing to mention figures," he said with a sigh, sweeping an arm over a stack of pink and yellow complaint folders about everything from corruption to dereliction of duty. He wasn't talking about the number of complaints; he was talking about the budget to investigate them. "We feel shy, we are just doing a sacrificial job. At the same time, I don't want to make excuses. I want us to do the best job we can."

The northern office received less than four thousand dollars from the government each year to ferret out corruption and human rights violations, to keep the courts on track and the police honest, and to protect abused women and abandoned families. Seidu pulled out a file folder and extracted some typed white sheets stapled together, the budget for a two-day trip to visit four witch camps. It was an exercise in wishful thinking. Never mind the distance and the state of the roads; only twenty-five dollars had been budgeted for fuel. Two hospital visits had been tacked onto the program, as well as trips to two CHRAJ outposts. It would take another $125 to cover the cost of fuel for the trip, and a rip in the space-time continuum to accomplish the crowded itinerary.

"These are the tools. We don't need to put this in our stomachs," Seidu said, riffling the budget, his words an allegory for corruption. "This is what we need to do the job, to be effective, because the commission was set up because of the pressure on the courts. We are supposed to ensure the expeditious use of a case. How can we do that like this?" It was actually better than it used to be, he admitted. They used to receive only six hundred dollars a quarter.

As we were speaking of money it seemed an appropriate time to bring up the exorbitant fees being charged by the *gambarana* to secure a woman's release. When I asked Seidu if he was aware that the chief was charging up to fifty dollars to allow a woman to leave the witch camp, his jaw dropped open.

"Are you sure?" he whispered.

"Yes," I answered, slipping Ghanaian colloquialisms into my speech. "I have heard it from the families, and from Simon himself. He sometimes helps them pay. They come to him after they've spoken with the chief to say he has asked for this much and they have done this-and-this and what-and-what to get the money but have come up short. For a time Simon was helping them raise the money. He was giving them 100,000 cedis or so from the project."

Seidu sat for a minute. "Mr. Ngota has never mentioned this to me before," he said.

"I know," I said. "We talked about it in the truck on the way here and I think he feels uncomfortable being the one to go to you." Simon had made it clear that he worried his relationship with the chief would be jeopardized if the old man learned he had paid a visit to CHRAJ.

"We take this very seriously," Seidu said, vowing to investigate.

"There are so many things surrounding these rituals that we suspect might be blackmail." He thought families were bribing the *gambarana* to guarantee the bird would land in their favor. The chicken's slaughter is considered an "obnoxious custom" and therefore forbidden; it is a violation of the woman's right to a fair hearing, among other things, Seidu pointed out. But it's the only form of unbiased judgment most women can expect, since these cases are almost never sent to court. CHRAJ doesn't discourage the use of these kinds of traditional trial, he said. At the same time, it doesn't support them.

"Our position as a human rights institution is that the chief has the right to believe whatever he believes, but he has no power to subject a woman against her will to go through that process—and that's not just at Gambaga, but all authorities managing witch camps in the country," Seidu said.

He viewed the witch camps as the best means of dealing with a difficult problem. The camps offered asylum. The chicken's death might convict a woman, but it would also cool a community's rage and trigger a path to reconciliation and healing. CHRAJ took issue with forcing a woman to drink concoctions that might be injurious to her health, that might contain trace amounts of poison designed to induce vomiting or illness, but they weren't about to call for the camps' closure.

Few powerful Ghanaians, those revered for their education, their success, their business smarts, or their political drive, were willing to speak out against witchcraft, to denounce or belittle the belief or encourage believers to look elsewhere for the source of their problems. Charismatic church leaders, by contrast, were only too willing to fill entire sermons with doomsday predictions about the dangers of witches. It was a reflection of the country's attempt to straddle tradition and modernity.

"Our development paradigm is seen as a battle between tradition and modern. We put everything in black and white, good and bad, where tradition is bad and modern is good. It's not working," said Ben Kunbuor, the politician from the Upper West region. He embodied his words: he was dressed in the swirling traditional tunic of a northern man, but, like the lawyer and freedom fighter J. B. Danquah, had a mind shaped by the West. Kunbuor's father, a civil servant, had sent him to be educated in the United Kingdom; Kunbuor held a doctorate in legal anthropology, which he earned by studying the Masai of Kenya, the Jinja of Uganda, and the Maori of New Zealand. He'd contributed to a book on traditional and state law and the ways they helped and hindered land conflicts. He spoke about Ghana's development with a kind of poetry.

"We want to go to ballet dance in somebody's borrowed shoes. We cannot dance as well as the owner of the shoes, if we can even move at all. That's where we find ourselves," he said. "We are not traditional and we are not modern. We are not one or the other. We're neither."

The broken villages that fueled allegations of witchcraft were populated by people whose poverty made them most likely to believe. They were ripe for exploitation. It was taboo to talk about it, but that silence gave witchcraft its strength. The craft needed to be demystified. The choice was either to target witchcraft beliefs or the symptoms of the allegations. After living in a village plagued by witchcraft I felt the best solution was to develop these little villages until each was flooded with the electricity that witches feared, until they were free of the waterborne parasites that invisibly stalked their children, until a mosquito's bite no longer delivered a death sentence. They needed the security of proper harvests and the confidence that came with a full granary. Stronger bodies would be less susceptible to the illnesses most often attributed to witchcraft. If there were fewer deaths and illnesses to blame on witchcraft, there would be fewer accusations.

More important, from my perspective, was the fact that women needed a voice. They needed respect in their marriage, security in their status, and far more freedom to live. If they were better able to direct and control their existence in the physical realm, perhaps they wouldn't have the reputation for seeking out revenge in the spiritual one.

Seidu reminded me that reducing witchcraft's power over the people required patience. Where I saw only the negative, he saw progress, pointing to the evolution in the way women approached the violence that plagued too many northern marriages: "It used to be an abomination to report a husband in court, now we are inundated with cases. Is that not a good sign? Women were indoors, they were subservient. Now they have come out, they're aggressive and proactive. They do whatever they want." We both knew he was overstating the situation. "Things will change," he insisted.

I asked whether he believed in witchcraft. He told me he had never been a victim of witchcraft, nor had anyone in his family ever been accused of sorcery.

"Honestly?" he replied, practically whispering. "No. I've made it a policy not to assign unscientific reasons to my problems. I sit with the women, I talk to them, I hug them. I organize fora and they come and sing songs. When I come home, I don't fall sick. But I am not entitled to deprive people of their beliefs."

Seidu was one of the only northern Ghanaians I encountered who answered the question of belief with an unequivocal no. For him it wasn't the belief in witchcraft that was the problem; it was what people did to rid their families and villages of its practitioners.

"The entire society believes in what the chief is doing. If we attack it, we have to do it holistically, not in isolation." That meant the organization couldn't ban these traditional treatments without providing an alternative. They also couldn't investigate anyone who made an accusation of witchcraft if that meant it would leave the accused woman worse off. The solution wasn't easy.

"You are talking about democracy in Africa," he said. "It's a recent phenomenon. It's a gradual procedure that takes education and conscious effort.

"We may not achieve it in this generation, but maybe in the one that's growing," Seidu said. "My children will believe in rational thought. They'll believe in science. They'll believe in law."

CHAPTER FIFTEEN

Simon's motorbike kicked up a cloud of red dust as he steered southeast from Gambaga, piloting a narrow red path reduced to tire-churning sand by the dry heat. I held my breath and closed my eyes as he zipped over a footbridge barely wider than our tires. When I was startled by a particularly nasty bump, I instinctively grabbed him around the waist to keep myself from falling off the bike. I giggled out of embarrassment when I recovered my balance.

"Don't be shy," he said, to put me at ease. "You are like a daughter to me."

The path snaked through farmers' fields, skirting rows of stunted groundnuts and acres of wilted cassava plants. Here and there we caught sight of a man or woman bent double in a field, working in the cruelest part of the day in dark-colored clothes that faded into the landscape. Gradually a cluster of cone-shaped mud compounds came into view. The path merged with a wide, sandy road and we spun out, Simon barely managing to right the bike as we hit a skid of soft sand on the shoulder of the road. The bike could find no traction, so we walked into the village, Simon pushing his red motorcycle. When the path turned back into baked clay we hopped on and turned right, past a few rickety wooden stands selling sandwich baggie-size portions of pungent laundry detergent, bars of yellow soap, and a few boiled sweets. We veered left, then pulled the motorbike under a lean-to made of sticks.

We walked into a compound followed by a group of curious kids, kicked off our shoes, and settled ourselves on the immaculate concrete floor of a stuffy, airless room. In the middle of the room a few pieces of vibrant African fabric and some faded T-shirts had been thrown over a laundry line. Bags of grain lined one corner of the room. An impossibly thin woman sat by the door, shrouded by its shadow.

Simon and the ancient woman spoke for a few minutes in a language I didn't understand. We'd come looking for the old *magazia*, Hawa Mahama, the tall and statuesque Queen of Witches. For years the old chief at her village had refused to entertain the thought of Hawa's returning to Kparigu, convinced that she would destroy the place with her black magic. But when a new chief took his place on the royal goatskins Simon jumped on his motorbike and made his way across the footpaths to plead Hawa's case. After nearly four decades at the witch camp Hawa had returned home.

It had been more than a year since I'd last seen her. I sat quietly waiting for the graceful old woman to arrive, dip her head through the doorway, and settle onto the woven plastic prayer mat. I remembered her weak eyes and her patience as we played "broken telephone," relaying interview questions in three languages. Simon turned to me expectantly, waiting for me to begin asking questions. This, he said, gesturing at the emaciated old woman, was Hawa.

I was shocked. The person I remembered had shriveled into this whippet of a woman. Her gums were rotted and ringed with black. Her hair and eyebrows had turned snow white. Her eyes were runny. It seemed they had receded; there were no whites ringing the irises. She had gone completely blind.

I had to look closely for signs that this was the same woman.

She was skeletal, but she sang with the strength of a healthy woman. Her voice had always been her gift, and she warbled, occasionally swatting a microphone she couldn't see, as she clapped along. The room filled with her sons' wives, their friends, and their children, drawn by her song. She sang of putting one's trust in God, of having faith in the future.

She and Simon spoke for a few minutes. She held no bitterness, Simon said, and was happy to be reunited with her family at last. "It's a gift from God," Simon translated when I asked about witchcraft. "If you don't have it, you don't have it."

She had come to believe the accusation. "In the dream, the boy saw that she had his soul. She accepted it, she didn't deny it," Simon translated, "and she said because it was God that gave it to her and she misused it, so she agreed and also released the soul."

Her grandchildren huddled around her, four boys dressed in African-print button-down shirts and dark trousers and a girl who had looped a bolt of vivid red African fabric around her neck to make a sarong. They smiled shyly, eyes shining with excitement, waiting for what might come next.

Hawa had only one thing she still desired. "She's really praying that one day she will die a good death," Simon said.

I asked if she was sick, and he agreed she looked unwell, but he wasn't surprised. At the camp she didn't have to share her food with children and grandchildren. Whenever times were lean Catholic Relief Services sent food rations to the banished women. There was no help like that for the old women here, he said, reminding me that the maternal instinct to share one's portion with a hungry child doesn't diminish with age.

I took several pictures of Hawa, some with her grandchildren and one of her unwittingly staring directly into the camera, the swirling pattern of her white and turquoise head wrap repeated in the whorls of mud forming the walls behind her. I had to lay the picture next to the one taken years earlier at the witch camp and study them for similarities. In both photographs I saw a woman with a small mole near the tear duct under her left eye. Both had faint tribal scarring, vertical slits rubbed with burnt herbs to make black marks on both cheeks. But the woman in the first photo looked strong; the woman in the second photo looked as though she would join the ancestors before our conversation was finished.

When I asked Hawa whether Ghana's witch camps should be closed, she shook her head no, then spoke for several minutes. Hawa believed the camps offered protection from maltreatment. They were a sanctuary, not a prison. "When the person goes there, it serves as their refuge. So she would say that it's better it's there," Simon said.

Witchcraft had robbed Hawa of her family. It had led her to a life among strangers, to decades of hardship and insecurity. But it had also given her a strange kind of freedom, allowing her to live without the yoke of marriage or the battles of polygamy. It had given her a home, a title, and a small, tight circle of friends. She wouldn't call for its closure.

"We cannot say it shouldn't be there because witchcraft has no end," Simon said. "They believe."

EPILOGUE

THREE WEEKS AFTER I LEFT GAMBAGA THE LONG DROUGHT FI-
nally broke. The sky opened up, releasing an astonishing four and
a half inches of rain in a single day. It bounced off the tin roofs of
thousands of northern shacks with a deafening sound, like millions
of snapping fingers. Still the rain kept coming, as though all those
prayers and sacrifices had finally been heard. Nature responded
with cruelty. Nearly five inches of rain fell the next day. For five days
the rain poured as though it had burst from a swollen pipe.

By the time the clouds cleared, homes, crops, and livestock
had been washed away. Spillage from the Bagre dam in Burkina
Faso, Ghana's northern neighbor, caused the White Volta River
to breach its banks, putting hundreds of northern Ghana's farms
under water. Small bridges were caught in the swirling current
of raging rivers and carried away. More than thirty people died,
drowning in their homes, in their fields, in the flash floods that
roared through the dusty riverbeds where women washed their
children's clothes.

Already hungry and desperate, northern Ghanaians found themselves in a whole new disaster. Drought had turned to flood. More
than 70,000 hectares of farmland were destroyed. An estimated
140,000 metric tons of corn, sorghum, peanuts, yam, cassava, and
rice were washed away in the deluge. A three-month feeding pro-

gram was hastily established for 75,000 of the north's most vulnerable people, even though more than 330,000 people were thought to
be going hungry. Malnutrition rates jumped to include almost half
the north's population. Nearly 12 percent of children whose growth
and weight were already seriously stunted due to chronic hunger
were seen to drop weight and muscle tissue so rapidly they were
classified as starving.

More than 250,000 people living in the north were now home-
less. The longed-for rain had knocked over or partially destroyed
twenty thousand homes. As northerners began clearing debris left
by the flood, politicians in Accra announced the discovery of a
major cache of oil off the country's Atlantic shore. The south was
poised for another boom. Northern Ghanaians went back to zero.

CARLOS AKUKA EMAILED ASKING FOR A DONATION: HE HAD DE-
cided to seek out an appointment as the district's chief executive.
Most DCEs are young party faithful who control the awarding of
government contracts, leaving the position vulnerable to bribes and
favors. When Ghana elected the opposition party to power in 2008,
Carlos saw an opportunity to bring change. He reminded me that I
had once encouraged him to forgo preaching for politics. I sent him
two hundred dollars.

He campaigned vigorously for the appointment, but in the
end was disappointed when the party decided he did not bring
enough to warrant the nomination. A later email was soaked with
bitterness. The unfortunate reality of Ghana's political scene had
been laid bare for him. Carlos believed that unless he was willing
to prop up those who propped up others, he would find no niche
in politics. He believed that his ideals were not shared by the men
in control.

After completing his teaching degree Carlos opened a private
school in Gambaga.

AYISHETU BUGRE EVENTUALLY RAISED ENOUGH MONEY TO PAY
the chief for her freedom and returned home to her husband. Asara

Azindu also returned home to her family in Gushiegu, where she later died.

SIMON CONTINUED TO SEND EMAILS AND TEXT MESSAGES. HE called in the middle of the night, forgetting about the time difference or ignoring it altogether. Often he had no news, and the conversations were brief and bedeviled by a delay in the cross-Atlantic connection. He simply wanted to pass on his greetings to me, and my parents, and assure himself that we were still healthy and that "everything [was] proceeding normally."

The GO Home project closed; it existed in theory only. His emails spoke of suffering, of not earning enough to keep his children in clothes and schoolbooks. I forwarded his name to the journalists and researchers who contacted me looking for a fixer or translator for research on witchcraft or the witch camps. He limped along, scrounging for the next bit of work, the next small bit of pay, a situation that is the reality for so many Africans.

Nearly two years after I left Ghana Simon set aside his pride and asked for money. I sent two hundred dollars, worrying, unfairly, that it would be the first of many requests. A few months later he asked for ten thousand dollars in seed money for a witch-related charity that he planned to set up somewhere other than Gambaga. It was a sum I couldn't afford and a project I couldn't monitor.

Since then Simon has teamed up with a German academic who has taken on the task of setting up a foundation for Ghana's so-called witches and opening a bank account for donations coming from Europe and North America. Simon left Gambaga for Gushiegu, hoping to work with the foundation on programs and projects that grow out of Ann Thomson's initial investment.

I CONTINUE TO THINK ABOUT THE POWER OF WITCHCRAFT. When the witchdoctor who carried the spiritual AK-47 told me I had met a man who was interested in me and that this man needed me to make a journey, I thought he was right. After three years of writing and traveling in Africa I decided I was ready to leave and made plans to follow my heart to Timor-Leste. It was the craziest thing I had ever considered—moving halfway around the world to live with the Australian man I'd met on vacation—and I soothed my occasional feelings of panic by remembering my visit to the Langbinsi witchdoctor. "If you make this journey and you are with this man, you will be very happy. And everything will be in good working order," he had predicted. As improbable as it sounds, I found the words comforting. My rational mind knew they were just words, but the superstitious side of me saw it as a sign. Although there was absolutely no evidence to support it, I was willing to believe. I wanted this to be some sort of divine romance. The diviner's forecast warmed my cold feet and gave me the confidence I needed to go through with what otherwise seemed a wholly irrational move.

Six weeks after stepping off a tiny plane and into Timor's swaddling humidity I was on the verge of a breakdown, collapsing under the weight of loneliness and anxiety. My incompatibility with the Australian had been buffered by distance, but finally living together made it impossible to ignore. Our future may have been foretold by the shake of the cowrie shells, but reality broke the spell.

My friend Nicole, however, had the kind of experience that left me wondering. When she came to visit the witch camp I took her to meet the 120-year-old diviner who'd read my future and predicted that I would marry a man with a car and produce a son. She approached the diviner with reverence, closing her eyes as she meditated on the questions she wanted answered. The diviner rewarded her with a surprisingly specific reading. He told her she would have a long, healthy, and happy life. A "colored" man would become her husband. He spoke of a baby girl. He warned her that there were problems with her car and mentioned her father. There was money in her family and in her future, he promised.

Nicole was staggered: the diviner had touched on all the questions that had lingered in her mind, things that might not seem obvious to an African diviner. Her longtime boyfriend, Sanjay, is of mixed Indian and Japanese heritage. Nicole and her father are estranged, and she wondered if she would ever touch him again. The question of children hovered in the back of her mind.

She phoned Sanjay to share the reading, but he interrupted her with a sheepish confession: he'd been running errands and had dented her car.

Nearly two years after returning from Ghana, long after the memory of the diviner's predictions had faded from memory, Nicole announced that she was pregnant. In the final weeks before her delivery friends speculated about whether she'd produce a boy or a girl. The majority guessed it would be a boy, but then I stumbled across a passage about our visit to the diviner in my journal.

A month later Nicole and Sanjay welcomed a baby girl into their family.